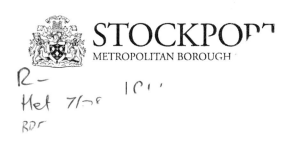

STOCKPORT
METROPOLITAN BOROUGH

Seven Seas, Nine Lives

A Royal Navy Officer's Story of Valour

SEVEN SEAS, NINE LIVES

A Royal Navy Officer's Story of Valour

Captain A W F Sutton CBE DSC*

Pen & Sword
MARITIME

First published in Great Britain in 2006 by
Pen & Sword Maritime
an imprint of
Pen & Sword Books Ltd
47 Church Street
Barnsley
South Yorkshire
S70 2AS

ISBN 1 84415 353 3

A CIP catalogue record for this book is
available from the British Library.

Typeset in 10/12pt Palatino by
Phoenix Typesetting, Auldgirth, Dumfriesshire

Printed and bound in England by
CPI UK

The author is grateful for permission to quote from *War in a Stringbag*
by Charles Lamb and published by Cassell PLC, a division of
The Orion Publishing Group.

Pen & Sword Books Ltd incorporates the imprints of Pen & Sword Aviation,
Pen & Sword Maritime, Pen & Sword Military, Wharncliffe Local History,
Pen & Sword Select, Pen & Sword Military Classics and Leo Cooper.

For a complete list of Pen & Sword titles please contact
PEN & SWORD BOOKS LIMITED
47 Church Street, Barnsley, South Yorkshire, S70 2AS, England
E-mail: enquiries@pen-and-sword.co.uk
Website: www.pen-and-sword.co.uk

Dedication

For Sue, for Gill and Garth, to the
memory of our first grandchild, Lily,
so fleetingly embraced by her
parents, Liz and Alastair.

Contents

Part One: Mutinous Fleet

Part Two: Spanish Interlude

PART THREE: ITALIAN JOB

PART ONE

Mutinous Fleet

Chapter One

Peer Pressures

Invergordon, Scotland, Monday, 14 September 1931

The midshipman glances at the picket boat's bow wave and frowns. He stares at the froth and fury of spray as the waters of the Cromarty Firth are thrust aside. He frowns again when he senses a shift in the accustomed rhythm of the boat's motion; the vessel lurches and groans as the sea slaps against the hull. He concludes, however, that the trouble is probably illusory, just a figment of his imagination. Normally thrilled by the sights and sounds of the seagoing life, Midshipman Alan William Frank Sutton is unhappy at present, unable to forget the immediacy of his invidious position. He gulps the sea air and shivers; he draws the protective layers of his navy-issue coat closer to his neck. In the distance beyond Invergordon, the early-evening light barely allows him to make out the line of high ground, although from time to time he can glimpse the hills of Easter Ross which, he thinks, look as uninviting as the Cromarty waters they overlook.

Midshipman Sutton knows that he must be strong-minded. Signs of weakness could lead to serious trouble; his personal doubts must be kept to himself. He has decided that his best course will be to display an air of quiet confidence – one of firm authority. He will make it understood that any acts of indiscipline, however minor, will not be tolerated. The matter, though, is not easy for a young man of just nineteen years, even one with a natural sense of leadership. This is, after all, his first posting with the Royal Navy. He is about to confront – be forced to confront – a situation which is hardly textbook for a new officer straight from his year of training as a special entry cadet at HMS *Erebus*, Devonport.

He glances once more at the bow wave. The gossamer lure of the sea seems surreal; the waters glisten and chatter as if in conversation with the gulls. He raises his eyes. For a moment he gazes at the gulls. He ponders about them, what curious creatures they are. He sees one of them dive towards the brass-funnelled picket boat and he recalls the advice given by an instructor at Devonport – Lieutenant Matthew

Slattery. 'Never refer to them as seagulls,' the lieutenant had said one time. 'There's no such thing, Mister Sutton.' The instructor had stared sternly at the young cadet. 'That's the kind of terminology used by ignorant landlubbers.'

So, muses Midshipman Sutton just now, what the hell are these then? Black-headed gulls, great black-headed gulls, herring gulls? Goodness knows. Scottish herring gulls, perhaps. They look a bit Scottish somehow. Maybe they eat haggis; they'll be wearing kilts next. The midshipman chuckles to himself and he momentarily puts present worries to the back of his mind. He remembers Lieutenant Slattery as an exceptionally good man: one of the old school, someone who would go far. As he surmises the prospects of the future Admiral Sir Matthew Slattery, and as he ruminates, Midshipman Sutton recalls the passing-out ceremony at Devonport last month. His mother had attended, and so had his brother, Dudley. Not his father, though.

If only . . .

But perhaps, in spirit, he had been there.

On that day at Devonport, Instructor Lieutenant Slattery had been a model host. He had known about Cadet Sutton's background, and with the natural urbanity of an officer and a gentleman he had welcomed the family into another family – that of the Royal Navy: bigger and broader, but a family nevertheless. Lieutenant Slattery was aware of the fate of Cadet Sutton's father, a soldier killed in the first Battle of the Somme. With quiet compassion the lieutenant had demonstrated his discernment of the devastation – the tortures – the cadet's mother must have endured. How does a young widow cope with such circumstances? 'Alan, I have something to tell you . . .' How do you explain to a boy of just four years about the loss of his father, a man they had revered, the man on whom so much depended?

'Look!' one of the crew members yells and points upwards. His reminiscences disrupted, Midshipman Sutton observes the restlessness of the gulls and he sees how their agitation is heightened when the boat nears the shoreline. His eyes narrow as he squints up at the birds. He discerns their impatient flutter against the backdrop of fractured stratus and he notices how occasional breaks in the cloud reveal the first of the stars, the brightest of the stars. What was he told at school? He remembers the teacher at the Christ's Hospital School, Horsham, who tried to explain about the muses: about Zeus and Mnemosyne; about their nine daughters. So which, then, was the muse of astronomy? Urania? Yes, that was it: Urania. He gazes at the heavens for some seconds; the stars in Scottish skies seem to have added clarity.

A determined gull looks aggressive, uncommonly so, as it squawks and swoops towards the picket boat; the midshipman feels an instinctive desire to duck. He must be getting edgy. He glances back at his mother vessel, HMS *Repulse*, a battle-cruiser at anchor in the outer reaches of the Cromarty Firth. He makes out the profile of the ship, the funnels and bridge structure, the guns fore and aft, the elegant line of the hull, how this disguises the mass of the 32,000 ton displacement. The *Repulse*, the twelfth Royal Navy ship to bear the name since first used in 1595, was built by the Clyde company of John Brown and was completed in August 1916. The ship, which is now farthest from his present position, is anchored off the town of Cromarty. He notes how the other ships are secured systematically in pairs until, between Invergordon and Udale Bay, HMS *Hood* and *Rodney* are set apart on their moorings.

He spots the navigation lights of the *Repulse*, then he checks around him to observe the lights of the whole fleet. He sees the sparkle of an Aldis communications lamp come to life; the operator winks some message to a fellow rating. He feels awed as he gazes at the grandeur of the largest of the ships within His Majesty's Atlantic Fleet; at present, the smaller craft are moored off Rosyth in the Firth of Forth. In the next day or so these elements are due to sail north to take part in the fleet's autumn exercises.

Despite the size and the splendour of the fifteen or so warships now in view, the midshipman realizes that the vessels become harder to make out in this fading light of dusk. He contemplates how the grey outlines seem deceptive: the exteriors disguise hives of activity within; the ships teem with an urgent and remarkable vitality. So many disciplines are contained within the depths of those hulls: engineers, gunners, administrators, marines, caterers . . . the cooks seem to work miracles under such conditions. He shivers again, and he wonders what will be on the menu in the midshipmen's mess tonight.

Not that he feels hungry at this moment; his sense of anxiety sees to that. The food, though, will be enjoyed eventually. At least the navy attempts to look after its people in that respect. The task must be Herculean; the numbers enormous. The *Repulse*'s crew is newly commissioned, and when gathered for arrival briefings he and his fellow midshipmen were told specifics about the ship's organization. Details of domestic requirements were explained: the complexity of arrangements to feed the ship's crew of 1,181 personnel. He remembers the conversations that followed: the midshipmen's incredulity at the figures; the subsequent discussions and the comparisons, so revealing, between naval rations and the now-famed provisions taken onto the liner *Titanic* . . . 75,000 lb of fresh meat, 40,000 fresh eggs, 1,500 gal of milk, 11,000 lb of fresh fish, even fifty boxes of grapefruit. The officers laughed; such luxury was unlikely to become part of a naval diet.

The midshipman peers ahead at his aiming point, the pier at

Invergordon. The outline becomes gradually more discernible and lines of streets, drab looking, become visible too. As he glances at the home of centuries of tradition and influence from the affairs of the sea, he feels the town's streets point towards him as if accusingly – antagonized by the years of boom and bust, of triumph and tragedy. At one time a great naval base, Invergordon now appears a shadow of former times.

Matters, he was told, were different during the Great War. The streets were filled with life and vigour then and the town's population swelled six-fold. Skilled labour apparently became so short that, for the first time, women were employed in traditional male jobs in the dockyards and in housing construction. And the housing problem was clearly acute; large numbers evidently had to be accommodated in three old warships. Those were the days when Invergordon was a boom town.

Then, in a moment of horror, came that event, that dreadful occurrence, on the very night of Hogmanay sixteen years ago. In mysterious circumstances one of His Majesty's ships, the *Natal*, blew up with the loss of over 300 lives.

Further tragedy followed. He was told how Invergordon was still trying to come to terms with the loss of the *Natal* when, within a matter of months, the townspeople witnessed the Royal Navy sailing for Jutland. A great naval engagement took place off the coast of Denmark, but the aftermath was felt along the coast of Scotland. In naval terms the battle's outcome was indecisive, but the impact on the people of Invergordon was clear enough: those were the people who had to cope with the immediate repercussions of over 6,000 sailors killed; the people who watched the ships limp back through the Cromarty Firth, and who saw a fleet of twelve ambulance boats take three days to ferry the wounded to Red Cross trains.

The sad affair seemed to mark the nadir of the town's fortunes. Nemesis followed: the inhabitants had had it too good for too long, now they would have to pay. The dockyard closed, the post-war depression set in, workers drifted away and the population declined. As he stares at the Invergordon pier, the midshipman wonders if the Royal Navy, the organization he has joined as a new and proud officer, should alone be held to account – exclusively blamed – for the hardships.

Just now, however, Midshipman Sutton is concerned about other troubles. He has to think about the present and about his imminent duty: to pick up thirty or so sailors on shore leave – liberty-men – and return them to HMS *Repulse*. In normal times this would be straightforward procedure, but he knows that tonight the matter will be fraught with potential problems. The ratings are in turbulent mood, their unpredictable behaviour sparked by the disclosure of pay cuts. The men have been informed that owing to the nation's financial difficulties the salaries of public servants will have to be reduced. As part of the process, Royal Navy remuneration will be decreased by up to 25 per cent. The lowest ranks will be worst affected: able seamen will have their pay taken down from 4 shillings to 3 shillings a day, ordinary seamen from 2 shillings and 9d a day to two shillings. Thus the basic salary of ordinary seamen will be reduced to around £3 a month, insufficient to pay their rent or to support their wives.

This news was announced with scant notice or advance explanation. Sutton, along with the *Repulse*'s other midshipmen, had overheard worried officers talk about their Lordships of the Admiralty and about how, for reasons of illness and absence on leave, key members had missed crucial meetings. Other admirals, including the fleet's commander-in-chief Admiral Sir Michael Hodges, had been away when the subject was discussed. For a variety of reasons, those left in charge had handled the matter ineptly. Whatever the background, the midshipman realizes that the effect was like dynamite: last weekend, new pay scales were posted in Admiralty Fleet Order No. 2239. The issue was matter-of-fact; the bombshell was presented as a *fait accompli*.

It was not as if the government and Prime Minister Ramsay MacDonald did not know what the likely reaction would be. The Prime Minister was made familiar – starkly so – with the men's feelings on the previous Saturday. As a guest on board the aircraft carrier *Courageous* to watch the Schneider Trophy air race, he had enjoyed a welcoming speech from the ship's captain. The entire crew was congregated in the carrier's hangar. After the speeches, the captain called for the traditional three cheers. 'Hip, hip, hip . . .' he cried as he raised his hat high. But silence ensued, followed by the blowing of a raspberry. The captain's face reddened. He tried again: 'Hip, hip, hip . . .' Another silence, then a larger number of raspberries.

Other signs of trouble were apparent too. On board the *Repulse*, the midshipmen had listened with serious expressions as officers discussed the embarrassment of Captain Custance of HMS *York*. When the fleet order was delivered, he had assembled his men so that he could read them the contents in person. The news was greeted with gasps of astonishment, especially from the married ratings who would be hit the hardest. When he had finished reading, the captain added: 'I'm sorry about this, but if you can't manage, your wives could be asked to take in washing to augment your pay.'

At this, a harsh and angry voice from the rear ranks shouted: 'You fat bastard! How would you like your old woman to crash out the dirties?' The shaken captain had immediately ordered the quarter-deck to be cleared and the ship's company to resume their duties. These, though, were undertaken with dissension and amid heated discussions.

So what, wonders the midshipman, was on the minds of their Lordships? And what about the commander-in-chief's number two, the man who would eventually shoulder much of the blame? Were these people so remote, so cemented to their ivory towers, that they did not consider the likely implications? Were the admirals sufficiently removed from day-to-day naval life that they did not realize the hardship that would be caused, how the ratings were bound to become inflamed and infuriated?

But some admirals, it seemed, were still rooted in the times of Nelson, the days when ordinary sailors had to sign their names with a cross. Evidently they had forgotten that modern ratings were educated individuals who could read newspapers and were informed about national affairs. The men would be aware that Ramsay MacDonald was now prime minister in name only, and that last week's demonstrations in London had led to violence and arrests. The men would know about, and worry about, predictions that the nation's impending financial collapse would lead to the abandonment of the gold standard and the temporary closure of the London Stock Exchange.

'A couple of minutes to the pier, Mister Sutton.' The rating's shout of advice is hardly needed, but the midshipman realizes that all the crew members have feelings as apprehensive as his own. Mutiny is an ugly thing; the very concept clashes with the instinct and natural pride of military personnel. For the Royal Navy, the senior service, the broad family, this is especially poignant. The scenario is akin to civil war, the most destructive form of warfare. How should an individual respond? Where are the true loyalties?

While he watches the pier loom, Midshipman Sutton has to supervise proceedings; he looks ahead as he monitors the coxswain's actions and judgement. A seaman of experience, the coxswain assesses the right instant to reduce the boat's forward speed. The pitch of the engine note begins to alter; the crew are gently tipped forward onto their toes. The effervescence of the bow wave starts to peter out; the inquisitive gulls stare down. The fish, too, seem interested: the midshipman thinks he spots some of them arch through the air before they dive back into the firth. For a moment he looks down to observe the sea's surface; he imagines the waters warmed by the currents of the Gulf Stream drifting south from Dornoch Firth, from Duncansby Head, from the perils of the Pentland Firth – feared by seamen but enjoyed by the porbeagle sharks, the halibut, the giant common skate. He checks again, but realizes that the fish have vanished. Perhaps, like other things this evening, their appearance was only in his imagination. He looks up, and once more he concentrates ahead as the boat closes onto the pier.

He now senses the increasing tension amongst his crew. As the picket boat chugs along at reduced speed, the five crew members – the bow man, the stern-sheet man, the stoker for the coal-fired reciprocating engine, the coxswain and himself – can make out unusual goings-on in the vicinity of the pier. Groups of ratings seem agitated as they wave their arms about. And the midshipman shares his crew's uneasiness; they watch the men ashore mill around as some of them point towards Saltburn to the east, then out to sea and towards the picket boat. The silhouettes of the Easter Ross hills, still faintly visible, look down in disapproval.

When the vessel's speed is further reduced, the bow man and the stern-sheet man take up station with boat hooks. The coxswain steers the craft towards an allocated section of pier; the midshipman, as a matter of routine drill, prepares his crew.

'Stand by for'ard.'

'Aye, aye, sir.'

'Stand by aft.'

'Aye, aye, sir.'

He observes the lights on the pier and around the locality; he sees how they cause distorted shadows which add to the sinister atmosphere. He stares at the lights and ponders the distinction: the half-hearted illumination, threatening and resentful, contrasts with the bold simplicity of the picket boat lights, the green for starboard and the red for port, which stand out firmly. He attempts to work out the number of men amassed and he tries to sound assured as he shouts: 'Steady as you go.'

'Aye, aye, sir.' The coxswain's voice, too, has a forced quality. The midshipman's call may have been superfluous, but the crew appreciate that the young officer has to display confidence – or at least an impression of confidence, of being in charge of the situation. They understand, too, that his true feelings must be suppressed. But his nervousness is real enough; he watches the activity ashore and he notes how distinct groups of men seem to have formed. He sees no signs of local men and none of women – even the types regular to harbour life.

'Steady as you go,' he repeats. This time the coxswain does not reply. As he sees the events of the pier at closer hand, perhaps his sympathies for the midshipman begin to wane. He must decide where his loyalties lie. Ratings, in any case, have an in-built caution when dealing with midshipmen – otherwise known as 'snotties'. Perhaps this one knows about Midshipman Sutton's non-naval background, how this must have led to difficulties at Devonport. And the non-commissioned ranks are highly critical of officers at present: officers are reckoned to have failed to support their men; officers, therefore, are perceived as the opposition. Although the routines of the sea have become more natural to the new midshipman – the port and the starboard, the semaphore signals, the bends and the hitches, the seamanship, the Morse code – the coxswain is in no mood to make allowances. He feels distaste – dislike – and he is disinterested in the young officer's problems.

It is, however, not the midshipman's finer feelings which cause the young officer to step back in a spontaneous gesture of alarm. The coxswain, too, feels his heart begin to pound as he observes a group of men surge towards the picket boat, and he yells: 'Watch out there! Watch out for that . . .'

CHAPTER TWO

Pier Pressures

Startled by the coxswain's shouts, the picket boat's crew pause in their duties for some seconds. The ratings gape in surprise at the coxswain and watch him warily; the midshipman, too, is caught off guard. An ominous hush follows. Anxiously, the crew listen to the contrast: the quiet creak of timbers as the boat rises and falls with the swell and bumps against fenders; the angry yells of the men ashore.

The midshipman grips his handrail with anxiety; he checks behind him, then he looks ahead. He knows he should re-exert his authority but just as he is about to shout another order, his attention is diverted; he stares towards a commotion at one end of the pier. Others are distracted too; all gaze at a particular area. Events are hard to make out in the shadowy illumination but excited cries can be heard; a scuffle has broken out.

The midshipman senses the now-urgent need to reinforce his authority. He shouts: 'Attend to those warps!' and the picket boat's bow man and stern-sheet man obey at once – discipline is inherent as the ratings resume their tasks, wielding boat hooks in attempts to grab mooring rings for the boat's rope warps. The crew, however, curse the lack of assistance from those ashore and while they struggle, the coxswain's skills, too, are tested: he revs the engine to manoeuvre and steady the vessel. The sound soars above strident voices.

'Stand back!'

'Grab that warp. What's the matter with you?'

'Throw him in the sea!'

'Hold it there, coxswain. Steady.'

'Careful, lads . . . remember the discussions at the canteen.'

'Okay, coxswain . . . that position's good. Secure those warps!'

'Passive resistance, remember . . . violence won't help our case. This will be a strike, lads, not a mutiny.'

'Wincott's right . . . we'll back each other . . . we'll pull together.'

'Says who?'

'Throw that bloody warrant officer in the water.'

'For God's sake!' This from a member of a naval patrol. His raised voice, his shocked and insistent tone, catches the crowd by surprise. The normally disciplined seamen hesitate as, in a particular moment, they seem to grasp the full significance, the heretic nature, of their actions.

Meanwhile, as the picket boat's crew secure warps to the mooring rings, members of the crowd look on; a few individuals whistle appreciation at the ratings' deft use of naval knots. With practised efficiency the crew work to secure the vessel to the landing stage, but they mutter further curses at the men who throng about the pier and who vent their frustration on accumulated debris: hawsers, rusted cans, discarded nets, general fishers' flotsam; all are moodily kicked aside.

Despite this provocation of his crew, the midshipman worries that his men may be persuaded to show solidarity with fellow ratings. He tries to work out what to say – what to do – if his ratings endeavour to leave the boat. Before long, though, he notes with a sense of relief that they are making no attempt to climb ashore.

The crew now observe events from the security of the picket boat. The midshipman glances at the goings-on at the pier end; the general illumination is still difficult but he can see that a naval patrol has been trapped by a large and unruly mob. Several ratings appear inebriated as they heckle the patrol and taunt the officer in charge. Patrol members have formed themselves into a ring of protection around their warrant officer; some hold up batons to ward off aggressors. 'I order you to stand back,' commands the warrant officer.

'Bastard!' shout the crowds, inflamed again. 'Throw him in the water.'

'Blame the government not the warrant officer,' yell members of the patrol.

From within the crowd a particular voice can be heard: 'Remember the discussions, lads . . . what we said at the canteen . . . we're all in this together . . . remember: passive resistance.' As they recognize the voice and listen to the exhortations, the crowds appear to falter again.

The midshipman looks around him to try to spot his liberty-men passengers. He has difficulty because the crowds, already large and confused, are progressively swelled as other sailors hasten towards the pier from the direction of the naval canteen at the north end of the town. Men argue and wave their arms in agitation; individuals belligerently point towards the picket boat and its crew.

The crew, before the picket boat's departure, were briefed by the *Repulse*'s duty officer; the two men discussed whether the midshipman might leave the boat temporarily in order to find the liberty-men and urge them to board. But the midshipman knows this is no longer realistic. The general mood ashore has deteriorated significantly. His first consideration must be for the safety of his vessel and crew; if the situation becomes further out of hand he may even have to order the crew to leave immediately and without passengers.

While the crowds continue to jostle and to grow, the midshipman sees more men form factions as various ships' crews join forces. Groups converse excitedly while they try to make plans. Snatches of information can be picked up as occasional words, caught in the breeze, drift across: 'Six o'clock tomorrow morning . . . remember the routine, lads . . . we'll cheer to victory . . .' And as he listens, he notes how the volume of voices ashore contrasts chillingly with the silence of his crew. His men glance at each other uneasily from time to time, but they say little. As a matter of routine drill the bow man and the stern-sheet man check the security of the fastenings to the landing stage and then, when they look around, their expressions reveal their discomfiture. And if the crewmen once were tempted to leave the boat, they know they have little option now but to remain firm as they hear the speeches and watch the milling crowds.

Their patience is tested for further minutes, but before long the crew's attention is drawn away from the disturbances ashore: the men hear squeals of objection from fenders as an increasing swell amplifies the vessel's rise and fall. With practised sea-legs they steady themselves. The midshipman listens to the steady put-put-put of the engine; the sound wavers eerily in the wind. He angles his head towards the breeze and notes that the strengthening gale confirms the Admiralty's recent shipping forecast: 'moderate breeze force five increasing to strong wind force six or seven, later reaching gale force eight or nine . . .' He considers that if, eventually, he does manage to locate his passengers, their present enthusiasm is likely to be dampened by a choppy ride back to the *Repulse*.

He looks up to observe the impact of this wind on the gulls. Their cries, though, remain derisive, their heads alert as they watch events around the pier. But the crowds disregard the gulls – the men are too preoccupied. The effect of all these shouts and jeers, thinks the midshipman, must be intimidating for local people. He glances at the line of a street marked by terraced houses, drab and grey-looking, which seem overshadowed by surrounding affairs. Occupants no doubt rely on locked doors for a semblance of security; worried faces peek from behind drawn curtains. Local folk, with their reputation for a gentle and soft-spoken approach to life, must have feelings as anxious as his own. Occasionally he hears stray sounds rise above the mob's roar: the cry of a child, the yelps of a frightened dog. He sees no sign of civil police and realizes that control of the crowds will be left to the tenuous authority of the warrant officer and his naval patrol. The men of the patrol, however, remain surrounded and impotent.

The midshipman hears the voices nearest the picket boat: 'It's not just us alone, lads,' says one man. 'Everyone's been affected; everyone's pay has been cut.'

'Is that the point?' says another man.

'Is it hell,' scoffs an angry voice.

'Our pay has been cut back the most.'

'More than the officers.'

'We won't even be able to afford our rent.'

'He's right.'

'We're hard up as it is.'

'Some of the wives can't even afford to buy food.'

'And they can't afford to clothe the bairns.'

'Spend less on booze then, Albert.' There's laughter at this.

'Bugger off.'

'It's no good.'

'Why should we put up with it?'

'We'll have to do something.'

'We fight for king and country; we put our lives at risk; is this the way we're to be treated?'

'We can't take this lying down.'

'We'll have to show them.'

'We'll show 'em all right!'

'Why don't the officers do something about it?'

'That's their job isn't it?'

'We'll make an example of this warrant officer and his bloody patrol.'

'Throw the bastard in!'

The voices, the midshipman realizes, are hardly those of raw recruits. He ponders the irony: he himself is the raw recruit yet he is expected to discipline experienced sailors, some of them seasoned veterans. He it is who, still a teenager, has to act as the representative of officialdom, the agent of authority. After one year of training at Devonport he finds himself the man in charge, the officer required to help control hardened individuals, seamen with years of service, now determined to disobey orders. 'Don't worry, Mister Sutton,' the *Repulse*'s duty officer had said benignly before the picket boat set off. 'I'm sure you'll manage.'

In normal times, the loyalty and the reliability of these men would be held in high regard but the midshipman feels increasingly unnerved as he senses the shift in attitudes, the decisive sea-change, taking place in front of his eyes. As more men join in the fracas and move towards the pier he sees how they work themselves up into greater states of fury and disaffection. His vulnerable position becomes more and more evident as the men, still determined to vent their frustration on the naval patrol, surge this way and that. The ratings try to provoke the encircled patrol; the warrant officer attempts to shrink behind the protective screen of his colleagues.

While he watches these events the midshipman notices other fateful signs. The ratings' state of dress, for example, seems unusually casual and careless: cap ribbons have been removed; the names of individual ships cannot be identified. The sailors' square collars – the normally smart traditional symbol from the days when tarred pigtails needed to be kept away from clothing – look askew and dishevelled. Some ratings insist on whistling loudly, a practice forbidden in the navy since the Nore mutiny of 1797 when whistling was the agreed signal for action.

'They'll send in the marines if we don't watch out,' says a cautious-sounding voice.

'What can the marines do?'

'Not much, and they're on our side anyway.'

'We must stick together; there's nothing they can do if we act together,' says the recognized voice. 'Are we to take the pay cuts lying down?'

'No, Wincott, we will not.'

'Will the fleet go to sea tomorrow?'

'Damned if it will!'

'Let's throw the warrant officer in the sea then.'

'He's between the devil and the deep blue sea,' cries a rating. Another ripple of laughter, then bouts of cheering.

'That's the idea, lads. We'll cheer ourselves to victory.'

'That'll be the signal tomorrow . . . remember to cheer, lads.'

The midshipman shudders. As he feels the growing chill of danger, he realizes how swiftly the invisible ties which bind men to the authority of their officers seem to break down. The discipline and loyalty so vital within the confines of a ship appear to disintegrate with extraordinary rapidity. Do the men really despise their officers to such a degree? Have all officers been tarred with the brush of aloofness and arrogance? Surely some are liked and respected. Should not these ratings blame the Admiralty and the government for the pay cuts? The officers can hardly be blamed: they received no advance notice or briefing. The Admiralty, it seems, failed to understand or properly think through the implications. And if a crew of 1,000 men decide not to co-operate with a handful of officers, what exactly, can the officers do about it?

The midshipman will be unaware, of course, of the number of options that members of the Admiralty and the Cabinet will discuss later in the week. His enthusiasm for a naval career might well be stifled if, at this moment, he were to be told that the use of force will be considered; that the government will discuss the example of Chile where a recent mutiny was quelled by the army; that senior members of the British hierarchy will seriously contemplate the use of bombs to attack the Atlantic Fleet.

'Behind us!' The coxswain shouts and points at more picket boats converging on the pier. The midshipman turns around to watch; he sees the sprays of bow waves effervesce against the grey background of the hull of HMS *Hood*, nearest to the pier. The tide holds the *Hood* in sequence with the *Valiant* and the *Nelson*. He thinks he sees unusual gatherings of men on the *Hood*'s forecastle, but perhaps this is a trick of the light. Gaps in the mooring arrangement are evident where the *Warspite* and the *Malaya* were positioned earlier in the day; these ships have left on exercise ahead of others. He notes the paradox of the neat and orderly line-up of vessels; how this conflicts with the state of mind of the crews. The Atlantic Fleet points towards the mouth of the Cromarty Firth and to the high ground of the North and South Sutor. The hills overlook the isolated position of his own ship, but perhaps the *Repulse* is glad to be set apart just now.

As the picket boats approach, the midshipman spots a further distraction. Another naval patrol – this time with additional officers – marches by the far end of the pier. A lieutenant commander, he thinks, is in charge. The midshipman realizes, though, that the officer is not shown the customary respect; the requirements of saluting are plainly absent. But the patrol ignore this as they hasten towards the direction of the naval canteen, their task evidently urgent enough to disregard the plight of their colleagues still surrounded and threatened on the pier.

The midshipman recalls Devonport, how he was lectured there on the structure of naval authority. That authority was taken as sacrosanct. The process had worked for Nelson, had worked for centuries, would continue to do so. The matter was incontrovertible. The midshipman sees the scenes around him as a reflection of the degree to which senior officers at Devonport and within the navy at large had failed to read the signs, to grasp the fact that the world had changed for ever. The Great War had seen to that. At one time the constraints of Britain's class-ridden society had fitted neatly into the constraints of life at sea: the upper and lower deck arrangement within ships had mirrored the days of servants and service; Disraeli's two nations were crystallized aboard. Now that will have to end. The men's loyalty can no longer be taken for granted. Allegiance to the navy is being remodelled into a solidarity of the lower deck.

'Six o'clock it is then . . .'

'Okay, lads. Stick together and we'll be all right.'

The midshipman listens to more exhortations. He knows that some men have been drinking; the unsteady sound of sailors singing 'The Red Flag' testifies to that. But as other men swarm onto the pier he senses how the atmosphere is charged with a particular and uncommon euphoria which is, perhaps, easy to mistake for drunkenness. The rowdi-

ness he had taken for inebriation he now realizes is, in fact, more akin to
exuberance.

'Don't forget, HMS *Valiant*.'

'Okay, *Nelson*. We'll be with you.'

The other picket boats reduce speed as they approach the pier. The
midshipman sees the faces of the crews gazing in his direction. He thinks
he recognizes another midshipman, a friend from his course at
Devonport. As the crews, with boat hooks at the ready, prepare to grab
mooring rings he notices the smart appearance of the vessels, the im-
peccable paintwork, the polished brass, the boats shipshape and
prepared with the navy's usual attention to detail. While he stares at the
vessels, for a moment he forgets the surrounding clamour; he yearns for
normality, a return to his desire for pride in his service, his new career.
Suddenly, though, he looks up; he hears the sound of a gruff voice from
the pier: 'Where are these bound?'

'Who knows?'

'What about this one? Where's this one going?' A rating kicks a rusted
can towards the picket boat.

'Careful, lads.'

'Okay, Len. We're with you.'

'This one's for the *Repulse*. Anyone seen liberty-men bound for the
Repulse?'

'Over there you blind bugger.'

'All right, all right.'

'Are you men agreed? Are you with us?'

'We're with you.'

'Six o'clock tomorrow it is then, lads.'

'The fleet won't sail.'

'Damned if it will!'

But while the midshipman listens to this bluster, while he watches the
activity, he thinks he is able to identify a number of individuals. Through
the dim light he begins to recognize the *Repulse*'s liberty-men as they
point and wave and as, still in debate, they make their way slowly
towards their picket boat.

CHAPTER THREE

Cruel Seas

While they work their way gradually towards the picket boat, the liberty-men find themselves jostled and impeded by the crowds. From time to time, when forced to stop, the men are drawn into impassioned discussions and quarrels although, as they near the boat, their spirits are lifted when they hear individuals shout last-minute cries of encouragement:

'Tomorrow morning then, *Repulse*.'

'Don't forget the routine, lads.'

'Okay, *Nelson*.'

'Good luck, *Rodney*.'

'We'll cheer to victory.'

As he listens to the yells, the midshipman glances anxiously at the picket boat's crew. The ratings, however, remain at their stations with inscrutable expressions, concentrating on their duties. In contrast, the liberty-men look around shiftily while they board and as the midshipman counts numbers . . . one, two, three, four . . . he watches closely as the tally mounts; it seems they are keen to avoid eye contact . . . seven, eight . . . and some of the younger faces appear especially apprehensive . . . ten, eleven, twelve . . . he notes that the men remain in earnest discussion as they leave behind the machinations on the pier . . . eighteen, nineteen, twenty . . . he detects certain characters displaying a deliberate carelessness of routine . . . twenty-two, twenty-three, twenty-four . . . and that a few men whistle loudly and persistently . . . twenty-five, twenty-six, twenty-seven . . .

When he sees the last man climb aboard, the midshipman makes a final check of numbers. He calls: 'Any more for the *Repulse*?' There's no reply. He yells again: 'Any more liberty-men bound for the *Repulse*?'

'I reckon that's it, sir,' says a nearby liberty-man. 'No more.'

The midshipman acknowledges with a nod and then, without further ado, he shouts: 'Stand by to cast off!' He watches his crew reach for the boat's mooring warps. He sees the men glance back as they anticipate the next order:

'Cast off for'ard.'

'Aye, aye, sir.'

'Cast off aft.'

'Aye, aye, sir.' The routine, proficient and practised, is observed by the passengers without comment although the midshipman senses the liberty-men's readiness to shout advice or abuse. But the bow man and the stern-sheet man detach the boat's warps nimbly from the mooring rings and the coxswain revs the engine; waters agitate and swirl while he manoeuvres the picket boat away from other vessels. He aims for a heading just south of east as he points the boat towards a gap in the Atlantic Fleet's mooring arrangement.

On the picket boat's port side now looms HMS *Dorsetshire*, the cruiser clearly distinguished by the triple funnel arrangement abaft the bridge. The midshipman muses that the three fingers point at the stars as if demanding recognition; the *Dorsetshire*, after all, is bound to have a sense of history, of naval tradition. It bears a name first used by the Royal Navy in 1694 and is now the third ship to bear the distinction. The midshipman assumes, however, that the ship, presently the headquarters of the admiral in charge of cruisers, Rear-Admiral Astley-Rushton, would view present disturbances with dismay. This evening the admiral will receive a visit from the captain of the *Norfolk*, the ship on which Able Seaman Len Wincott – the chief, if unofficial, agitator – is a member of crew. With anxiety the admiral and the captain will discuss rumours and reports which have reached them. The two men will have additional talks when, later on, they dine with Admiral Tomkinson on HMS *Hood*.

HMS *Hood* is on the picket boat's starboard beam. The light is still deceptive but the midshipman is now convinced he can detect men massed on the forecastle. He knows that to achieve the most direct route for the 4 mile run to the *Repulse*, his coxswain will aim to pass near to the *Hood*. The men on the picket boat, therefore, will be able to witness activities on the *Hood*'s forecastle at closer range. As the picket boat moves away from the pier, and as interference with small vessels diminishes, the coxswain begins to open up the throttle. The coxswain is less concerned about disturbance to the large ships of the Atlantic Fleet; even at a maximum speed of 12 knots, the influence of the picket boat's bow wave on these warships will be insignificant.

Before long, when the picket boat approaches the *Hood* – the ship said to be the embodiment of British sea-power and of the British Empire – the midshipman confirms his earlier suspicions: the unusual gathering of men on the forecastle is no mere trick of light. He sees how the sailors walk around and point, their manner similar to that of the men on the pier. He thinks about the contradictions: the pier, littered with the gentle flotsam of fisher folk, contrasts with the decks of the *Hood* which bristle with weapons of war, with guns and antennae. The seamen, though, are heedless of both and in turn the *Hood* displays an impression of detachment. Perhaps, with that elegant and symmetrical hull line, it cannot avoid an aura of loftiness – an unwillingness to become involved with these impertinent seamen and their troubles.

The picket boat now passes between the *Hood* and the *Dorsetshire*. The midshipman has a sense of awe as he stares in turn at the two ships and as he ponders the disparity: the *Hood*, with a displacement of 42,100 tons towers over the *Dorsetshire*'s 9,975 tons. The ships may be at different ends of the operational spectrum but there is one equivalence. The *Hood* is the third Royal Navy ship to bear the name (honouring a family which has produced four famous admirals) and the *Dorsetshire* is the same. The *Hood*'s dominance, however, is irrefutable. By reputation she is the world's largest and fastest warship. She uses 1 ton of oil to travel half a mile at a speed of 32 knots, carries eight 15-inch guns mounted in pairs – sufficient firepower to destroy a small town – and at 868 ft, is in length over five times the height of the Statue of Liberty from the torch's tip to the statue's base.

The midshipman recalls his admiration for the 'mighty *Hood*' when, as a boy of eleven and with the particular enthusiasm of a youngster, he had followed the ship's progress during an eleven-month world tour in the early 1920s. In company with the *Repulse* and five cruisers, the *Hood* had visited South Africa, Zanzibar, Ceylon, Singapore, Australia, New Zealand, the Pacific islands, San Francisco, the Panama Canal, Jamaica, Canada and Newfoundland. Her arrival with her escorts caused huge crowds to gather; the pages of the local press were filled. A woman in Melbourne wrote: 'Every road and pathway was thick and many families were making a day of it, taking out the children and carrying hampers of food and bottles of beer. The bay was dotted with sailing boats. It was a wonderful sight – something I shall never forget, everyone cheering and the kids running up and down and the sirens of all the ships going off.'

Millions of people must have seen her, hundreds of thousands must have gone aboard. Visitors no doubt fingered her brass-work with admiration, gawped at the 15-inch guns, walked the decks and climbed the superstructure. When her admiral gave a missing boy scout a free lift to San Francisco, the Mayor's words ricocheted around the world: 'We surrender our city unto you. We capitulate.'

This evening, however, with those admiring crowds replaced by disgruntled sailors, the navy's attitude has veered from pride to embarrassment. No wonder the Admiralty will be keen to avoid leakage of details to the press and the public.

There are further problems. As the sailors move about, as they agitate and point and focus on their immediate troubles, perhaps some are mindful of another factor: the *Hood*'s design weakness. Her top surfaces are known to be vulnerable to enemy shells and this shortcoming is recognized by the navy. But the government, in spite of warnings, fails to provide funds to rectify the fault; for reasons of economy the decks will not be strengthened. The surfaces now trampled by angry sailors will be the source of disaster to come, the Achilles heel which will trumpet the ship's demise.

In ten years' time two admirals, the British Admiral Holland, the German Admiral Lutjens, will face each other like duellists. When the mighty *Hood* attacks the German ship *Bismark*, both will have large numbers of duellists' seconds – back-up teams of some 1,500 men each. In all probability these individuals will have no feelings of antagonism towards each other. Perhaps, in different circumstances, they would prefer to recognize each other as colleagues.

However, on 24 May 1941, at a tender and ethereal start of dawn, the lunacy of war will prevail. The duel will last a mere matter of minutes before one of the *Bismark*'s shells – possibly by chance – will score a direct hit against the *Hood*'s top surfaces. The shell will pass through the decks which should have been strengthened but which were not, and will explode deep inside the ships vitals.

On the *Hood*'s bridge, Signalman Briggs will hear the officer of the watch report that the compass has gone; the quartermaster will yell that the steering has been lost; the captain will order a switch to emergency power.

After this the ship will lurch violently sideways.

Able Seaman Tilburn on the boat deck will see the man beside him killed and another man's intestines ripped open by a splinter. The able seaman will move to one side of the deck to be sick and as he does so, he will realize that the deck is level with the water.

In other parts of the ship, men will watch dials calmly, monitor pressures, adjust levers, reload guns. All will be absorbed with the performance of their duties but before they can really understand what has happened, they will be lifted off their feet. They will hear rivets crack and plates and bulkheads around them collapse as an overwhelming force consumes the ship. In an eruption of light – a sudden brilliance at once glorious and horrific and esoteric – for a fragment of time the men will sense the futility of further activity. For perhaps a number of seconds, perhaps just a fraction of a second, they will know that the fight has been lost.

The captain of the *Hood*'s cohort ship, the *Prince of Wales*, will order hard a'starboard to avoid wreckage. Commander Jasper, the gunnery officer on the German ship *Prinz Eugen*, will be watching through his range finder as the side of the *Hood* rears up from the water. Inside will be hundreds of men tossed around like rag dolls in the darkness of shell-room and magazine. 'Poor devils, poor devils,' the commander will say aloud as he echoes the sentiments of those around him.

Four Royal Navy destroyers will be sent to rescue survivors. Preparations will be made to receive shell-shocked and shattered men: blankets will be drawn from stores, dry clothing will be made ready, soup will be heated in galleys, medics will be braced to deal with casualties. The destroyers will come across patches of oil on the water, occasional pieces of wood, scraps of documents, a few personal effects. The ships will locate three Carley life rafts with one man in each. 'There *must* be more,' the engineering officer will say, 'there can't be only *three* of them,' and the search will continue for a long time. The destroyers will find pathetic flotsam – minor pieces of wreckage, a hat with the number RMB X738, but little else, not a single corpse.

The *Hood*'s three survivors will be taken on board HMS *Electra*, where wet clothing will be removed and the men wrapped in blankets. But they will have feelings of guilt: why should they have survived and others not? Admiral Holland, Captain Kerr, ninety officers and over 1,400 men will lie a thousand fathoms down entombed for ever within the *Hood*'s remains. Why should these three alone be chosen to live?

When questioned later, Midshipman Dundas will report how he climbed out of the upper bridge window to escape. Signalman Briggs will recall how he evacuated by the starboard door of the compass plat-form, noting as he left that Admiral Holland made no attempt to save himself. Able Seaman Tilburn will go over the ship's side but his sea boots will become trapped by aerials as the *Hood* rolls over. He will use a clasp-knife to cut off his boots under water. All three men will find separate Carley life rafts. They will try to bind the rafts together but the cold and the shock and the trauma will cause their fingers to shake too violently.

Able Seaman Tilburn will think himself bound to die; he will close his eyes in anticipation, thinking that would be a pleasant way to go. He will, however, obstinately stay awake and two hours later the *Electra* will appear.

All three of the *Hood*'s survivors will talk about the uncanny silence which follows the roar and the confusion of battle.

Three hours after the start of the engagement, when the dawn mists have developed into the symbiosis of a spring morning, the destroyers will give up the search.

Three days later, after torpedoes have been dropped by Swordfish aircraft and after an unprecedented effort and determined action on the part of some 100 Royal Navy ships, the *Bismark* will be sunk.

HMS *Dorsetshire* will pick up around eighty of the *Bismark*'s survivors, the *Maori* a handful of others. But the iron fist of fate will deliver more cruelty yet. During the rescue process, the captains of the *Dorsetshire* and the *Maori* will suspect that their ships are in imminent danger of attack from a German U-boat. The captains will ring for full speed ahead. *Bismark* survivors almost on board the *Dorsetshire* will be bundled over guard-rails onto the deck. Those halfway up ropes will find themselves trailing astern until, one by one, they will drop off. Sailors in the water will claw frantically at the paintwork as the ship's side slips by. One man, whose arms have been blown off and who survives by gripping a rope between his teeth, will be lost in the turmoil of foam and bubble induced by the exertion of the *Dorsetshire*'s screws at full power.

The *Bismark*'s crew, who have endured so much and who think they are within centimetres of rescue, will suddenly realize that they are to be abandoned. The cries of hundreds of men – seamen, chaplains, chefs, doctors, admirals, marines, stokers – floundering as they fight for breath will endure within the minds, the hearts . . . will monopolize the dreams of the *Dorsetshire*'s crew and those already rescued for the rest of their lives.

'See up there?' The picket boat's coxswain directs the midshipman's gaze to the *Hood*'s forecastle. Now at closer range, both men spot the sailors who mill about and point and wave at the *Repulse*'s liberty-men. As the picket boat moves beyond the moorings of the *Hood* and the *Dorsetshire* the coxswain and the midshipman see signs of disturbance amongst their liberty-men: the activity on the *Hood*'s forecastle appears to have stirred up their feelings.

On their port side now looms HMS *Norfolk*. If they maintain their present heading, the vessel will pass through a convenient gap in the fleet's mooring arrangement created by the *Warspite*'s earlier departure. A mile or so ahead is the *Valiant*. Some distance on the picket boat's starboard side is the southerly line of the mooring arrangement, but the boat is well clear of these ships.

The midshipman now gives an unexpected order: 'Turn starboard thirty, coxswain.'

'Starboard thirty, sir?' The coxswain glances at him; such a change will take them away from a direct course to the *Repulse*.

'Turn starboard thirty,' repeats the midshipman.

'Aye, aye, sir.' As the coxswain nods acknowledgement and turns the picket boat onto the required heading, he begins to appreciate the young midshipman's line of thought. The boat now moves towards a head sea; instead of an oblique angle, it attacks the waters directly. The vessel's movement alters from a rhythmic ride to a disagreeable series of jolts when the bow crashes against waves. Added to this is the effect of increased winds – the gales felt at the pier – now evident in the central areas of the Cromarty Firth. Each jolt causes salty waters to be flung up to the heavens before being caught by the breeze, generously fermented, then hurled at the picket boat in the form of torrential rain.

The liberty-men, attempting to protect themselves from the elements, fall silent as they huddle together. As the atmosphere becomes saturated, the conversations dry up. Similarly, the whistles, the pointing, the overall exuberance, become subdued. Issues of pay and general discontent are now subordinate to the vexation of the sailors' more immediate situation.

'Hold this, coxswain.' The midshipman, as he says this, sneaks a glance at the coxswain. The coxswain, in turn, looks briefly at the midshipman. Both men think they detect a look of amusement in the other's expression. No doubt both appreciate the benefit of this naval way of coping with a naval situation.

However, they themselves are not immune from the ferocity of nature. The picket boat's framework and their navy-issue clothing help to protect them, but both men wince as they feel the raw seas bite against fingers and hands, against ears and cheeks and other exposed areas of the face. All the crew grip the handrails tightly to steady themselves, although the men are hampered as the sprays compel them to half-close their eyes. As he tries to squint ahead, and as he struggles to wipe the waters from his face, the midshipman muses on how the frailty of humankind – even within the protected confines of the Cromarty Firth and despite best efforts – ultimately will succumb to the potency of the seas.

On one occasion as he mops spray from his eyes and, for a second or two, glances up to observe the skies, he is surprised to discover that even the ubiquitous gulls have vanished by now. They seem to have been devoured, their cries at once pitiful and haunting, swallowed into the mystical void, their lives cast aside like pieces of flotsam, existentialists absorbed into the greater mystery and now about to face the revelations of higher secrets: the enigmas of Neptune, of Poseidon, of the high-born Achilles, of his cruel mother the sea-nymph Thetis. He is shocked when he ponders this; how the once-boisterous gulls have been squandered to the gods, consumed by the elements without a trace of their former existence and this, it seems, for reasons as arcane as they were pitiless and heroic.

CHAPTER FOUR

Return to
HMS *Repulse*

The outline of HMS *Repulse* is by now merged with the sunless background of the South Suter hills. The coxswain steers the picket boat towards the ship's navigation lights but even as the boat draws near, *Repulse* is hard to make out in the grey of dusk. The evening light may hamper his efforts but gradually, framed within the illumination around the decking, the midshipman can identify the ship's profile – the masts stretching above the twin funnels, the six guns of 15 inch calibre, the extensive lines of portholes. More readily discernible is the twinkle of lights to the south which mark the town of Cromarty.

The midshipman has ordered a resumption of the picket boat's direct course; away from a head sea the vessel now rides the waves with ease. However, the liberty-men's spirits remain as damp and as miserable as their clothing. The midshipman sees how his passengers' expressions reflect their thoughts: the men glance at each other despondently from time to time although individuals, he thinks, still seem keen to avoid eye contact with him or with other members of the crew.

Before long, as the coxswain reduces speed, the engine's note dies down and the effervescence of the bow wave starts to peter out. The coxswain steers the boat towards the *Repulse*'s quarterdeck where, on the lee side, a landing ladder has been placed. The boat's bow man and stern-sheet man prepare to grab landing warps. With boat hooks at the ready the crew listen out for the midshipman's calls.

'Stand by for'ard.'

'Aye, aye, sir.'

'Stand by aft.'

'Aye, aye, sir.'

The ratings respond to his orders but, as he supervises the activities of his crew, the midshipman now begins to discern an unusual gathering on the *Repulse*'s deck. In normal times he would expect to see the quartermaster, distinguishable by the whistle attached to the chain around his neck (his bosun's call), act as the sole member of the reception party. The quartermaster, as the midshipman knows, would use the whistle in the event of difficulty: two quick blips would summon assistance from the duty officer. However, tonight it appears that trouble has been anticipated: the duty officer is there already. His figure looks tense as, with arms held smartly and formally behind his back, he stands with a number of marines near the top step of the landing ladder.

Soon, when the picket boat's crew have secured the vessel, and when the liberty-men have been ordered to disembark, the men climb up the ladder gloomily. Individual liberty-men, their attire still as sodden as their attitude is sullen, are noted by members of the reception party. Eventually, when the last passenger has stepped away from the boat, orders are given for the ladder to be hauled up and for derricks to be positioned for the picket boat stowage drill. Meanwhile the duty officer beckons the midshipman to one side.

'That run seemed to take rather longer than normal, Mister Sutton,' he says curtly. 'I assume you had one or two problems?'

'I'm afraid there was a considerable delay at the pier, sir.'

'I think I warned you that might be the case,' says the duty officer.

'At one point I was worried we may have to leave immediately and without the liberty-men.'

'Without the liberty-men? That would have been a little drastic would it not?'

'There was a state of anarchy ashore; the pier was overrun by crowds of sailors and the men were very unruly. They had worked themselves up into a state of fury as they discussed these pay cuts. I was concerned about the safety of vessel and crew.'

'Were there no patrols?'

'There was one patrol on the pier.'

'Surely they offered you assistance?' The duty officer lowers his voice and steps nearer to the midshipman to avoid being overheard.

'But the patrol itself was in difficulty; the members were surrounded.'

'Surrounded?'

'By irate ratings. The patrol members had to hold up batons to protect themselves. The warrant officer, in particular, was in danger; the mobs were threatening to seize him and to throw him in the sea. They wanted to vent their anger on someone. The nearest officer became their target.'

'My God . . . is that so?' The duty officer frowns as he deliberates. 'And was that the only patrol?' he asks at length.

'Another patrol appeared eventually but they were too far away and the light was too weak for me to see clearly. From nearby comments I gathered that a lieutenant commander was in charge. They hurried

towards the naval canteen at the north end of town; they seemed to
ignore the problems on the pier.'

'They must have had orders to close the canteen as quickly as
possible.'

'I think so.'

The duty officer falters; he seems to struggle with his thoughts before
asking: 'Were there any other picket boats?'

'Other picket boats were arriving as we left.'

'And your liberty-men turned up all right?'

'They took their time.'

'Was your run back uneventful?'

'Not exactly, sir.' The midshipman watches the quizzical eyes of the
other. 'We went close to the *Hood* and although it was hard to make out
at first, eventually we saw groups of sailors on her fo'c's'le. They were
milling around and pointing – similar to the men on the pier.'

'Are you sure? This light can be deceptive.'

'There was no mistake; we passed close by.'

'Of all ships . . .' says the duty officer shaking his head slowly.

'Why the *Hood* do you think?'

'Who knows?' This with a shrug of the shoulders. 'The *Hood* is
Admiral Tomkinson's flagship. Perhaps that was the point.'

'The situation does not look promising, sir.'

'No, indeed not. Admiral Tomkinson plans to have the other admirals
and all the captains to his dinner table tonight. Perhaps they'll decide
what action to take – how to handle this mess before things get further
out of hand.'

'They'll have a difficult task. The men are in belligerent mood.'

'And frankly there's not much Admiral Tomkinson can do without
support from the Admiralty and the government. But have you anything
else to report?'

'Just that . . .' The midshipman stops mid-sentence, interrupted by the
clatter of derricks being repositioned.

'Well?' says the duty officer after a pause.

'As we went by the *Hood*, and as the men on the fo'c's'le waved and
pointed at us, our liberty-men began to get unsettled.'

'They don't seem too bad just now.'

'But the matter was rather different as we passed by the *Hood*. The
passengers became agitated.'

'Inebriated perhaps? I'm afraid you have to get used to that sort of
behaviour Mister Sutton.'

'But it was more than that. It's true that some of the men were
the worse for wear, but there was something else as well; their attitude was . . .'

'So what did you do about it?'

'An old trick – a seaman's ruse – seemed to help the situation.'

'An old trick?' asks the duty officer. 'To calm down the liberty-men?'

'An alteration of course, sir.'

'What about it?'

'I ordered the coxswain to alter course – to aim for a head sea.'

'Oh,' says the duty officer with a nod. 'I thought that you all looked a bit damp and dejected. So who told you about this old trick?'

'It was mentioned at Devonport – one of the members of staff told us.'

'I see,' says the duty officer whose solemn expression breaks into a grin. 'I'm glad to hear that you paid attention at Devonport, Mister Sutton. Well done.'

'But I didn't expect this quite so early in my career.'

'To survive in the navy you'll have to learn to be adaptable.'

'I'm gaining that impression, sir.'

'But I think your duties have finished for today: you've surely done your bit. You'd better consider yourself off duty.'

'Thank you, sir.'

'You should get going now, ' says the duty officer brusquely. 'You'd better change out of that wet clothing.'

'Yes.'

'But one more thing before you leave. In view of these troubles, the captain has given specific orders: from now on you and the other midshipmen, while on duty, will be escorted by marines. Captain Cochrane is concerned that some of the ratings may try to molest junior officers. He's hopeful that this escorting routine won't have to last for long – that matters will quieten down soon – but he's deemed it a necessary precaution for the present.'

'That's understood, sir.'

'Now may I suggest that you get ready for this evening. Midshipmen have been invited to the wardroom to join officers for pre-dinner drinks. You've got about half an hour before the officers start to assemble. The dress, as I expect you know, will be mess undress. No doubt I'll see you in the wardroom later.'

'Shall I help with the picket boat stowage drill?'

'Don't worry, Mister Sutton. The crew will see to it.'

The midshipman salutes before he hurries away. He makes first for a designated drying area where he peels off his outer clothing, his oilskins and his duffel coat, before he drapes them next to heated pipe-work. He then sets off for the midshipmen's living quarters in the gunroom sector below the quarter deck. As he wends his way through chest flats to find his allocated space – a chest of drawers for his personal belongings and a place where his hammock can be slung – he comes across a number of other midshipmen now donning traditional naval dress for pre-dinner drinks. The atmosphere, he realizes, is more convivial than elsewhere; he hears excited laughter and badinage as the young officers prepare for the formality that customarily accompanies an invitation to the ward-room.

'Alfie?' says a fellow midshipman as he spots his colleague and, with a grin, uses the sobriquet first coined at Devonport (one which will stay with Midshipman Sutton for the rest of his naval career). 'You look a bit bedraggled, old chap. What have you been up to?'

'Well, well,' says Alfie coughing lightly, 'I've been here and there in my picket boat – one man's attempt to keep His Majesty's Royal Navy afloat. Someone has to do it.'

'I knew it; I always knew you had it in you. And did you get on all right?'

'There was trouble at the Invergordon landing pier.'

'There's trouble everywhere, Alfie.' He pauses. 'But no more bad news – I've heard nothing but gloomy news all day. Let's talk about cheerful things. Did you see any beautiful girls?'

'Beautiful girls? At Invergordon?'

'You know, those delicate creatures with . . .'

'You've been dreaming again, Charles.'

'Have I?' Charles' eyes narrow as he stares into the distance. 'But just think . . .' he hesitates. 'Fair of face – kindred souls to summon the best of things: life's riches . . . the green fields under cloudless skies . . . the warmth of an open fire . . . the colours of an autumn sunset . . .'

'You *have* been dreaming again.'

'Are you certain, Alfie? How disappointing.'

'I saw plenty of disgruntled sailors.'

'I can believe it.' Charles grimaces. 'The world has become topsy-turvy.'

'But when it comes to beautiful girls, Charles, what makes you so sure about Invergordon?'

'Actually, I'm not so sure; I've never looked at the place properly. Presumably there are some Scottish lassies in the vicinity . . . there are bound to be some, aren't there? They'll be there to help with celebrations – Robbie Burns and all that.'

'Never heard of the fellow. Or have I?'

'Didn't he join the navy and write poetry?'

'The navy? I don't think the navy appreciated his poetry.'

'So what did he do, Alfie?'

'Perhaps he became a customs official instead.'

'Now I recall . . . *The dei'ls awah with the exciseman . . .*'

'By Jove!' says Alfie. 'Did he have a serious face and a beard?'

'Everyone had beards in those days.'

'Does this affect the Burns' night celebrations?'

'We'll have to wait until January and by then the beautiful girls will have disappeared – taken by others.'

'Take heart, Charles, and remember this: if you're to succeed in the navy you'll have to learn to be adaptable. Ask the duty officer; he'll tell you about it.'

'I've heard rumours that he doesn't approve of kilts – that they don't look good under navy-issue duffel coats.' Alfie's expression turns to a smile, but Charles continues with a serious face: 'And I've heard that he's not keen on Burns, that he can't stand bagpipes, porridge makes him feel sick, whisky gives him a headache and he couldn't, apparently, care less about Scottish dancing. It seems that he'd rather whirl to the paso doble or the Charleston.'

'Then we'll have to hope he avoids this latest fashion for the sailor's hornpipe *sur les pointes*. But what about the haircut?' says Alfie. 'One, say, with a tartan emphasis?'

'Tartan or Spartan?'

'Either.'

'Possibly not. No, definitely not. Too ostentatious.'

'Or beard?'

'Not even that; and I don't think I like the sound of the navy any more, Alfie. Where's the fun?'

'You could grow a beard of your own.'

'I'm trying to do that already.'

'Just keep trying, Charles.'

'Thank you.'

'Will the captain allow it?'

'Allow what?'

'Allow you to grow a beard?'

'The question,' says Charles looking bashful, 'is theoretical *pro tempore*. But you must be hungry after your picket boat duties; have you heard what's on the menu tonight, old fellow?'

'Are the cooks still working?'

'If the cooks decide to mutiny we're in real trouble.'

'I think, Charles, that I'd like a change from bully beef.'

'Perhaps we'll be given a naval treat this evening.' Charles assumes a pensive air. 'Maybe the beef will be in the form of *Boeuf Bourguignonne* – lightly seasoned with herbs and garnished with cubes of bacon, small onions and mushrooms.'

'Why do we always have to eat bully beef?' says Alfie. 'Shouldn't we be given more variety? What, for example, about braised venison with julienne strips of parsnip and carrot?'

'Not bad, not bad. And for your first course?'

'Perhaps a soup of chanterelle and leek.'

'Is that ideal for September, Alfie?' Charles' eyes glaze over as he peers into the distance. 'Maybe a feuilleté of mushroom and cheese would be more appropriate.'

'I'm not so sure.'

'What else then?'

'We're entitled to pork once a month but only in the winter months. There's something about an 'r' in the month.'

'Then September should count.' Charles brightens as he says this.

'Come back Mother Beaton – we'll forgive you for everything.'

'Anyway, I fancy—'

'One must stop this dreaming, Charles, it won't get us anywhere.'

'But I fancy—'

'Never mind that. Tell me, though, Charles: what made you join the navy?'

'It's the same all over, isn't it?' Charles sighs. 'The icy blast of economic reality.'

'Was that the only reason?'

'I confess, in truth, it was the main reason.'

'So you were forced into the navy by press gangs?'

'The modern-day version of the press gangs, I suppose.' Charles ponders for a moment or two before he continues: 'At the turn of the century my grandfather was something in the City – a successful financier – but our family fortunes began to decline after the Great War. We had to move several times; we lived in a series of homes, each one smaller than the last, and we had to shed servants on the way. In the end my father – he's a doctor – had to sell his car, his treasured possession, to help pay my boarding school fees.'

'And when you'd finished at school, did he insist that you joined the navy?'

'He didn't want me to become mixed up in the world of the rich and indolent. He said he couldn't afford to support me. He thought that their lifestyle was immoral in a country with so many on the poverty line and with more than two million unemployed. He told me, Alfie, that one of my forebears used to be a captain in the navy under Nelson. He felt it would be an appropriate career for me.'

'But you were not keen on the idea yourself?'

'Yes and no.'

'What about the selection board?'

'What about it?'

'Did they ask searching questions?'

'It was probably the same with you, Alfie. The selection board were interested in where I went to school, about my family background, that sort of thing. And the officers' eyes lit up when I mentioned my ancestry; I was soon given the nod of approval. As for the medical examination, when the doctor scrutinized my notes and when he spotted that my father was a doctor, he said: "There can't be much wrong with you, young man," and he didn't bother to examine me further.'

'You look fit enough to me, Charles.'

'Nevertheless, as I left the medical examination room I turned to him and said: "My father, by the way, is not a medical doctor. He's a doctor of chemistry."'

'And what was the reaction?'

' "Oh well ," he says, "it's too late now. You'd better disappear quickly before I change my mind." '

'It's hardly our fault, Charles, that the timing is poor. This must be the worst of times to start a naval career.'

'From my present perspective,' says Charles gloomily, 'the rich and indolent life looks an attractive option.'

'Cheer up, Charles. Things are not that bad; remember we live in exceptional times.'

'Are they that exceptional? Or is the navy in the process of changing for ever? Perhaps those disturbances at the Invergordon pier were a sign of things to come.'

'They were ugly scenes, it's true. But this business cannot go on; surely things will improve before long.'

'Unless, that is, this country goes to war. Is the navy – is the country – well enough prepared for another war? It makes you wonder, Alfie, especially with these signs of trouble in Germany brewing up again.'

'So if the country does become embroiled in another war, how would you feel then about being in the navy?'

'I wouldn't mind that, actually – I'm not afraid to do my bit for king and country.' Charles glances at the other. 'But how would you feel, Alfie? What made you join the navy?'

'A number of reasons, I suppose.' Alfie angles his head as he reflects. 'I happened to meet Admiral Beatty one time. I was at a tea party he attended; it turned out to be a fortuitous meeting.'

'What did you think of the grand gentleman?'

'He was grand; a powerful character; he made me think about the prospects of a life at sea.'

'Did your father insist that you joined?'

'My father was killed in the Great War.'

'I'm sorry, Alfie. I didn't realize . . .'

'It's all right, Charles. There are many like me, are there not? And incidentally, your family was not alone in suffering financial hardship. The fortunes of my own family were squandered by spendthrifts, so the idea of a naval officer's income had appeal for me.'

'With these pay cuts we're unlikely to be in a position to get very far.'

'But we must hurry now, Charles. Time presses and I must clean up before changing for dinner.'

'I trust your shirt isn't crushed?'

'Or my monkey jacket or my trousers. How are we supposed to keep spruced up and shipshape with kit stored in these chests?'

'It's part of the challenge.'

'The challenge?'

'Yes, the challenge.' Charles looks smug as he goes on with a chuckle: 'And remember this, Alfie: you'll have to learn to be adaptable if you're to survive in the navy.'

'Thank you, Charles. Thank you for those few kind words.'

CHAPTER FIVE

Wardroom Worries

A rmed marines escort the group of midshipmen from their living quarters to the wardroom. The young men – amongst other matters anxious that their regulation mess undress should be correctly adjusted – appear apprehensive when they enter the anteroom area of the *Repulse*'s wardroom, by now crowded with officers. The 'snotties' nurse – a lieutenant commander assigned to oversee the general training and welfare of the eighteen or so midshipmen – walks across to greet them: 'Good evening, gentlemen. Your bow ties, I trust, are pukka and not pre-made up? Are your trousers smartly pressed, your shirts uncreased? That's good; well done. But don't huddle together now; help yourselves to a glass of sherry if you wish, then try to mix with the other officers.' He waves his hand towards the assembled company. 'As you know, we're a newly commissioned crew on this ship and we must make an effort to get to know one another. Unfortunately there are no ladies present this evening but you're no doubt aware that we do invite ladies on occasions. The navy prides itself on good hospitality. These formal wardroom functions are part of our tradition; they're a necessary – and hopefully pleasurable – side to your naval training. Officers are glad,' he says with a courteous bow of the head, 'to invite midshipmen to join them in the wardroom from time to time. At least it will make a change from your normal routine in the midshipmen's mess.'

Midshipman Sutton detaches himself from the group and heads for another area of the anteroom. A lieutenant commander is speaking: 'One can hardly condone these disturbances,' he says, 'but in many respects I feel sorry for the men. There are cases of real hardship. Individuals often have no choice but to supplement their naval incomes by other means.'

'They have to rely on their wives, for instance?' says an officer.

'That seems to be the upshot for many. But there are various opportunities – the *dhobi* firms for instance. Some of the men do quite well out of them.'

'The schemes can be most ingenious but it's hardly right that the men should have to depend on them.'

'May I ask, sir,' says Midshipman Sutton with a polite cough, 'about the navy's attitude to these *dhobi* firms?'

'Why, good evening Mister Sutton,' says the lieutenant commander turning to face the midshipman. 'I hear you've been gadding around in your picket boat in an effort to sort out our liberty-men.'

'That was the general idea, sir.'

'You had problems I understand.'

'The Invergordon landing pier was in a state of uproar.'

'Yes, so I've heard. The duty officer has briefed us about your experience. I gather the place had been taken over by unruly seamen.'

'There were some unpleasant scenes, I'm afraid.'

'It's most worrying,' says the lieutenant commander shaking his head. 'But I was told that you coped well with the situation, so full marks for that. As for tomorrow morning, I suppose we'll just have to wait to see what happens. It's not looking hopeful, though.'

'The men seem quite determined.'

'One can hardly blame them really; a lot of the men are severely hard up. Hence these *dhobi* firms of course . . . and to answer your question: no special permission is needed for the time-honoured *dhobi* system – taking in other peoples' laundry.'

'There are other schemes?'

'It's astonishing what goes on within a large ship.'

'With a crew of a thousand or more, I suppose a warship is the equivalent of a small town,' says the midshipman.

'Just keep your eyes open, young man, and you'll be amazed by what goes on.' The lieutenant commander's voice becomes confidential . 'Some of the activities are pursued, shall we say, in a discreet way. Nowadays, though, men can apply for permission to run all kinds of so-called firms. Permission is usually granted as long as there's no interference with duties. Some of the men show creditable enterprise – darts, cards, barbers, fortune-tellers, footwear shops, goodness knows what. All at a price, of course. As a new crew, things have yet to settle down on this ship, but elsewhere in the navy I've seen extraordinary diversity.'

'On my last ship,' says an officer cheerily, 'we had a skilled artist. He would set up shop in a particular gun emplacement and sell his paintings to shipmates. His portrait work was first-rate and he became well known for his line in photographs, birthday cards, Christmas cards, that sort of thing.'

'Then there's old Scratcher Sam.'

'Scratcher Sam?'

'There's normally one on every ship: a tattoo artist. Although in some cases I'm not so sure that 'artist' is a very appropriate term.'

'You'll even come across the "court sort" on some ships – so-called legal beagles who'll help write wills, check hire purchase agreements and sort out typical sailors' problems.'

'I heard of a court sort recently,' chuckles an officer, 'who was, as they say, caught short.'

'Perhaps he should have been referred to the Stinker Stevens-types of this world.'

'Good old Stinker; we mustn't forget about him.'

'What the deuce . . . ?' says the midshipman.

'On second thoughts perhaps you *should* forget about him.'

'We had a leading hand on my previous ship,' says an officer, 'who was a cigarette maker. His cigarettes were somewhat eccentric – in fact they tasted, well—' he gesticulates with one hand, '—as if they'd been nurtured in the backyard of a Baghdad brothel. But at least they were cheap.'

'Tapestry work is another favourite,' says the lieutenant commander. 'It's amusing to see the reaction of some of the younger men: they'll laugh at the artistic flair of long-service colleagues. The three-badge "Barnacle Bills" will clout the youngsters for cheek, but then needs must; the old hands will be highly proficient when they get down to work with needle and thread and sewing machine.'

'I suppose they've been taught tricks of the trade by their wives.'

'Some of the experienced sailors show astonishing dexterity.'

'Their wives will have to rely on it, no doubt. In certain cases the women are in desperate situations; the husbands have little choice but to run some sort of a firm, *dhobi* or otherwise,' says an officer grimly.

'It's true that the married men are the worst off.'

'Especially if they're aged under twenty-five. These men receive no marriage allowance and a number of them find it well-nigh impossible to make ends meet.'

'Aren't the Admiralty aware of what's going on?' asks the midshipman.

'The Admiralty seem to take advantage of Nelson's proverbial blind eye. The situation is a disgrace, actually.'

'A lot of the men,' says an officer, 'have to buy furniture on hire purchase and they become locked in to dubious deals.' He frowns and goes on: 'There are plenty of unscrupulous salesmen around the home ports.'

'In my experience,' says the lieutenant commander, 'these hire purchase arrangements are a common cause of serious trouble.'

'Some of the families end up being chased for money by bailiffs. And with these pay cuts it's quite likely that furniture will have to be repossessed. It wouldn't surprise me if some families are faced with eviction and the wives will have to apply to a naval charity for help.'

'Naval charity?' asks the midshipman.

'There are a number of naval benefit and welfare societies. For instance, there's the Royal and Ancient Order of Buffaloes. Then the Royal Navy Benevolent Trust tries to help out where it can.'

'Until recently,' says the lieutenant commander, 'our commander's writer – clerk – helped to run the Chatham branch of the RNBT. He said he had to deal with pitiful cases; some of the wives were in a terrible state. He was authorized to hand out five shillings a week for up to six weeks, but after that the wives had to return to fending for themselves.' He shakes his head slowly. 'Many of the women were practically penniless; they had to resort to dire measures to feed their children.'

'It's well known what goes on in Plymouth.'

'Some of the landladies there are appalled by what they see. The kind-hearted ones offer free Sunday meals to the wives and children.'

'I sometimes wonder,' says an officer, 'why any woman would want to marry a sailor.'

'Perhaps it's to do with the uniform.'

'I can't think of many other reasons.'

'Oh, I don't know. Just think of the dash and the panache.'

'I've been married for eleven years,' says an older officer brightly. 'My wife and I have managed all right. Mind you, some of the foreign commissions have been difficult. You can be away for a couple of years and it can be very unsettling when you hear about problems at home and you're unable to do anything to help. If the navy reckon you make too much fuss, there's a black mark on your record. I've had to strive hard to avoid blotting my naval copybook.' He turns to the midshipman to explain: 'I came up through the "hawse hole" – the link between the fore-castle and the quarterdeck in a traditional wooden ship. In other words, I started life in the lower decks and worked for promotion to commissioned rank.'

'Not many seem to make it,' says the lieutenant commander with an approving nod. 'So due credit to you.'

'In general that's the outlook of other officers. Unfortunately, though, the lower decks don't have the same attitude. Men feel that I've strayed into territory where I don't belong; that I have delusions of grandeur. It can make matters difficult, especially at times like these and with the events of today.'

'I'm sure the men respect your overall experience in the navy,' says the lieutenant commander. 'And surely the incentive of commissioned rank encourages individuals to work hard. Amongst other things, there's the opportunity to resolve financial problems.'

'I've been attempting to save up to buy a car,' says the officer. 'But I'm not so sure that I'll manage it now.'

'Because of the pay cuts?'

'Partly that, but also thanks to that ridiculous Road Traffic Act which, if you recall, the government introduced in January.' He frowns. 'Why are our politicians so inept? Why do we have to be lumbered with such hopeless characters? Their recent announcement about petrol tax was just about the last straw.'

'What's the cost of petrol now?'

'One shilling and fourpence halfpenny will buy a gallon of the stuff. The situation is absurd: to fill a car's tank you'll need about half the weekly wage of an able seaman.'

'Do you intend to buy a Bentley or something?' says the lieutenant commander.

'That would be ideal, wouldn't it? The perfect machine . . . apart from one small problem.'

'A problem with a Bentley?'

'Bentley Motors went into receivership in July.'

'Then you could buy a Rolls-Royce instead.'

'A Rolls-Royce? Actually I had a Ford T in mind.'

'A Model T?'

'Why not?'

'They stopped Model T production four years ago.'

'There are plenty of second-hand machines.'

'Have you thought about reliability?' chuckles an officer. 'You might be keen to complete your journey one day.'

The group laugh and the midshipman, as he looks around the ward-room, spots a flicker of illumination from the town of Cromarty. He glances through a nearby porthole to observe the sparkle of the town's lights: the isolated brilliance clashes with the general air of exterior gloominess. He stares through the porthole for some seconds. As he returns his gaze back to the wardroom, he notes the comfortable furnish-ings – the pictures of sailing vessels, their dignity quietly apparent as hulls slice elegantly through the seas of yesteryear, the pieces of mess silver placed on furniture tops, the neat rows of newspapers and maga-zines on the top of a polished mahogany table.

He discerns the wardroom's particular ambience, how this conforms with the correct-looking figures of officers who stand in groups, their demeanour well groomed, their voices appropriately calm as they chat about varied subjects. He ponders the disparity: the officers' world so many leagues away from the conditions of the lower deck. He sees the marines who stand placidly in different parts of the room as, in their secondary role, they now act as mess stewards – wardroom attendants. These are trusted men; sworn men who, unlike the seamen, do not have to remove headgear when they receive their pay. These are the officers' bodyguards who, in the days of press gangs, were seen as a necessary buffer between decks.

Marines do not perceive themselves as being in the navy. They are members of a regiment and their mess deck is referred to as 'barracks'. Ratings of old used to joke that officers without the protection of marines were in danger of being eaten up by the lower decks. But are matters so very different just now? The captain, after all, has had to give these orders to prevent molestation of junior officers.

Midshipman Sutton would be shocked to know that tomorrow on certain ships marines will barricade themselves to avoid violent confrontation. On one battleship, when the captain of marines attempts to extract his men from barracks, he will be ordered back by other officers: 'You'll be killed if you go in there,' he will be told.

'And how about you, Mister Sutton?' says the lieutenant commander.

'Sir?'

'Do you harbour ambitions to buy a car?'

'Not really, sir. I'd like to afford a motor cycle eventually. A Triumph or a Harley Davidson would do the trick nicely.'

'Questionable machines these motor cycles, if you ask me,' says an officer. 'And I'm not so sure that owning one is the done thing, don't you know? Especially, that is, for a naval officer. You could always,' he adds with a wink, 'think about joining the air force. I'm sure that air force types would have no objection to your owning a motor cycle.'

'Well, well,' says the lieutenant commander, 'until they sort out this pay shambles it's all fairly hypothetical anyway.'

'Talking about the air force,' says an officer. 'Has anyone been to one of these air pageants at Hendon? They hold them in the summer months and I took my young son to one recently.'

'That was a bit rash, was it not?'

'I would recommend it: the Royal Air Force fellows put on an excellent display. Some of the de Havilland Moths took off and performed aerobatics with, as the saying goes, strings attached: their wings were tied together.'

'Tied together? Surely that was even more rash?'

'At one point we saw a kite balloon being brought down in flames and then there were mock dogfights between aircraft.'

'I've had joyrides in civil aeroplanes,' says the midshipman, 'but I'd like to have a flight in a military machine. It would surely be an exciting experience.'

'Great Scott, man, I was only joking just now. You'd better have another glass of sherry. Steward?'

There's more laughter from the group as a marine attendant, who clutches a silver salver laden with filled glasses, is beckoned across. The midshipman sees the man's serious expression as he offers drinks to the officers. What, he wonders, must be running through the marine's mind just now? The officers enjoy the banter but they understand that the expressions of joviality are, in part, an expedient to relieve the tensions of the moment.

As the midshipman speculates on the feelings of the marines, he realizes that the aloofness often attributed to officers – that sense of being a class apart – has a further unattractive twist: the officers stand accused of not caring about their men. Ships' captains, for instance, are notoriously detached, not even dining with their fellow officers unless by special invitation. They have to rely on their commanders for the efficient day-to-day running of ships. A good commander will bring a ship's company together, but crew morale will deteriorate swiftly in the hands of a poor one.

Once a week, usually on a Sunday, the captain will walk around his ship on a tour of inspection and then ratings, if they are lucky, may catch a glimpse of their exalted leader. Otherwise the captains will remain in their quarters, in lonely isolation, until needed on the bridge. Their link with the rest of the crew is often achieved through contact with servants: a good messenger boy will relay ship's gossip to the captain. Captain Custance of HMS *York* was severely embarrassed last weekend, but over the next few days other officers will be appalled to learn of the extent of the ratings' aversion towards captains.

Even the divisional officer system – whereby ratings may apply in writing to speak with their divisional officer – is seen as flawed and unpopular. Applications have to be vetted by the master-at-arms and the divisional petty officer before access to a divisional officer is permitted. A divisional officer may have as many as 150 men on his division, and a busy officer will not welcome his time being taken up. If a sailor wishes to complain, he has to go through the officer of the watch, who will make a note on the commander's report before the complaint is passed to the captain. Further discouragement is generated by Admiralty Orders: a complainer has to be warned that there must be reasonable grounds for his grievance, otherwise he is liable to be treated as having made a 'frivolous or vexatious complaint which is deemed to be an act to the prejudice of good order and naval discipline.'

'Good God,' says an officer as he lifts up his sherry glass to study the contents. 'Call this sherry? Where do they manage to drag up the stuff?'

'You'd better stick to the rum, old chap.'

'And what's on the menu tonight, I wonder?'

'We were discussing that in the midshipman's quarters,' says the midshipman.

'I trust you approve of naval food?' says the lieutenant commander.

'There were mutterings about bully beef.'

'Were there indeed? You'll have to get used to such delicacies in the navy, you know.'

'There's this new general messing system,' says an officer. 'Supposedly it will improve the quality of our food.'

'It's probably another economy measure. Economy, economy; that's all we hear about these days.'

'We'd better watch out in case the cooks have poisoned our food,' says another officer half-jokingly.

'We could try out the food on the midshipmen first.'

'Good idea.'

'Thank you,' says the midshipman. 'I'm sure we are keen to our duty.'

'That's the idea, my lad. Just do your bit for king and country and you won't go far wrong.'

'Oh look,' says an officer as he spots a senior attendant enter the ante-room from the direction of the dining room. 'Grub's up.'

The hum of conversation temporarily quietens as the senior attendant announces that dinner is served. The assembled officers glance up before they resume their conversations and then, in a leisurely manner, start to ease their way towards the dining room. The conversations, notes the midshipman, continue regardless. Most officers, it seems, are determined to put the immediate problems to the backs of their minds, to deprecate the lower-deck trouble that is about to engulf them. The frenetic scenes at the Invergordon pier, the calm urbanity of the wardroom conversations – the midshipman sees how, at this moment, latent fractures within the naval structure are revealed.

These officers, though, should hardly be blamed for the navy's inadequacies. They are individuals who have inherited a system handed down through generations and who, haplessly, are about to be placed on the spot. Nonetheless, in the next few days they will be made directly aware, in some cases cruelly so, of the new naval realities. The morale of many will become shattered. No doubt this will include the officers who, on certain ships, will have the comfort of their sleep disturbed by the turmoil below deck. Some will feel obliged to keep revolvers concealed under pillows. Some may even feel the need to keep fingers loosely clasping the triggers of those service-issue weapons.

CHAPTER SIX

Night of the Knives

'It's hard to know what to make of the fellow . . .' the officer near Midshipman Sutton falters as he enters the gunroom. The midshipman and his colleagues, whose invitation to pre-dinner drinks in the wardroom did not extend to dinner there, all withdrew when dinner was announced. Now they are making for the dining area of the midshipmen's mess. A few officers, including their lieutenant commander in charge – the 'snotties' nurse – have been invited to join their protégés. The dining tables in the gun room have been prepared by marine attendants: folded napkins, carefully placed cutlery, polished glasses, a few items of mess silver give a smart impression to replicate wardroom life. 'Except that . . .' The officer hesitates again as he looks around the midshipmen and their guests standing behind their chairs. A few conversations persist but eventually peter out when the lieutenant commander bangs a gavel and calls: 'Grace please, padre.'

'For what we are about to receive,' says the padre with head lowered, 'may the Lord make us truly thankful.'

'And so say all of us,' mutters the officer next to Midshipman Sutton, 'especially tonight of all nights.'

An experienced-looking lieutenant glances around amiably as he says: 'Was there talk of gallant young midshipmen tasting the food before their guests?'

'Will that do any good?' says Midshipman Sutton's neighbour, a member of the naval education branch. 'Won't it take five days or more for the effects of poison to be felt by the average midshipman?' He chortles and sneaks a glance at Midshipman Sutton. The midshipman bows his head in response to the general laughter. 'No,' continues the officer, 'I see little alternative. We'll all just have to take our chances. By the way,' he goes on, 'there'll be a bit of a delay before our food is served tonight. There's been a spot of trouble in the galley, though it seems the cooks are working as normal. The wardroom will get their food first, then us. Never mind; we're surely allowed to talk a bit of shop under these – um – exceptional circumstances. We'll have to make good naval conversation while we're waiting. What were we discussing a moment ago?'

'Something about Mr Churchill?' says Midshipman Sutton.

'Oh, yes; so we were. It's hard to know what to make of the fellow, isn't it? What did they tell you about him at Devonport, Mister Sutton?'

'They told us that he was just thirty-six years old when he was made First Lord of the Admiralty in 1911.'

'Did they indeed? I suppose that was a fair point. Clearly the man was talented, but then some of the measures he introduced . . .'

'He started, in effect, a revolution,' says the experienced-looking lieutenant.

'Nothing to beat a good revolution,' says Midshipman Sutton's neighbour with a wink. 'The French are especially good at them, don't you know. Round and round in circles, what?' He grins.

'When Churchill became First Lord of the Admiralty,' goes on the experienced lieutenant, 'he was determined to upgrade the capability of the navy's battleships. The *Dreadnought* story, for instance, puts the matter in context.'

'Ah! The *Dreadnought* story,' the education officer sighs nostalgically.

'It was some time before Churchill became First Lord,' says the lieutenant, 'but I remember the occasion when the *Dreadnought* first slipped out of Portsmouth Harbour for sea trials. It was exactly a year and a day after her keel was laid in October 1905.' The lieutenant's expression becomes far-off. 'I was just a lad in those days, but I still recollect the fuss created by the *Dreadnought* episode. New techniques were used to speed up her construction and when she was launched, all the older battleships were rendered obsolete at a stroke. Not only did the *Dreadnought* have ten twelve-inch guns capable of firing a broadside twice the weight of any previous battleship, but she was the first warship of her size to be powered by turbine. Even so, Churchill sought a further revolution when he appeared on the naval scene: he was determined to improve on the potential of the *Dreadnought*. He wanted to make battleships as far ahead of *Dreadnought* as that ship had been ahead of her predecessors.'

'Was that when another class was created?' asks a midshipman.

'Indeed it was,' says the lieutenant with a nod of approval. 'The Queen Elizabeth class introduced a fast division of five battleships. One ship took the name *Queen Elizabeth*; the others were named the *Warspite* and the *Malaya* – which, as you know, left for exercises earlier today – then came the *Barham* and the *Valiant*. You can perhaps recollect, Mister Sutton, the particular innovation of these ships.'

'Something to do with the armament, sir?'

The lieutenant nods again and goes on: '15 inch guns were introduced, although there was a certain snag: the greater weight of the new guns meant the sacrifice of one turret. However, there was powerful compensation: eight guns in a broadside could throw shells weighing a ton or more an incredible distance – about 20 miles.'

'I suppose we've become used to the idea nowadays,' says the education officer, 'but at the time the thought of flinging a massive shell over such a distance was indeed revolutionary.'

'But then Churchill was worried about developments in other navies,' continues the lieutenant. 'In particular the well-armed, well-trained German High Seas Fleet was itself revolutionary.'

'Although the British and the Germans were supposedly on friendly terms at that stage.'

'Indeed they were, and it was presumably with this in mind that, just before the start of the Great War – and three years after he became First Lord – Churchill authorized a fleet visit to Germany. That visit, if you cast your minds back, became an opportunity for the Royal Navy to witness a most extraordinary event: the famous Kiel regatta of 1914.'

'They briefed us about it at Devonport,' says a midshipman.

'I wonder if they told you about the Austrian countess?'

'I don't think . . .'

'Again, I was just a lad, but I still recall the tale,' says the lieutenant. He leans forward on his elbows and looks around. 'I haven't met the fellow,' he continues, 'but I have a friend who knows him: Lieutenant King-Hall from HMS *Southampton*. He was one of the officers to observe at first hand the dramatic events of the Kiel regatta. He was invited one afternoon to a tea dance as a guest on board a German battleship. He told how, at about five o'clock, the band suddenly stopped playing and the ship's captain marched onto the dais. With a sombre expression he announced that Archduke Franz Ferdinand, heir to the Austro-Hungarian Imperial Throne, had been assassinated at Sarajevo. There was a stunned silence during which the quiet weeping of an Austrian countess could be heard.' The lieutenant hesitates.

'Sir?' says a midshipman meekly.

'Sorry,' says the lieutenant, 'I was lost in thought for a moment. This countess was seated at the same table as King-Hall. When the news of the assassination was announced, and with her eyes full of tears, she said to him: "We shall never meet again. This will mean war."'

'How correct she was,' says an officer quietly, 'how tragically correct.'

'Was that the end of the fleet visit, sir?' asks a midshipman.

'Not exactly.' The lieutenant leans back in his chair. 'The Kaiser, who was taking part in a sailing race, ordered that the race be cancelled but that other social engagements should be allowed to carry on. The commander of the British squadron, Vice-Admiral George Warrender, subsequently attended a party given by the Royal Navy for their German hosts. He seemed to get a bit carried away: he climbed onto a table from where he gave an enthusiastic speech about the friendship of the two nations, Britain and Germany. His speech ended with three cheers for the German navy and he shook hands with his German counterpart, Admiral Mauwe, amidst much hand-clapping and foot-stamping.'

'With the benefit of hindsight,' says an officer, 'it all seems so ironic.'

'The fleet visit wound down after that, and The Times reported that it "had been a great success and gave fine proof of naval comradeship the world over and of German hospitality".'

'And then,' says the education officer glancing at his listeners, 'came that famous signal.'

'Famous signal?' says a midshipman.

'As the British squadron steamed out of Kiel harbour,' says the lieutenant, 'Admiral Warrender – he was known as 'Gentleman George' – radioed a parting message to his hosts and brothers in arms. In view of the critical international situation of the time, his message must go down as one of the most unguarded signals in history. He said: "Friends in past and friends for ever."'

'It was the last day of June, 1914,' says the education officer. 'And within five weeks the two navies were at war.'

'I wonder—' says Midshipman Sutton but he is interrupted when a marine attendant leans forward to place a bowl of soup on the table.

'Ah! Soup at last,' cries the 'snotties' nurse.

The attendant positions the bowl carefully then withdraws his hand. The midshipman notes the attendant's impassive expression. The men have exchanged their marine uniforms for the white coats of stewards and unsmiling faces betray a no-nonsense attitude as the marines carry out their duties. With their bulk – most are over 6 ft tall and heavily built – the men seem to make unlikely waiters. The midshipman muses that if anyone is going to eat up the officers, these individuals look like ideal contenders. The stewards, though, act under the close supervision of a marine sergeant.

'You were wondering, Mister Sutton?' says the lieutenant, eyebrows raised.

'I just wondered about Churchill's reaction to the Kiel saga.'

'I suspect Mr Churchill had other things to worry about.'

'He was, I seem to recollect,' says the education officer, 'in the habit of eccentric pondering.'

'At least there was a politician who gave thought to matters.'

'Bath!' cries the education officer.

'Bath?'

'He was in the habit of ruminating in his bath.'

'And why not?'

'There was the episode when he was caught out if you remember. He had to be summoned from his bath to the war room.'

'You're right,' says the lieutenant. 'It was just before the first Christmas of the war and the Germans had decided, in their wisdom, to bombard Scarborough.'

'Scarborough?'

'Well, Whitby and Hartlepool too. The enemy raiders, so recently eulogized by Gentleman George, appeared out of the early mists of that December morning and began to launch an attack on our people. Hundreds of shells were directed at innocent civilians. After the events at Kiel this was considered—' the lieutenant shakes one finger sternly, '—most ill-mannered. Children were on the streets and on their way to school. Shops were opening up; life was in the process of stirring. Naturally there was panic – one moment peace, the next chaos, with mayhem raining down from the skies. If my memory is correct, I think over 100 souls were killed and 300 wounded. It was a terrifying and terrible incident.'

'No wonder Churchill was summoned from his bath in a hurry.'

'When an officer rushed from the war room to Churchill's bathroom with news of the bombardment, the First Lord grasped the note with shaking – and dripping – hand. He jumped out of his bath, pulled clothes over his damp body, and dashed downstairs to the war room.'

A buzz of amusement spreads, then the conversation subsides as the officers and midshipmen begin to consume their soup. Midshipman Sutton, as he observes the officers, considers wryly how the pact for first tasting by midshipmen appears to have been overlooked. He notices, too, that most of the officers hold their spoons in a particular manner. He ponders the fierce requirements of social etiquette. A person's upbringing, he thinks, can be cruelly revealed by table manners. Perhaps, out of interest, he should try something unusual. He could test the officers' reaction. Would anyone, for example, notice if he turned his spoon the wrong way up? Possibly . . .

'Are you enjoying your soup, Mister Sutton?' The 'snotties' nurse glances across.

'Vegetable soup, sir? Yes, very—'

'Who said anything about vegetable?'

'I thought . . .'

'If anything remotely resembling a vegetable has been waved at this pot – even fleetingly – it would surely count as a miracle.'

'Then what . . . ?'

'Don't ask, young man. Think about things naval rather than about the food in front of you. It will be a lot safer.'

'And a lot more interesting,' chuckles the education officer.

'Quite right,' says the experienced lieutenant. He puts his soup spoon down and goes on: 'Which means we should finish the tale about the east coast raids and the untimely conclusion of Churchill's bath.'

'I believe the Germans were pursued,' says a midshipman.

'The background to the pursuit is of particular interest,' says the lieutenant. 'A month or two before the raids, a new branch of the Royal Naval Intelligence Division – hand-picked individuals – had tried without success to decipher German wireless signals. Then, by chance, they received a piece of vital information. A German light cruiser, the *Magdeburg*, had run aground in the Baltic. To avoid the capture of her code book, it was weighted with lead and a sailor was ordered to take it away in a rowing boat and drop it in deep water. The sailor, though, was killed in the process and his body, still clutching the code book, was washed ashore. From that moment we had the key to successful decoding of enemy signals.'

'Was that when the renowned Admiralty Room 40 was set up?'

The lieutenant nods. 'Yes, and the staff in Room 40 worked in the greatest secrecy. They were a brilliant and strange mix of men and women from various disciplines. They worked tirelessly to provide advance information about German fleet movements. The Admiralty, therefore, had some prior warning of the east coast raids.'

'Could they not have prevented them?'

'There were cruel twists of fate,' says the lieutenant. 'Royal Naval squadrons from Scapa, Cromarty, and Rosyth were ordered to meet up and to steam south. Even as the east coast towns were suffering under German shells, Admiral Warrender's squadron and Admiral Beatty's battlecruisers approached the German line of retreat. But there was considerable confusion. Telegrams from naval stations along the coast and from ships in the vicinity poured into the Admiralty; staff were swamped with an excess of information. There were orders and counter orders. When Admiral Warrender finally realized that he was between the enemy and their base, he turned to catch them but the weather was against him. Mist drove across the sea, visibility fell, and the Germans escaped. The Admiralty were dismayed at the lost opportunities, and – interestingly – the German admirals were critical, too, that their fleet commanders had not achieved more.'

'The attitude of the leaders in Berlin was rather different,' says an officer.

'The German leaders boasted about their fleet's successes. However, in Britain there was outrage. This was not helped by Admiralty bulletins – the Admiralty staff evidently as inept in those days as now – which effectively said that east coast towns must expect to be bombarded and there was nothing that could be done about it.'

'I suppose the true story could not be told,' says Midshipman Sutton.

'The staff in Room 40, to their chagrin no doubt, had to keep silent,' says the lieutenant. 'Nonetheless, the following month, when the German navy emerged again, Room 40 gave due and exact warning. The result was a clash between capital ships and although Admiral Beatty was disappointed with the outcome, the British press claimed victory and the German hierarchy looked for scapegoats: the commander-in-chief of the German High Seas Fleet was replaced. The new commander-in-chief, though, remained greatly puzzled by the uncanny ability of the Royal Navy to appear out of the blue whenever major forces of the German navy put to sea.'

Midshipman Sutton becomes aware of the marine attendant leaning across to remove the now-empty soup bowls. His expression still impassive, the marine performs a balancing act as he stacks bowls, one on top of the other. How, wonders the midshipman, would this man react if their roles were reversed? Would he appreciate this conversation? He probably has considerable experience of naval life. Perhaps he, too, had observed the launch of the first *Dreadnought*, remembered about the Kiel regatta, the east coast attacks, the interruption of the First Lord's bath.

'The Germans weren't the only ones to suffer eruptions at the top,' says the education officer. 'The circumstance of Churchill's eventual resignation was another remarkable saga. He left office under an unexpected cloud.'

'The war was certainly at a crucial stage when he resigned,' says the experienced lieutenant.

'Wasn't there misunderstanding between Churchill and the sea lords?' says a midshipman.

'The young Churchill and the First Sea Lord – Admiral of the Fleet Lord Fisher – were often at loggerheads,' says the lieutenant. 'The cause of the resignation of both men centred around the ship we were discussing just now – the super-dreadnought *Queen Elizabeth*. Lord Fisher wanted her sent home from the Dardanelles despite Lord Kitchener's plea that it would look as though the navy was deserting the army.'

'So who won the argument?'

'Lord Fisher got his way, but Kitchener was not reconciled. Further reinforcements had to be considered. Churchill and Fisher worked to reach an agreement but their differences in age, outlook, and – as much as anything – in their working hours caused another rupture.'

'Working hours?'

'The older man (Fisher was in his seventies) started at dawn and left work before his colleague. Churchill, however, began late and worked until after midnight. One day, at about five in the morning, Fisher received several memoranda written by his political master the previous evening. In one of these Churchill appeared to go back on his word. This was the last straw for Fisher. He resigned immediately, even though Room 40 had warned that the German fleet was about to appear. Prime Minister Asquith appealed to Fisher to stay but the petulant old sailor skulked in a London hotel. He was anxious not to meet Churchill, whose eloquence he feared he may not be able to resist.'

'But Churchill's eloquence failed to save his own job?'

'The resignation of a First Sea Lord does not generally give rise to a political crisis,' says the lieutenant, 'but in this case it did. A coalition government was formed and there was a press campaign not to let Fisher go. The old man, though, insisted on conditions which were absurd – preposterous. Churchill was to be left out of the cabinet; the entire Board of Admiralty was to be replaced. He made several other demands and to these he added his now-famous postscript: "The sixty per cent of my time and energy which I have exhausted on nine First Lords in the past I wish in future to devote on the successful prosecution of the war ... " Prime ministers are not accustomed to be told who they must exclude from their cabinets, and Asquith therefore accepted Fisher's resignation. Churchill struggled to retain his own position but resigned with dignity the day before Fisher.'

'I believe,' says a midshipman, 'that Asquith found good men to replace Fisher and Churchill?'

'Arthur Balfour became First Lord and Sir Henry Jackson First Sea Lord. But without the focused energies of Fisher and Churchill to develop new weapons, the Royal Navy had to do its best with the tools at its disposal. The result was—' the lieutenant looks up sharply. Men stare towards one end of the dining room. The hum of conversation subsides as they pick up a drift of words: '—an unauthorized gathering of men on the fo'c's'le has been reported, sir.' A chill of apprehension seeps into the room as others overhear too. The lieutenant commander 'snotties' nurse, after some seconds of further discussion, slides back his chair. He glances at the other officers before he hurries from the gun room.

The awkward atmosphere lingers. Gradually, however, the conversation picks up as those remaining attempt to regain normality. But their efforts, muses Midshipman Sutton, seem half-hearted. Perhaps the enormity they have tried to put behind them can be forestalled no longer. Reality is about to strike, the inevitable must be confronted. But what reality? Surely this is the hardest aspect to bear: the sense of uncertainty, of not knowing where they stand. He gazes at the cutlery on the table: the soup spoons have disappeared but potential weapons, knives, remain. He glances at the marine attendants who bustle around as they prepare to serve the next course. If matters get further out of hand perhaps they will have to shed their white jackets and re-don their marine uniforms. But whose side will they join? Will they fight mutineers or affiliate with them? Do the marines themselves yet know? He contemplates the ordeal of Louis XVI: the pursuit to Varennes before he and his family were overwhelmed by the mobs; the dreadful vulnerability they must have endured; the parallel dreads now perceived by the officers of the Atlantic Fleet. Midshipman Sutton shudders. He realizes that he and other personnel of the Atlantic Fleet will have to face up to a troubled, fearful and sleepless night. A night, even, of long knives.

CHAPTER SEVEN

Noises Off

TUESDAY, 15 SEPTEMBER, 1931

The shriek of a reveille bugle rouses Midshipman Sutton with a predictable lack of enthusiasm. He is at once glad and annoyed to be liberated from the fitful pattern of his dreams. Through the mists of his memory, and as he attempts to shake off his early-morning slumbers, he instinctively takes in the time: 0500. He is aware of another intrusive din – a distant and distinctive rumble which reverberates through the ship's structure. As the significance of this registers in his mind – initially in the subliminal, then within his evolving consciousness – he feels a sudden sense of surprise. He realizes that they are the signs of activity within the bowels of the vessel. The four-shaft geared turbines designed to achieve an output of 112,000 shaft horsepower must be in the process of preparation; even if other elements of the ship's crew have become disaffected, the engine-room staff, at least, must be at their posts as normal.

He glances at the hammocks of his fellow midshipmen but sees few signs of the others wishing to stir. Through the blur of a single drowsy eye he catches sight of the metal rings at each end of his own hammock; the flimsy-looking devices on which his slumbers and their contentment rely. To manage a reasonable night of sleep, he has to follow strict hammock-slinging procedures. As a first step he has to ensure that he gives the centre nettles 1½ inches more scope than the side ones. Then he has to check that the length of the nettles reduces gradually towards the sides, and that the ends of the nettles are plaited neatly in threes. The bight of the lanyard has to be placed over the hammock hook, and the end roved through the hammock ring. Finally he has to trice the hammock up to the height required and to secure the end with a jambing (Blackwall) hitch.

The steady throb of the ship's turbines persists; the source is far off but nevertheless pounds and clatters through the ship like a giant's heart-beat. Midshipman Sutton glances once more at his colleagues, though he still sees a lack of keenness to stir. He gazes at the ship's pipework above his head, thinking about his worries from last night. He recalls his experiences at the Invergordon pier. His report was accepted calmly enough by the duty officer, but in truth he knew that a person had to be present himself – to witness events at first hand – in order to understand properly the atmosphere of rage and resentment. And the midshipman could see clearly how strong were the grievances, how deeply held were the feelings. The ratings may have been misguided in the way they threatened the warrant officer and the naval patrol, but the midshipman, though apprehensive, was not greatly surprised: the mood of exasperation was patent – and potent. He knew the men wanted to vent their frustrations and he appreciated that the displays of anger were hardly groundless. He was made manifestly aware that some ratings were about to find themselves in desperate situations. Many of the married men and their families would be plunged into dire and dangerous circumstances. The situation, he realized, was intolerable.

The duty officer's attitude to Midshipman Sutton had been one of understanding even though he had seemed a little terse. But he, no doubt had his own difficulties, which must have reached a peak when, presumably, he was summoned last night at the same time as the 'snotties nurse'. The transformation of the atmosphere in the midshipmen's dining room at that juncture had been stark. The marine attendants had carried on with their duties, but private worries about their loyalties, about which side they would decide to support, had nagged at the backs of people's minds. As matters turned out, the marines' behaviour during the evening had been exemplary, as had the execution of their escort duties between the wardroom and the gunroom. But while he watched the marines perform their tasks, Midshipman Sutton could not avoid thoughts about the divisions between the upper and the lower decks. These were strong indeed.

The messing arrangements for the ratings, for example, meant that individuals were restricted to cramped seating around rough tables suspended from the ceiling. The tables were designed to be swiftly dismantled in the event of action stations, just as in a wooden man of war. Within the last few years ratings have been allowed the privilege of eating with cutlery, and the men now use cups instead of unsavoury drinking bowls. Even so, the casual visitor to the lower-deck messes would see an undifferentiated mass of humanity crammed into an absurdly small space. What would the visitor make of such conditions? And more interestingly, what would the visitor make of such conditions compared to those of the wardroom? The polished mahogany tables, the comfortable chairs, the waiter service, the gracious items of mess silver . . .

Midshipman Sutton thinks he sees signs of life from his neighbour. 'Charles, are you awake?' he says.

'God, no. God knows.' Charles' drowsy eyes peek out from under his bedding. 'Where am I? What's going on?'

'Shake a leg, Charles. It's time to get up.'

'I thought we had an unofficial lie-in today.'

'Listen to that sound . . . the turbines have been fired up.' Alfie hesitates. 'The ship's being made ready.'

'Ready for what?'

'Come on, or the duty officer will turn the hoses on you.'

'What hoses?'

'It'll save you having to go under the shower, I suppose.'

'A shower?'

'A shower before breakfast might do us all a favour.'

'Breakfast? Ah, breakfast.' Charles attempts to sit up in his hammock. 'I could do with some of that. Will it be bully beef again?'

'Bully, bully, bully . . .'

'Alfie, you're a bully.'

'You'll thank me for it one day.'

'What's the time?' Charles collapses back into his hammock again. 'What's the point? Oh God, what's going on?'

Midshipman Sutton ponders the lashing requirements for his hammock. Having jumped clear of his hammock, he will have to distribute the bedding evenly over the whole length. He will then pass the lashing with seven turns, the first being a running eye and the remainder marline hitched. (In the event of fire, however, he will use just three turns and trice the hammock up to the beams or stow it in nets as ordered.) He will have to stand with his right arm against the hammock looking towards the head before he passes the end of the lashing over the hammock with his left hand. He will have to be careful that the turns are equidistant and that the first and the last turns are clear of the bedding. As a final step, he will lay the hammock on the deck before he twists the clews and tucks them under the lashing towards the centre.

He thinks about the boy seamen who, having lashed their hammocks, have to struggle the length of the ship below decks as they carry the sausage-like bundles on their shoulders. The youngsters will have to duck and weave under sleeping sailors and try not to bump them; this would bring forth a string of curses. The boy ratings – who have a separate mess deck and who, for their moral protection, are not allowed to mix with or even speak with the men – will wend their way aft. Eventually they will emerge onto the quarterdeck (officers' territory – always to be saluted, always to be crossed at the double) where the bundle will be inspected. If the lashings are not precisely spaced, the boys will be ordered to take their bundles back to their mess deck, remake the lashings, and return for a further inspection.

The voice from the adjacent hammock sounds plaintive as it croaks: 'Is it raining, Alfie?'

'I don't know. I can't see outside . . . it's too dark.'

'I'm sure it must be raining.'

'Why?'

'It's always raining in this godforsaken place.' Charles snorts. 'I join the navy to see the world and look where I end up.'

'That's not what you said the other evening.'

'Other evening?'

'We saw the aurora, didn't we? You don't often see such sights in Surrey.'

'Old Boris was it?'

'Borealis, do you mean? Remember how it started?'

'I don't remember a thing.'

'We saw that eerie glow on the horizon from the quarterdeck. Then, if you recollect, we were startled by the follow-on display – those auroral forms.' Alfie hesitates. 'The sight interrupted our conversations. We were all amazed as we watched the arcs . . . the bands of colours . . . how the creations flared up to illuminate the night sky in criss-cross patterns – greens and reds, ghostly greys and whites. It was as if we were tiny elements of a bigger scene; unwitting witnesses to heaven-sent fireworks.'

'I remember it now,' says Charles brusquely. 'What was going on?'

'Something to do with electrically charged particles from the sun bombarding the earth's atmospheric gases.'

'Sounds quite vulgar. No wonder you can't see such things in Surrey.'

By now several of the midshipmen have emerged from their slumbers. As they jump from their hammocks and prepare for lashing up, the young men chatter and debate anxiously. They are conscious of restricted space as they perform their hammock-lashing routines. Men have to be mindful of neighbours as each co-operates with the next. At length, when the hammocks have been stowed, they concentrate on additional domestic matters. Uniforms and general appearances have to be fully up to naval standards, and the young officers, as they wash and shave, are aware of the navy's attitude. Beards are not permitted unless approval has been given by the ship's captain. Normally, unless for medical or exceptional reasons, permission will not be granted to midshipmen. The navy, however, attaches importance to personal hygiene. Some midshipmen have showers before dressing appropriately for their duties of the day. While they do so, the young men continue to discuss the ongoing clatters from the *Repulse*'s engine room. These echo through the ship's structure with increased vigour, and as the implications become unmistakeable, the midshipmen, in their excitement, make every effort to hasten.

Further afield in the Cromarty Firth, as other personnel of the Atlantic Fleet are awakened by the reveille calls from ships' buglers, men begin to feel the growing air of suspense. From admiral to able seaman, from regulating petty officer to boy seaman, all find their thoughts dominated by the uncertain prospects of the day ahead.

If officers have spent an uneasy night, members of the lower decks have been disagreeably affected too. Reactions have varied, but on some ships the dangers have been more than mere fantasy; threats of violence and intimidation have been rife. Sailors reluctant to spoil their good records have been coerced by burly seamen and stokers; they have been told that they will be thrown over the side if they do not conform. A boy seaman with the volunteer reserve has had nightmares. His dreams, he later writes in a diary, were about 'the crowds on the fo'c's'le, the hoarse orators, the cheers, the dark waters lapping, the singing, the beams of searchlights directed at the pier and canteen. It was all so strange.'

Admiral Tomkinson, Senior Officer Atlantic Fleet, has spent a particularly disturbed night. After his dinner party on HMS *Hood*, his senior guests prepared to return to their own ships. All of them, however, were embarrassed as they saw liberty-men returning. The ratings' manner was quarrelsome and obnoxious as they approached the ship. They sang 'The Red Flag' at the tops of their voices; they were careless about the respect normally shown to senior officers. Eventually the *Hood*'s commander managed to persuade the ratings to board quietly, but this was an exercise in considerable tact rather than discipline. And the men, when expected to head for their quarters below, decided instead to join others amassed on the fo'c's'le.

Shortly before midnight, Admiral Tomkinson had summoned Admiral Astley-Rushton back to discuss the situation. Tomkinson was now considering the cancellation of fleet exercises. Astley-Rushton, however, was of the opinion that this would be a mistake. Tomkinson, after some deliberation, eventually decided to follow the other's advice; he would later write that he felt it probable 'if certain ships proceeded, others would follow'. However, he remained irresolute and dispirited. At one hour and twenty minutes after midnight Tomkinson sent a further signal to the Admiralty: 'I am of the opinion that it may be difficult to get ships to sea for practice this morning, Tuesday. I have made the following general signal to the Atlantic Fleet in company. Begins: The Senior Officer Atlantic Fleet is aware that cases of hardship will result in consequence of the new rates of pay. COs are to make a thorough investigation and report to me typical cases without delay in order that I may bring the matter at once to the notice of the Admiralty.'

Just now, some forty-five minutes after the reveille call, Able Seaman Wincott of HMS *Norfolk* speculates on his best course of action. As with everyone in the Atlantic Fleet, he finds himself in an unwelcome state of uncertainty. He decides to take himself from the *Norfolk*'s lower decks to the forecastle. He regards himself as the leader of the activists in his own ship and the initiator of action in other ships. He wants to see for himself what is happening, if there are signs of trouble, sounds of activity. He hopes to see evidence of signalling, perhaps some cheering. There may be other positive signs. As he looks around the fleet, however, he feels a surge of disappointment. In the developing light of the September dawn he is filled with suspicion. The agreements of the previous evening were, he fears, no more than empty posturing, worthless rhetoric. 'I'm not going through with this just to hold the baby for others,' he is heard to mutter when he returns to the lower decks.

The activities on HMS *Repulse* will not have given Able Seaman Wincott encouragement. As that ship makes ready for sea, members of her crew carry out duties as normal. However, Wincott is not aware that the *Repulse* is the only ship in the Cromarty Firth currently proceeding as normal. Elsewhere in the fleet the efforts of the petty officers are thwarted as they try to rouse their crews. Seamen, stokers, boys, even marines, generally refuse to budge, preferring instead to remain in their hammocks – especially when encouraged to do so by harangues from the activists.

A ship, though, is a closed community. Within their own community personnel will be aware of activity – or lack of it – but they cannot be sure about what is happening elsewhere. Last night, when ratings agreed on the actions to be taken, these actions were intended to embrace the fleet as a whole. In practice, however, each ship will act independently. For this reason, members of the *Repulse*'s crew fail to appreciate that they are alone in performing their duties.

An hour and a half after hearing their reveille call, and as the *Repulse*'s anchor-weighing drills are carried out, Midshipman Sutton and his colleagues still listen to the distant hum produced by turbine propeller shafts. The ship's crew wait for the vessel to move as the throb of the turbines pulsates through the structure. On instructions from the captain – 'Slow ahead' – the engine room crew respond and then the ship gradually, majestically, steams away from her position between the South Sutor and North Sutor hills. The noise from the engine room rises but now another sound, even more powerful, even more meaningful, starts to rise too.

The crew of the *Repulse* are unaware, without doubt, but as the ship leaves her moorings at 0630, exactly as planned, an uproar of booing from other crews in the fleet echoes across the waters of the Cromarty Firth. This is the noise which, as much as anything else, will entrench attitudes. For this is the noise heard by most people in the Atlantic Fleet which makes them realize that the fleet, after all, will not be sailing.

CHAPTER EIGHT

Sea Sore

The *Repulse*'s crew, though clearly oblivious of the wrath they have left behind them, will be appalled when told later about the reaction of others in the Atlantic Fleet. Captain Cochrane and his officers, who may at present feel relieved at the ship's timely departure, will be equally shocked. But just now the captain, a tall Scotsman with a grave and headmasterly air, concentrates on his immediate tasks as, from the ship's signalling bridge, he supervises proceedings. He is supported by a number of duty personnel, including Midshipman Sutton, assigned to his station by the 'snotties' nurse who, amongst other matters, arranges the midshipmen's rota. Today, the midshipman has received specific instructions: he is to assist with, and learn about, the complexity of work performed by the ship's signals section. Together with the signals officer and backed by trained petty officers and ratings, he will gain experience in the management of flag signals, semaphore, and Morse code messages. Additionally, he will co-operate with the radio room staff below decks – the personnel who attend to the constant flow of Admiralty and other messages. For today's duty, however, he rarely ventures below decks and on the ship's bridge he is ideally placed to gain an overview of general operations. As the *Repulse* gains momentum he watches the North and South Sutor hills fade gradually into the mists of the September morning.

He glances at Captain Cochrane. The young officer realizes that his captain will expect high standards. He will have to apply in practice the principles learned from regular classroom lessons below decks, and he knows that he will be required to manage Morse code messages at speeds up to eight words a minute. Already he has mastered his own name (dit-dah, dit-dah-dit-dit, dit-dit-dah-dit, dit-dit, dit) at higher speeds and in due course he will be expected to achieve proficiency in Morse code (communicated by means of heliograph, siren, signal lamp, whistle, fog horn, flag, buzzer and wireless telegraphy/telephony) at speeds as high as twenty words a minute.

In the classroom he has been told about the navy's enthusiasm for coloured flags and pennants. These, he has been taught, are made in six different sizes according to the purpose and normally will be employed in groups. From the letter 'A' (alternate diagonals of red and white) to the blue and white chequers of 'Z', words and numbers will be spelt out for rapid interpretation by expert signalmen. If the ratings become overloaded, the midshipman has been authorized to refer to signals books to decode messages.

He has been taught the fundamentals of another naval partiality: the use of semaphore. He knows that a transmitting ship will make initial contact with the ships she wishes to signal by hoisting the flag 'E' (either singly, or inferior to fleet numbers or distinguishing signals). At the same time the arms of the semaphore sender have to be positioned to form the 'alphabetical' sign (right arm extended vertically, left arm to meet the right horizontally). As soon as the receiving ship has hoisted the answering pennant close up (this pennant has a white inboard segment with a red outer section), the semaphore sender will proceed promptly with the message. If a word is missed, the midshipman has been briefed that the answering pennant should be dipped; the transmitting ship will then repeat the word until the answering pennant has been hoisted close up again.

He has been instructed on the requirement to monitor signalmen during semaphore messaging. The sender should make his signs accurately: arm, wrist, and hand-flag should be controlled as if in one continuous line and moves from sign to sign should be by the shortest route. A common tendency for the sender to bend his elbows should be discouraged. The hand-flags should be kept clear and should be presented at the proper angle. The sender's arms, as well as being held straight, should be swung through the vertical plane. The sender should ensure that his body is steady and square to the direction of signalling. His arms, when disengaged, should be dropped smartly and held in front of his legs.

Some senders will resort to unofficial techniques. These include a system of short-arm semaphore and some signalmen, when observed through binoculars, can communicate by the manipulation of fingers alone. The midshipman has been briefed, however, that the navy does not in general approve of such methods. The actions of bookies at a horse race meeting are seen as inappropriate for members of the Royal Navy. His instructors have stressed that accuracy is the first priority, speed is secondary. Signalmen, therefore, are trained to resist the temptation to rush; messages made at six words a minute are of greater use to the navy than rushed messages at twelve words a minute. Hastily sent messages can lead to misinterpretation and misunderstanding.

'W/T message coming through, sir,' a nearby signalman attracts Midshipman Sutton's attention.

'Thank you.'

'It's a repeat message, sir. The original was corrupted.'

'Okay,' says the midshipman. He takes a slip of paper and scans the contents. He moves across the bridge towards a lieutenant commander. 'This has just come through, sir.' The midshipman hands across the slip. 'An Admiralty gale warning for the Pentland area later today.'

'Thank you, Mister Sutton.'

The midshipman returns to his allocated bridge station where he observes how the following wind assists the ship's progress. The *Repulse* now approaches the outer reaches of the Moray Firth, and with practised sea legs crew members brace themselves against the motion of a developing swell. By this stage the landmarks of the Cromarty Firth have shrunk out of view and Captain Cochrane, having stipulated a north-easterly course for the rendezvous planned with the target tug *St Cyrus*, orders a further increase in speed. His instructions are relayed below decks; those on the bridge glance up as the clang of the telegraph system reverberates across the area. In the vitals of the ship this sound is antici-pated by the engineers who hasten to execute orders. The pitch of the turbine whine soars. The engine-room personnel monitor temperature and pressure gauges. The *Repulse*'s bow and stern waves pile high as quadruple screws dig into the leaden surfaces. Men listen to the wind tear and snatch at halyards, and see how the smoke and vapour forced up through the twin funnels signal the ship's position.

Midshipman Sutton knows that the ship's four-hourly watch system is about to be brought into operation and that, having handed over to the duty watch, Captain Cochrane and his senior officers will leave the bridge. The midshipman glances at these officers as they confer together in confidential voices. He sees how they and others on the bridge treat the proceedings as routine, without the apprehension felt by in-experienced personnel as the ship progresses towards deep waters. His sense of nervous anticipation escalates in sympathy with the ship's pitching movement. On her present course, about to exchange the rela-tive calm of the Moray Firth for the boisterous streams of the North Sea, he feels a thrill of excitement. As he sees sprays hurled up by the move-ment of the bow, he muses that these same waters have been plied by seafarers through the centuries. From fishing sloops to men of war, from giant commercial carriers to diminutive tug boats, from corvettes to battle-cruisers, the diversity of vessel must be as extensive as the needs of an island nation and her reliance on mastery of the seas.

He recalls last night's conversations. He ponders the discussions about the Great War, about Churchill and Fisher, the east coast raids, the curious events at Kiel before the war. Just two years later, at the Battle of Jutland, that island nation faced unparalleled danger. And this – despite the midshipman's sense of a different era – a mere fifteen years ago; fifteen years since members of the British Grand Fleet had feelings of nervous anticipation surely greater than his today. Bow waves and stern waves must have piled even higher as the might of the Royal Navy was mustered and as diverse elements were ordered to rendezvous off the west coast of Jutland at maximum speed. He considers the ironies: the mutual expressions of goodwill at Kiel, the unguarded farewell message on the last day, the swift and dramatic turn around in attitudes. The move from friendship to hostility revealed harsh realities; hollow rhetoric was soon forgotten. The British Grand Fleet and the German High Seas Fleet had, in reality, spent years equipping themselves for confrontation.

And the outcome, when that confrontation finally materialized, was of critical significance to the island nation – more so than to Germany with its land borders. The midshipman had learned how Churchill described the commander-in-chief, Admiral Jellicoe, as having responsibilities 'on a different scale to all others. It might fall to him as to no other man – sovereign, statesman, admiral or general – to issue orders which in the space of two or three hours might nakedly decide who won the war. The destruction of the British battle fleet would be final. Jellicoe was the only man on either side who could lose the war in an afternoon.'

The midshipman wonders about the nature of such challenges; how nights must have been long and sleepless; how a fellow admiral had said of Admiral Jellicoe: 'I am struck with his marvellous alertness and precision . . . No unsound, however attractive, proposal has a rabbit's chance when he runs his searchlight brain on it – it's riddled by a dry fact or two that he knows but no one else seems to.'

On the last day of May 1916 – two years and one month after Kiel – when off Jutland the world's first and last gun battle between ships of the dreadnought era took place, the midshipman knows that a signalling error caused the British Grand Fleet to encounter early difficulty. A signalling error! And the hazards so recently stressed by his instructors. He glances at a nearby signalman and wonders how this man would have coped. He speculates how he himself might react in the heat of battle. The instructors talked about the need for accurate signalling, but their lectures were delivered in the calm of the classroom. Classroom comforts versus the pressures of battle; advice can be easy to proffer but hard to practise in extreme conditions. So it was that at the start of the battle on that May afternoon, four Queen Elizabeth class ships were erroneously signalled to steer in the opposite direction to that intended.

However, the officer in charge of battle-cruisers, Admiral Beatty, was impatient to press an attack against five German battle-cruisers. Perhaps he consulted with others, but perhaps not. In any event, his decision not to wait meant that the four Queen Elizabeth class ships were still 10 miles away at the start of the attack. Nonetheless, Beatty considered the six ships at his immediate disposal were, ship for ship, 'superior to his possible opponents'. At 1548 he gave the order to open fire. The ships of both sides ran on parallel courses 9 miles apart as salvo after salvo crashed out in swift succession. But the afternoon light was not in Admiral Beatty's favour. The superior German stereoscopic range-finders soon found their range and about fifteen minutes after the commencement of firing, HMS *Indefatigable,* at the rear of Beatty's line, was struck by shells from the *Von der Tann.* The *Indefatigable* settled by the stern and began to fall out of line. She was hit by two more projectiles, this time near the bows. Confusion reigned. There was an explosion. An observer recorded how 'an immense column of grey smoke with a fiery base and a flaming top stood up on the sea where *Indefatigable* should have been. It hung there . . . and then a hole appeared in this pillar of smoke through which I caught a glimpse of the *Indefatigable* lying on its side. There was a streak of flame and a fresh outpouring of smoke. Then the ship quickly rolled over and disappeared beneath the waves taking 800 men with her. German light cruisers passing the spot later found just two survivors.'

A chilling numbness gripped watchers. Perhaps there was a moment of silence, but the quiet spell was short-lived. Ships on both sides soon resumed firing with renewed vigour. Their efforts, though, proved inconclusive until, at 1608, the balance of favour appeared to tilt towards the British when the Queen Elizabeth class ships at last caught up sufficiently to open fire at long range. But the Germans still had light in their favour – Beatty's gunnery officers had no aiming points other than red flashes from enemy guns concealed within the obscurity of mists. The German ships found their targets more successfully than the British and at 1625 the *Derfflinger* caught HMS *Queen Mary* with a salvo. A column of smoke 1,000 ft high was propelled into the air as the *Queen Mary* broke in half. The crew of HMS *Tiger* had the unnerving experience of steel and woodwork crashing down onto the decks around them as the *Queen Mary* disintegrated. Within what appeared to be a matter of seconds she vanished. All but twenty of her crew of 1,280 men went down with the ship.

Admiral Beatty had lost two of his great battle-cruisers within the space of minutes – 'there seems to be something wrong with our bloody ships today' he famously remarked to his flag captain. Despite further losses over the next two or so hours, the admiral so admired by

Midshipman Sutton did not lose his nerve. His tactics and his timing were skilled when, in late afternoon, he ordered a turn due north. He planned to lure the enemy towards Admiral Jellicoe's ships as they steamed urgently south-east. As one German officer later recorded: 'We were filled with the proud joy of victory ... We had acquired an absolute confidence in our own ship ... It seemed out of the question that our proud ship could be shattered in a few minutes like the *Queen Mary* and the *Indefatigable*.' The Germans took the bait. As they headed towards Jellicoe's Grand Fleet with 40,000 men at action stations the commander-in-chief of the German High Seas Fleet, Admiral Scheer, was not warned of the danger until it was too late.

Now Jellicoe peered ahead from the bridge of his flagship – HMS *Iron Duke*. He could hear the great guns in the distance but the visibility was reducing and he received too few reports of enemy positions. He was desperate for information: he pressed Admiral Burney on the right wing for clues. Burney was vague: he could report only 'gun flashes and heavy gunfire on the starboard bow.' Jellicoe signalled another enquiry. At 1814 hours Admiral Beatty responded; he reported the enemy bearing south-south-west, but he failed to give a course. Jellicoe's next order would be crucial: he could not afford to keep his dreadnoughts bunched in a cruising formation, but a badly timed instruction would allow the Germans to concentrate on each division as it turned. Jellicoe stared at his compass for a full twenty seconds. His judgement, however, was admirable. He signalled a deployment on the left wing and six columns of battleships turned with precision to form one long line that stretched for 6 miles. British guns were trained where the enemy was expected; the decision by the British commander-in-chief now gave him the benefit of position and light.

The British fleet's advantage, however, was lessened by deteriorating visibility. Admiral Scheer was horrified to find British ships in front of him and expecting him, but as Jellicoe later reported, 'At this time, owing to smoke and mist, it was most difficult to distinguish friend from foe ... The identity of the ships on the starboard beam was not even sufficiently clear for me to permit fire to be opened.' It was not until the leading German ships were just 12,000 yards away that the *Iron Duke* opened fire. Now the British had the advantage of light and it was the turn of the Germans to rely on gun flashes from the mists. The German shooting became ludicrously bad. Scheer could not allow this situation to continue so in a tactical move which his men had previously rehearsed he ordered a 'battle turn-away'. The German line reversed direction; with laudable precision each ship turned when the one behind was seen to be turning, a tricky manoeuvre in battle conditions. Simultaneously, German destroyers ran between the two fleets to lay smoke screens. The targets disappeared; the guns fell silent. Scheer had saved his fleet for the moment.

Fifteen minutes later, however, he unwisely decided to turn back. He blundered into the middle of Jellicoe's battle line and once more the High Seas Fleet was in a desperate position. For a short while it seemed that Jellicoe had the enemy at his mercy but Scheer responded with iron resolution: he ordered his battle-cruisers to charge. With the flag signal that became famous throughout the world's navies he ordered: 'Battle-cruisers at the enemy! Give it everything!' At the same time he ordered his main fleet to execute another 'battle turn-away' and in the seesaw of fortunes so typical of the battle, fate played once more into German hands. In the feeble light of dusk Jellicoe failed to spot Scheer's manoeuvre and lost contact with the enemy. Scheer's withdrawal was managed 'in a very masterful fashion out of the closing jaws of Jellicoe.'

The price for Scheer, though, was the destruction of his battle-cruisers as an effective fighting force. Although none was sunk, these ships were damaged beyond the point of battle usefulness; some struggled just to stay afloat. Scheer now had little choice but to return to the safety of his fleet's home port 80 miles away. He estimated that by first light he would be close to mined areas where paths could be swept that were wide enough for his ships to enter, but too narrow for the fleets to manoeuvre and fight. To achieve this, Scheer knew he would have to risk driving his force through elements of the British fleet. He reckoned, however, that the fast-approaching nightfall would give him the respite he needed so urgently.

The British commander-in-chief now had to reposition his fleet to intercept the enemy by daybreak before safety was reached. In the subsequent night mêlées, both sides suffered further casualties. Searchlights were used with paralysing effect, brilliant star shells were thrown up to illuminate an enemy as far away as 3 miles. The Germans nevertheless managed to drive through the British fleet and by 0300, just as dawn was breaking, Scheer's ships were positioned a few miles from the mineswept channel he sought. He was as good as home.

Sick with disappointment at the lost opportunities, Jellicoe turned his fleet away and headed towards Scotland, thinking, perhaps, of how the Battle of Jutland was so painfully concluded, so painfully inconclusive. The Germans had lost eleven ships, the British fourteen – roughly 10 per cent of each fleet. The numbers of dead were 2,551 German, 6,097 British. By noon the next day the battered remains of the British Grand Fleet had reached various bases in Scotland. At Invergordon, where twelve ambulance boats would spend three sad days ferrying the injured to Red Cross trains, the insane nature of man's inhumanity to man was brought home in a sense both literal and figurative.

In the judgements that followed, the Admiralty exonerated Jellicoe. So who was to blame for the failures? The charismatic Beatty? But he could do no wrong in the public eye. Was it the officers, their training, the naval system? Some thought so, and Midshipman Sutton knew that in the subsequent analysis no sea battle except for Trafalgar was the subject of such abundant literature. As an American newspaper commented: 'The German navy has assaulted its jailer but is still in jail.' Scheer understood how near he had come to disaster. He advised the Kaiser that Germany could not win the surface war in the North Sea. The German fleet remained in port until, with guns disarmed, the ships were sent to the bleak waters of Scapa Flow at the end of the war.

'Sir?' Midshipman Sutton overhears the officer of the watch speak with the captain. Conversation follows and the midshipman picks up the order 'Maintain this course and speed.'

'Aye, aye, sir.' The officer of the watch is obsequious as he receives further instructions. The captain asks for questions. There are none. The captain nods acknowledgement and prepares to leave the bridge. All stand as a mark of respect and as he leaves, Midshipman Sutton muses that his headmasterly presence can create an austere atmosphere. The midshipman stares at the seas ahead as, with a sigh, he considers the significance of the Battle of Jutland and how, for the survivors, the stings their ordeals remain to be relived: sea salt in sea sores. He gazes sombrely at the movements of the ship's bow, the rush of spray. He turns. The signals officer is opening the bridge door from outside.

'Everything all right, Mister Sutton? Any problems to report?' the signals officer strides across.

'A few W/T messages, sir, otherwise quiet at present.'

'Have you had breakfast yet?'

'No, sir.'

'Why don't you do that now?'

'Thank you, sir.'

The midshipman glances around the bridge before he leaves the area. He is followed by a marine escort as he hastens down steps, along corridors, past pipework, through passageways. Soon he reaches the gunroom where his colleagues are tucking into their breakfast. He joins the conversations as the young officers discuss the ship's timely departure. Were last night's worries exaggerated?

However, these midshipmen remain ignorant of the true state of affairs. In time they will learn that Admiral Tomkinson, still steadfastly stuck in the Cromarty Firth, has signalled the Admiralty: 'Situation 0900 today, Tuesday. HMS *Repulse* has proceeded to sea for exercises, other ships have not and considerable portions of ships companies have absented themselves from duty.'

When Midshipman Sutton leaves the gunroom, he returns directly to his station on the bridge where he is greeted by the signals officer. As part of the midshipman's training, the officer will give additional briefings and guidance on signals procedures. It is during these discussions that he is interrupted: a message from Admiral Tomkinson is about to come through. The message is urgent and must be seen by the captain immediately

Captain Cochrane seems ruffled when he hastens back to the bridge. He finds an expectant hush amongst his bridge staff. The captain reads the message. He coughs and glances around irritably before he relays the gist: Atlantic Fleet autumn exercises are cancelled with immediate effect. HMS *Repulse*, along with the *Malaya*, the *Warspite*, and the *St Cyrus*, is to return to harbour forthwith.

The time is 0931, exactly three hours and one minute since the *Repulse* left behind that outbreak of booing which so disturbed the tenuous tranquillity of the Cromarty Firth. The boos from present troubles, the cheers for heroes past, the same trepidation felt by both. And witnessed, muses Midshipman Sutton, so coolly by the seas he now observes. He gazes again at the rhythmic plunge of the bow. He imagines the hiss of sprays thrown aloft, the ferocious demands of such seas. As if created from the blood of Uranus, like the daughters of Gaia, these waters challenge the spirits of conscience, punishment, and retribution. Do they seek other challenges too? Is it clemency they yearn? Or signs of compassion? The midshipman recalls the excesses of the past, the enormity of their consequences, and he is shocked to realize how such signs have been so surely and sorely conspicuous by their absence.

CHAPTER NINE

Mutiny

In no position to ignore his admiral's summons, Captain Cochrane nonetheless appears reluctant to take his ship back to harbour. And if the captain seems dispirited, his feelings, notes Midshipman Sutton, are reflected by others on the bridge; most view with dismay the prospect of returning to a disaffected fleet. He realizes that the uncertain mood, the air of apathy, which now afflicts those on the bridge is mirrored throughout the ship. But the question of choice does not arise: the admiral has to be obeyed, the matter is final. The captain barks an order and from their elevated position, bridge personnel feel the lean of the ship as she changes course through 180 degrees. While the *Repulse* is steered back towards the Cromarty Firth, the crew note that a strengthening headwind will hinder the ship's progress as she steams for harbour.

The navigation officer, having calculated that the ship's return will take in excess of six hours, is matter-of-fact when he informs Captain Cochrane. The captain, however, seems untroubled: the longer the better as far as he is concerned. He is irritated by the admiral's order which, he feels, is misjudged. The *Repulse*'s timely departure raised his hopes of a return to normality. Indeed, his ship might have been seen as an example to the rest of the fleet. He and his officers would have received due credit. But now such aspirations have been dashed. Furthermore, he has received instructions that the passage back should be taken as an opportunity to explain to his crew about the pay cuts. Is this, he wonders, really prudent? As the events of last night proved, the men are well enough acquainted with the facts and the captain sees little point in stirring up strong feelings again. The admiral, however, has directed that individuals who claim they will suffer undue hardship should be encouraged to speak with their divisional officers. Details should be signalled to the chief of staff, who has been instructed to compile a dossier of grievances to present to the Admiralty. The chief of staff is due leave for London on the lunchtime train.

Captain Cochrane, having instigated the necessary arrangements, decides to remain on the bridge. From that position he will receive input from his officers as divisions are mustered and briefed. As predicted, however, the divisional officers find themselves unhappily placed. If an officer attempts to soften the blow, he merely sees the men further inflamed. The facts speak for themselves – officers cannot ameliorate the harsh, in some cases ruinous, impact of Admiralty Fleet Order 2239: chief petty officers' pay down from 8 shillings and 6 pence to 7 shillings and 6 pence a day; leading seamen from 5 shilling and 3 pence to 4 shillings and 3 pence; able seamen from 4 shillings to 3 shillings, ordinary seamen from 2 shillings and 9 pence to 2 shillings. When the divisional officers have read out the new scales, the reaction, as at the Invergordon meetings, is one of outrage. The wrath of the older men is especially poignant; for years they have been promised that their more favourable pre-1925 pay scale would be treated as sacrosanct. Now the Government has reneged on that promise. The shabbiness of such treatment infuriates the ratings, as does the biased form of the cuts. A lieutenant commander, for example, will lose 3.7 per cent of his pay, an able seaman 25 per cent. How is the lieutenant commander divisional officer supposed to justify such disparity?

Amidst this atmosphere, and having relayed the admiral's instructions on hardship cases, the divisional officers dismiss their groups. As they return to duties, the ratings make no attempt to hide their fury at the Admiralty's inept handling of the situation. The men feel bitterly betrayed. However, when divisional officers are approached by individual ratings, it becomes clear that the troublemakers – those who see an opportunity to turn the situation to their advantage – are the ones to come forward. Those with genuine grievances seem unwilling to discuss family problems with officers. While the ship wends her way back to harbour, Captain Cochrane and his officers realize that the present disaffection at harbour is more or less bound to be taken up by ratings on the *Repulse*.

Midshipman Sutton, as he glances at the captain, sees how the tall figure seems to shrink in stature. The captain leans forward in a particular fashion; his shoulders become hunched as he responds to feedback from his divisional officers. He seems wearied by the burden of responsibility. While the extraordinary events unfold, the ratings' determination and anger seem to gather momentum. The captain nods curtly as more information is relayed to him. His cheerless expression – gradually grimmer at his growing lack of control over men and events – he finds hard to conceal. It is as if, thinks the midshipman, he is the unwitting director of a production gone mad; a tormented and isolated figurehead thrown without due preparation into a maelstrom of unforeseen pitfalls. 'Well,' as Feste would say, 'God give them wisdom that have it; and those that are fools let them use their talents.' So how, wonders the midshipman, will Captain Cochrane fare? The performance of his fellow captains to date has been, to say the least, hardly impressive. When the captain of HMS *Malaya* addressed his men and said that he, too, was putting up with a pay cut, he was met with howls of protest. The effect was disastrous. Eventually the ship's commander had to take over to calm the situation while the captain was forced to retire to his cabin.

But mutiny, muses the midshipman, is an action of such gravity that few captains will care to consider in advance how they might cope. As a mechanism of last resort, mutiny can produce many losers, few winners. When navies do become embroiled, history's memory will be long. To this day, the Royal Navy feels the repercussions of the Nore mutiny of 1797. The decade before that, when the enigmatic Lieutenant William Bligh was commissioned to take HMS *Bounty* to the South Pacific, the affair led to the famed events of Tuesday, 28 April, 1789. Midshipman Sutton recollects how the Bounty's crew, with their objective of collecting breadfruit for onward conveyance to the Caribbean, knew that the voyage would be a long one with years away from home. At an early stage, however, the naval tradition of divisions became apparent in more than one sense. As the voyage proceeded, and as bad weather, bad leadership, bad temper, and bad luck dogged the lives of the crew, the petulant style of Captain Bligh created escalating resentment and dissatisfaction. The lamentable atmosphere smouldered and spread as the months went by until, on that April morning, Master's Mate Fletcher Christian and twelve crew members decided they would take no more. Action was agreed: Christian and his men would seize control of the ship. At dawn, Captain Bligh was woken by the weight of hands pressed upon him. His arms were bound behind his back; he was bundled up a staircase as he screamed 'murder' at the top of his voice. On deck there was a blur of confused activity; voices shouted, mocked, gave orders. Some two and a half hours later the ship's launch was in the water with Fletcher Christian directing men to enter it. Bligh later wrote about Christian, 'Of all diabolical looking men he exceeded every possible description.'

As he was pushed towards the launch Bligh pleaded with Christian: 'I have a wife and four children . . .'

'That, Captain Bligh,' retorted Christian, 'that is the thing . . . I am in hell . . . I am in hell.'

'Never fear, my lads,' Bligh cried out as the 23 ft launch with nineteen men aboard was cast adrift. 'I'll do justice if ever I reach England!'

Fortunately, thinks the midshipman, modern navies are more advanced; they have become professional as the affairs of the world have moved on. Modern styles of leadership have revolutionised attitudes. Or have they? Apart from the pay issue, the problem of divisions between decks is surely at the heart of present-day frictions: Disraeli's two nations crystallized aboard. And is this issue, he wonders, restricted to Britain alone? The Royal Navy has difficulties, but are Disraeli's divisions experienced abroad as well as aboard? The midshipman recalls the Russian Revolution – preceded by the sickening events on the cruiser *Potemkin* – and the recent disaffection amongst the fleet in Chile. He remembers that even the Kaiser's navy faced heresy when, just fourteen years ago, the High Seas Fleet suffered food shortages towards the end of the Great War. He recollects how the German officers were given privileged rations, which caused furious resentment amongst the men. As the agitation persisted, the ringleaders delivered an ultimatum: they 'would gladly eat whatever food was given to them as long as the officers do the same'. When the ultimatum was ignored, disaffection spread swiftly from ship to ship.

The Germans suffered other problems. The elitist U-boat service had few qualms about stockpiling prizes requisitioned from enemy ships, and this caused malice amongst ratings in other sections of the fleet. When a visitor wrote about a typical U-boat scene, he encapsulated the mood: 'The crew in their leather kit and among them the officers keeping strict order. On board a medley of boxes and chests of cocoa, coffee and expensive tea, sacks of wonderful American meal, fresh butter, fine white English bread, English marmalade, ham, bacon, beans, tobacco . . . all these things removed from a few paltry enemy fishing boats while in Germany the women and children are starving and dying from inanition or supporting life on vile, injurious and almost inedible food substitutes.' And while the U-boat men thrived, the rest of the High Seas Fleet seethed as they starved. The upshot of this, perhaps forgotten in the turmoil of greater events but remembered by men of the sea, was gruesome. Old hands would shake their heads when they spoke about it. They would talk about the German officers who struggled to cope, how these officers resorted to extreme measures – two ringleaders hanged, three sent to penal servitude. However, this action, combined with a conciliatory increase in the bread ration, finally brought the mutiny under control.

So how, speculates the midshipman, would those in the Cromarty Firth react to such treatment? He cannot, of course, be aware of the drastic proposals that will be discussed tomorrow by the Board of Admiralty and by the Cabinet. He cannot know of the personal involvement of King George V as efforts are made to resolve the impasse.

Meanwhile, the seamen in the Cromarty Firth have settled into unusual and unpredictable patterns of life. As the *Repulse* contends with headwinds on her westerly course back to harbour, normal routines on other ships in harbour have been cast adrift. On some ships there has been a comprehensive collapse of official authority; ratings will recall this day with awe: 'We spent the morning on the upper deck joining in with the lads, cheering other ships in the fleet. We came down for the midday meal, and then in the afternoon they called for volunteers: the baker needed flour and asked for men to go to the stores; the galley wanted meat brought up from the cold store room. There was never a shortage of volunteers. They played the piano – a bit of a singsong – they played "The Red Flag" very often. Leaders stood up on the fo'c's'le with some of the crew around, giving morale-boosting speeches. Stick together – we don't want this pay cut – if we all stick together they're bound to give in eventually. That was the theme. Then they would call for three cheers to the nearest ship.'

As the morning progresses, Able Seaman Wincott on HMS *Norfolk* assumes an increasingly significant role. His captain, anxious for a written statement of the men's grievances to present to the admiral, approaches the commander's writer (clerk) to act as a go-between. The commander's writer later speaks about Wincott's reaction, "Statement? I'll give them a statement all right . . . Clear lower deck! Everybody on the fo'c's'le!" . . . in a moment of panic you'd have thought it was abandon ship; there was a mad rush to get on to the fo'c's'le deck.' A table, a typewriter and chair are brought and the entire ship's company watches while Wincott dictates a document which bears comparison with the petition made by the Nore mutineers: 'We, the loyal subjects of His Majesty the King, do hereby represent to My Lords Commissioners of the Admiralty our representations to implore them to amend the drastic cuts in pay that have been inflicted upon the lowest paid man of the lower deck. It is evident to all concerned that this cut is the forerunner of tragedy, misery and immorality amongst the families of the lower deck, and unless we can be guaranteed a written agreement from Admiralty, confirmed by parliament, stating that our pay will be revised, we are still to remain as one unit, refusing to serve under the new rate of pay.'

Eight copies of this statement are produced. One copy is placed in a lieutenant commander's cabin; one finds its way to the offices of the *Daily Herald*. Others are distributed surreptitiously around the fleet by the *Norfolk*'s picket boat in the course of delivering mail and official documents. Souvenir copies are made by a calligrapher on the *Norfolk*. After this flurry of activity, however, there is little for the fleet to do but wait. Ratings discover that a mutinous day can be a dreary day. The men have to make an effort to bolster morale; regular cheering from ship to ship is accompanied by short-arm semaphore messages which say in essence: 'Still holding out all right.'

Despite the lack of official control, routine harbour duties continue to be carried out in certain ships, although others are less well organized. Common to all ships, though, is the main sign of abnormal activity: crowds of men on forecastles. As captains attempt to keep abreast of affairs they find themselves treated with disdain. Some, reluctant to leave their cabins, plead for their messenger boys to be returned. Strike leaders (the word mutiny is avoided) leave it up to the boys to decide. Officers in general seem to be treated with respect and are given their meals in wardrooms as normal. On some ships, however, there is little or no dialogue between officers and men. Marines find they are awkwardly placed; some try to make themselves scarce, some erect barricades around their barracks. In two ships the marines agree to join the strike. Petty officers adopt a generally neutral position, although most show strong sympathies for the men.

When the Chief of Staff, Rear-Admiral Colvin, sets off for London at lunchtime he takes with him a dossier of accounts. Some of these have made a deep impression on senior officers. The captain of HMS *Nelson* adds a poignant postscript to his report: 'For some of the men the proposed cuts mean not hardship, but ruin.' When Colvin and his secretary are taken past the ships in the admiral's barge, he is greeted by a mixture of jeers and cheers from the men on the forecastles. He tries to make the best of the situation by waving breezily as he passes.

Shortly after lunchtime, at 1330, Admiral Tomkinson sends a further signal to Admiralty staff. He is desperate to prompt them into giving him more concrete help. He highlights the effect of the cuts for ratings on the old scale; he points out the short interval before the reductions take effect; he seeks clarification about the old scale of pay which was promised to those affected for the whole period of their service. He goes on: 'I do not consider that the men will feel they have received justice unless reductions are more in proportion to their pay . . . I would urge a very early decision should be communicated by their Lordships. Unless this is received I regret that in my opinion discipline in the Atlantic Fleet will not be restored and may still further deteriorate (ADM 178/129).'

Two hours later, a particular cheer from the men on fo'c's'les replaces earlier jeers when they spot HMS *Repulse* return to harbour. Midshipman Sutton is aware of Captain Cochrane's gloom as he surveys the crowds that now wander the fleet's forecastles with impunity. The midshipman, though, is kept busy as the *Repulse*'s approach to harbour produces a flurry of semaphore signals. Captain Cochrane is told that Admiral Tomkinson still awaits a reply from the Admiralty to his lunchtime signal and that strike committees are being formed around the fleet.

As the *Repulse* approaches her old position between the North Sutor and South Sutor hills, preparations are made for her mooring drills. The midshipman watches keenly as the classroom theories on mooring – the release of two anchors at a distance one from the other so the ship's stem is midway between anchors with cables taut – are now applied in practice. He has been told that a ship properly moored has freedom to pivot on her stem when swinging round with tide or wind, and that whenever possible anchors should be laid in line with the prevailing elements. In the strong tides of the Cromarty Firth, cable officers ensure that cables are veered until the swivel lies on the bottom; the combined weight of the cable and swivel thus act as a restraint to relieve the stress on the anchor itself. During this procedure, Captain Cochrane orders the speed of the ship to retain 'advance' while the first anchor is let go. Meanwhile, the senior cable officer judges the tautness of the first cable before he orders the second anchor to be released.

When the mooring drills have been concluded, the captain decides to retire to his cabin. It is not long, however, before he is summoned to return to the bridge. The duty officer's expression is grave when he briefs Captain Cochrane that their earlier fears have materialized: the ratings on the *Repulse* have downed tools for a meeting on the forecastle. The captain observes the assembled company with dread, his sense of powerlessness heightened when his men receive support from others who visit by picket boat and who shout messages of encouragement through megaphones.

He watches for some time, but perhaps recognizing how his position on the bridge emphasizes his impotence, he decides to retire to his cabin once more. As he leaves, he gives instructions that he should be kept abreast of significant developments and that he wishes to be informed when the Admiralty's reply to Admiral Tomkinson's signal is received. This, however, does not arrive until the evening and although the signals staff of individual ships are not normally direct parties to the admiral's personal signals, the message is relayed around the fleet. 'The Board of Admiralty will give their earnest and immediate consideration to representations of hardship. Meanwhile, impress on ships' companies that existing rates of pay remain in force until 1 October and that their Lordships confidently expect that the men of the Atlantic Fleet will uphold the tradition of the service by loyally carrying out their duty (ADM178/129).'

Captain Cochrane and his fellow captains realize that this anodyne signal will not help Admiral Tomkinson in the least and that, if they are not aware already, most will appreciate the extent of the admiral's frustration at the Admiralty's lack of perception: 'The Admiralty expects that the programme of exercises should be resumed as soon as your investigations are complete.'

Just before 0100, the sleep-deprived Admiral Tomkinson contacts the

Admiralty again: 'I must emphasize that the situation at Invergordon will not have been met until definite decisions have been communicated. A continuation of the exercise programme is out of the question in the present state of mind of a considerable proportion of the crews.' Having sent this signal, he dispatches a message round the fleet to say that he anticipates no action from the Admiralty for a day or two. He adds that he expects men, meanwhile, to 'carry out their duties'. However, he must realize that such an expectation is a lost cause. He is aware without doubt that the fleet is destined for another bad night, a night of heightening tension on board all ships and, in the worst affected, one of violence and danger.

CHAPTER TEN

Resolutions

WEDNESDAY, 14 SEPTEMBER, 1931

The absence of this morning's reveille bugle may give Midshipman Sutton some minor respite, but any benefit proves short-lived; stirred by an inner restiveness, he wakes at the usual dawn hour. He has an immediate sense of anxiety. He lies still in his hammock as he tries to confirm a particular noise, an unfamiliar din from a distant part of the ship. He strains to identify the sound, then realizes with growing alarm that the routine clatter from the engine room and other areas has been replaced by an alien noise: the pitch of raised voices. These echo through the ship's structure and originate, he estimates, from the direction of the lower decks. Although far off and spasmodic, a threat is discernible; he hears voluble arguments followed by intervals of quiet. It is the latter, he thinks, that have the greater impact and add so ominously to the ship's general atmosphere of suspense. As he ponders the ironies, the unusual circumstances of his first posting in the navy, he recalls the unnerving revelations of two men, Christopher Isherwood and Edward Upward, who told of their panic when, as undergraduates, they discovered the 'other town' below the real Cambridge, of how their obsession with a place of mystery became apparent only when darkness fell. The ship's character, too, appears to change during the night hours.

When the other midshipmen start to stir, Sutton begins to appreciate that his feelings of anxiety are shared by colleagues. The dawn hour may not be well liked, but nervous conversations indicate that few are keen to linger; the young officers decide to leave their hammocks promptly. As they follow their domestic routines, Midshipman Sutton notes how everyday chatter seems uncharacteristically restrained this morning. But if the midshipmen are subdued, their sense of relief is clear when they spot that the armed marine guards remain at their posts at the entrance to the gunroom. Plainly these men, at least, continue to obey the captain's orders.

In other parts of the ship, however, there has been a less enthusiastic approach to duty. Midshipman Sutton and his colleagues will discover that a number of black eyes testify to the extent of force and intimidation. The *Repulse* may have been affected, but violence has been evident in other ships too. Agitated by the lack of a response to their action, crews held discussions on board a number of ships during the night. There have been reports of activists touring lower decks to remind ratings of their obligations. If commitment to the cause was doubtful, acts of 'persuasion' were arranged in a swift and autocratic manner by strike leaders. As the strictures of a well-regulated ship's society evaporated within the cloak of darkness, as the Naval Discipline Act was cast to the September winds, so the air of tension and fear began to rise. From the revolvers of certain officers to the bare knuckles of men in the lower decks, everyone soon discovered the need to use any available means to fend for themselves. Later in the day, Midshipman Sutton will reflect on how the presence of armed marines ensured that he and his colleagues were better placed than many. He will realize that the marines themselves must have appreciated the ability to defend fellow marines and others with weapons that were issued officially. He will consider, too, the vulnerability of the individual; the sense of loneliness triggered in a once-orderly society which has become suddenly and substantially lawless.

As he and his fellows carry out their hammock slinging and other domestic chores, they receive directions from their 'snotties' nurse: all midshipmen should remain in their mess until further notice. In the afternoon Midshipman Sutton will be tasked with specific picket boat duties, but for much of the morning he and his colleagues will be confined to quarters in the gunroom. At one point a flustered 'snotties' nurse attempts to bolster their morale. His agitation, though, is obvious: his visit hardly reassures his protégés, who glance at each other in bewilderment when he eventually hurries from the gunroom with muttered excuses. The room subsequently quietens for a spell until morale is boosted by other visitors: personnel from the ship's galley deliver breakfast amidst universal sighs of relief. Thankfully the cooks as well as the marines continue with their duties. The midshipmen's meal is leisurely until interrupted by a terse message from the 'snotties' nurse: he intends to start classroom lectures shortly. Before long, however, the marine guards deliver a further message: the lieutenant commander has decided to cancel lectures and the midshipmen will be required to assist instead with a project to paint the ship's side. At length the midshipmen receive a follow-up message: plans to paint the ship's side have been cancelled because large numbers of ratings have failed to turn to.

The fleet's midshipmen may be confined to their messes, the officers to their wardrooms, but the overall scene in the Cromarty Firth indicates that most ratings are rather less inhibited. Men decide to take advantage of the morning's exceptional circumstances. A marine corporal on HMS *Valiant* will later report: 'The industry of the ship got under way this morning. Behind one breakwater you'd find a chap soling shoes, behind another the sewing firm – the sailors' sewing firm, one with a machine, the button boy sewing buttons on, another making buttonholes. Then there'd be a photographic firm – a couple of fellows with a good camera to photograph shipmates. Each gun is separated by an armoured bulkhead, and behind there'd be the master of his trade. Haircuts, 3 pence a time. In my casemate, for'ard with a gangway, there's a dartboard. The lads are up there, eleven o'clock in the morning, playing darts, which they didn't ought to have been.'

Moored just to the south of the *Valiant* is HMS *York*, one of the ships where men held meetings in the night. The ratings on the *York* were shamed by yesterday's taunts from the *Valiant*'s crews: 'Y-O-R-K YELLOW.' Today her crew wish to demonstrate solidarity with others in a more visible manner. Ship's colours are hoisted at 0800 after which a hundred or more ratings congregate on the forecastle. They begin to cheer nearby ships, the *Valiant* to the north, the *Exeter* and the *Adventure* to the west and east respectively. The captain, afraid of prompting a confrontation between seamen and marines, decides to read the articles of war to crew members whom he considers loyal. He asks the men to use their influence on others but as one rating later points out: 'The articles of war make you think a bit, but they couldn't hang the lot of us.'

As the morning progresses, the man in charge of the fleet's cruiser squadron, Rear-Admiral Astley-Rushton, chooses to visit the ships under his command. An arrogant man with a reputation as a bully, he is deeply upset by what is going on. Perhaps aware of the influence of Able Seaman Wincott, his first port of call is HMS *Norfolk*. A boy with the Royal Naval Volunteer Reserve watches Astley-Rushton's performance with fascination: 'A red-faced admiral comes aboard from a picket boat manned by petty officers and we are summoned to the quarter-deck. This is usually done at the double but the men just saunter there. The admiral stands on a gun turret and harangues us in an explosive fit of angry words mixed with curses. As a young man I feel shocked to hear a senior officer curse like that. And as he shouts, men just drift back to the forecastle without permission.'

Astley-Rushton has misjudged the mood badly. When his picket boat approaches HMS *Adventure*, ratings line the rails of the mid-ships gangway and start to jeer. Despite appeals, the men refuse to allow him aboard. A marine records how the admiral 'looks as if he is almost in tears. He speaks through a megaphone. "Please, men, go back to work.

We'll get it all sorted out eventually. I know it's hard for you, but it's three hundred years of tradition going down the drain if you carry on like this." '

The efforts of the Atlantic Fleet's senior officers may prove pitiful, but some of the ratings begin to feel uneasy as the morning's unprecedented scenes unfold. As one man will explain later: 'I remember feeling – as I saw the disorder – that when discipline breaks down anything could happen. So many men felt panicked. I remember feeling quite scared that anything could happen. Boats were being lowered and people messing about, communicating and all that sort of thing . . .'

The men's uneasiness, however, would no doubt increase tenfold with revelations about the morning's talks in London. The Board of Admiralty, whose members meet at 0930, have an hour and a half to prepare advice for the Cabinet. Rear-Admiral Colvin is invited to present his dossier of typical hardship cases. Having listened to these, the Board members have to discuss their options. Aware that stories of the mutiny are in the morning newspapers, they know as well that lack of coverage in the continental press will afford some respite from the whims of foreign bankers. They perhaps sense undue pressures from these money-men. Possibly, as well, there's a growing awareness of panic within the government. Perhaps they are off-colour, inclined even to bouts of cerebral storm – key individuals have absented themselves on sick leave already. Whatever the background reasons, and despite the shrouds of confidentiality which make facts hard to discern, disturbing truths will be disclosed by some of those present. The details will lead to an uncomfortable analysis: certain Board members believe that decisive military action could settle the whole matter before the foreign bankers start to lose confidence, that bombardment of the Atlantic Fleet with heavy howitzers from the hills around the Cromarty Firth could resolve the crisis.

Moves to launch a military assault on the fleet using marine artillery or naval aircraft would need formal government authorization and the approval of the King. The First Lord of the Admiralty is Austen Chamberlain, a politician who prefers the contemplation of political issues on the grand scale and who is uneasy with his backwater job. He regards his position as a 'caretaker one which is suddenly to become a centre of danger and interest'. He considers that the admirals around him have brought little humour or imagination to their posts and scarcely any of the foresight and understanding now required. He tells these men of his discussions yesterday with his brother Neville, the Chancellor of the Exchequer, and with the Lord President of the Council, Stanley Baldwin. He explains that in his opinion the idea of military intervention would have approval at the highest levels of government.

And while the Board agonize over the prospects of such an incredible scheme, it is the First Sea Lord, Admiral Field, who eventually proposes a fresh line of thought. He is an accomplished conjuror and a member of the Magic Circle, and from his admiral's hat, he now produces a white rabbit of lifesaving potential, one which ultimately will provide the solution to the trials and tribulations of a tired and troubled Board. He suggests that by refusing to sail on exercises the men have got themselves into an impossibly entrenched situation. However, their main concern, especially the more moderate amongst them – surely the majority – is for their families. Most men would be unlikely to resist the opportunity of an early return to their wives and children. The answer, says Admiral Field, is to persuade the men to sail directly to their home ports.

At 1100 the Cabinet meet as planned. Austen Chamberlain hastens to this meeting and reads out the telegrams received from Admiral Tomkinson. The Cabinet, it seems, are willing to sanction an attack on the fleet but Chamberlain tells them of another possibility. At this point Admirals Field and Colvin are brought in. While Colvin explains his notion that an order to return to home ports may not work and that some financial concession might be needed as well, a further signal is received from Admiral Tomkinson headed 'MOST IMMEDIATE'. The message is taken into the cabinet meeting: 'I am of the opinion that the situation will get entirely out of control unless an immediate concession is made . . .'

The session lasts for over three hours. Towards the end, another signal is received from the fleet. Again headed 'MOST IMMEDIATE' the message reads: 'Situation 1400. Fleet informed Cabinet sitting at noon. More ships have ceased ordinary harbour work and men are massing on forecastles at intervals. Adjacent ships cheering each other. Interference with running machinery and forced inter-ship communication may be the next step.' However, in spite of this message, a number of Cabinet members apparently remain undecided; there is significant pressure for the use of force. Finally, though, common sense prevails. The Cabinet agree that some form of financial help should be considered, especially to classes of men suffering real hardship. The time is past 1400 when the meeting breaks up.

Admiralty staff are informed of the cabinet's decisions at once. Officers are instructed to pass on the information without delay: 'The Board of Admiralty is fully alive to the fact that amongst certain classes of rating special hardship will result from the reduction in pay ordered by HM Government. It is therefore directed that ships of the Atlantic Fleet are to proceed to their home ports forthwith to enable personal investigation by commanders-in-chief and representatives from the Admiralty with a view to necessary alleviation being made. Any further refusals of individuals to carry out orders will be dealt with under the Naval Discipline Act . . . (ADM178/129).'

It is during these high level machinations that Midshipman Sutton receives a summons from the 'snotties' nurse. By now the time is around 1700, and the midshipman finds the lieutenant commander in a state of excitement. 'Mister Sutton,' he says briskly, 'I'm sure you'll be glad of a little fresh air, so I have a small task for you. The captain wants various documents and other items delivered straightaway. As you did such a good job the other day, I'd like you to take charge of the picket boat for a couple of hours.'

'Thank you, sir. I'll be happy to do that.'

'You're perhaps aware of the news just in?'

'The Admiralty has instructed us to sail for our home port at Chatham?'

'Yes, but it's not just us. The whole fleet has been ordered to return to home ports. Admiral Tomkinson has set the fleet's sailing time for twenty-one hundred this evening.'

'Will this do the trick, sir?'

The lieutenant commander shrugs and says in a confidential tone: 'I'm sure the importance of persuading men to accept this order is understood by all in the fleet. We have just four hours left to comply – and hopefully to bring this trouble to an end.'

'And if the men don't comply?'

'I dread to think what might happen.' The lieutenant commander waves one hand. 'I can only assume that officers and ratings know that the future of the navy – even of the country – is in the balance.'

'The country?'

'You've heard these rumours about the gold standard?'

'That the country's linkage to the gold standard may have to be ended?'

'Exactly.' The lieutenant commander frowns. 'Contrary to popular belief I am not omniscient and I don't pretend to be a financial wizard, but I'm told that the consequences of abandoning the gold standard could be very serious.'

'Perhaps the men are too wrapped up in their own problems to see the larger picture.'

'I'm sure there's an element of that, Mister Sutton, but even so this situation has been handled so badly that, frankly, it's hard to blame the men for the stand they've taken. Nevertheless, one can't help worrying about the larger picture as you put it, and as for this latest twist . . .'

The midshipman gesticulates the length of the ship as he says: 'What's been the reaction here, sir?'

'A very good question,' says the 'snotties' nurse. He continues with lowered voice: 'I mustn't speak too soon, and fingers crossed and all that, but to be honest I have the impression of an air of relief. Men perhaps welcome an end to this atmosphere of uncertainty. However, having said that, what happens on this ship will not necessarily be replicated elsewhere.'

'How do you mean?'

'No doubt the men on some of the fleet's worst-affected ships realize that they're in a strong bargaining position just now. They may feel that once they put to sea their position of advantage could be lost – that anything might happen. Perhaps, therefore, they see the home ports order as a trap.'

'But not on this ship?'

'Let's put it this way, Mister Sutton. We had no difficulty in raising the picket boat crew. The men responded without argument and your crew make the boat ready as we speak. I suggest, therefore, that you gear up as quickly as possible then report for duty.'

'Yes, sir.'

'And the best of British, Mister Sutton. Remember to keep your eyes and ears open on your travels. We'll wait to hear what you have to say. The duty officer will take your report when you get back. Good luck.'

The midshipman hastens towards the drying area to retrieve his gear. In his mind, he goes over standard picket boat procedures. He decides to don oilskins before he hurries to the ship's picket boat area. He arrives to see the boat already lowered in the water and with davits being detached. While the crew carry out further checks, the duty officer hands across documents and detailed instructions. Midshipman Sutton double checks the names of the ships to be visited, then nods acknowledgement before he steps on board the picket boat. He takes up position next to the coxswain. He cries:

'Stand by to cast off!' The crew members seem glad of the opportunity to escape the *Repulse*'s oppressive atmosphere. The men respond to the routine commands, and the coxswain opens up the throttle as he steers away from the *Repulse* to head due west towards Invergordon. The crew relish the wind in their faces as the vessel is directed towards the first of the fleet's ships to be visited.

Some two hours later, when Midshipman Sutton and his crew have completed their task, the 2 miles from HMS *Nelson* is soon covered. The picket boat is manoeuvred towards the *Repulse*'s landing ladder, then secured. The crew climb the ladder and as they do so, men sense a change of atmosphere. A businesslike air has replaced earlier lethargy as the *Repulse* is made ready for sea. The duty officer has left instructions for the midshipman to report to the bridge immediately.

When he pushes open the bridge door, the midshipman glances

around with a sense of disappointment. Staff appear too absorbed with their duties to notice his presence. Eventually the duty officer looks up and bustles across impatiently to take the young officer's report. 'Welcome back, Mister Sutton,' he says. 'As you see we're rather busy at present, but how did you get on?'

'The reaction of ships varied considerably, sir. On some we saw quarrels, sometimes even fights – we were waved away before I had a chance to deliver the documents. Other ships seemed all right. We had no difficulties, for example, with the *York* or with the *Rodney*.'

'That ties in with the information we've been getting from other sources. It seems that officers on some ships have had to convince their ratings that the Admiralty order is *bona fide* and not some kind of trick. Fortunately our own crew on the *Repulse* seem to have accepted the order at face value.'

'We shall be sailing for Chatham as planned?'

'That's the way it looks.' The duty officer nods. 'But have you anything else to report?'

'No, sir, that's all.'

'In that case you can change out of your gear, then the 'snotties' nurse wants you back on the bridge to resume your duties.'

The midshipman acknowledges and hurries away. On his return he finds the bridge staff with binoculars trained on HMS *Adventure*. That ship is moored on the fleet's southerly rank, next in line after the destroyer HMS *Shikari*. By now the time is approaching 2000 and the *Adventure* has an important charge: she is the first of the fleet scheduled to sail. However, she is one of the ships that refused permission for Midshipman Sutton's picket boat to pull alongside. Despite this, current signs suggest that her engine room is working and that the captain has ordered his officers to take the ship to sea in spite of the ongoing arguments between ratings. Tension rises as everyone in the fleet monitors her progress. At length there are excited comments as, at 2020, she leaves her moorings as planned. Staff on the fleet's bridges now debate anxiously whether she will be alone as the *Repulse* was yesterday. Two cruisers soon provide the answer: the *Exeter* is seen to weigh anchor followed by the *Dorsetshire*. If the officers breathe sighs of relief, they do so quietly. The next ship due out is HMS *Norfolk*, whose crucial role has seen lower-deck squabbles flare into sporadic acts of violence. Eventually, however, Able Seaman Wincott's control and his strike committee's imperious rule begin to ebb away. At that point Wincott pronounces ruefully: 'The home ports order could be a ruse, but it's a risk we've got to take.' And when the *Norfolk* is seen to weigh anchor, when she slips out of harbour under the scrutiny of the rest of the fleet, all now realize that resistance has crumbled. The mutiny is over.

Three days later, when the ships have docked in their home ports, the crews are permitted shore leave in watches.

When Midshipman Sutton is issued with a rail warrant, he decides to begin his journey home without delay. He boards a train bound for London with hopes that a spell at home might ease a feeling of fatigue, help restore a sense of equilibrium. As the train, in a frenzy of steam, pulls slowly out of the station he surveys the peaceful Kent countryside with an air of weariness. The train blusters past the towns of Rochester, Gravesend, and Dartford on its way to London for the first part of his journey. He sees his fellow passengers studying newspaper articles under headlines like: 'Gold Standard to be abandoned – Ramsey MacDonald must think the unthinkable.' The people around him will be unaware of his connection with the dramas that engineered such news. He speculates on the reaction of the ratings in the Atlantic Fleet. He assumes the men will find theories about the gold standard less interesting than issues about their pay. But will their actions, he wonders, have achieved their objectives? In time he will learn that the government's decision to limit pay reductions to 10 per cent will have only a minor relevance for most ratings. For the majority of men, cuts in their allowances will bring their total loss of pay close to the amounts originally intended.

But apart from matters of pay, what about broader aspects? Has his baptism of fire – perhaps with a dash of flood – dampened his enthusiasm for the navy? That service of tradition, of awareness of its history, is about to change for ever. In future, welfare will have to be taken seriously, men will have to be led, not driven. He recollects the dangers of discipline breakdown, the unexpected consequences – the sense of an enemy at once everywhere and nowhere, an enemy within. As he ponders, and as he realizes the justness of the ratings' case, he recalls the acts of belligerence. He remembers the worries of the officers, the violence and the vacillations of the lower decks, the fear felt by all.

He glances at the serious faces in the carriage. He muses that a little good humour can go a long way; resolution becomes harder as positions become polarized. He closes his eyes to calm the turbulent scenes that rush through his mind. But the flashbacks persist – images that disturb and shock him, although he will be amazed to learn the truth when the repercussions are explained fully. Eventually, however, he will begin to understand. It will take a long time – a matter of months, even years – but ultimately he will come to realize the implications of recent events, how their significance will prove to be as profound as his career will prove to be diverse and remarkable.

PART TWO

Spanish Interlude

CHAPTER ELEVEN

Spithead to Spain

SAINT-JEAN-DE-LUZ, FRANCE, JUNE 1937

Lieutenant Alan William Frank Sutton is impatient as he glances around his cabin. He has much to do and he is eager to proceed with his tasks. Before he starts, however, he must check his cabin for domestic and other preparations. He bends to inspect the clothes chest below his bunk and confirms that his kit has been stowed by his seaman steward. As he spots the neatness of layout, he gives a nod of approval. He makes a mental note: he must remember to thank the steward, to praise the reliable man's efforts. Officers used to be careless about such matters but attitudes have changed in recent years. The gulf between officers and their men still exists, although perhaps not to the same degree or in the same sense as in the past. Officers have learned new perspectives. He ponders the ways in which outlooks have altered since he first joined the navy. Officers now realize the need to care for the men and to demonstrate the reasons why they care. The Royal Navy's divisional system has been remodelled; efforts are made to keep the men well informed, and priority is given to welfare these days. Ratings appreciate this and the officers have to make positive attempts to avoid the air of mistrust, the examples of poor leadership so painfully evident at Invergordon six years ago.

The lieutenant now tests the safe stowage of his bunk. This is hooked against a bulkhead to allow extra space in his small cabin (approximately 6 ft square). When he is satisfied with the security of the arrangement, he grabs the back of the solitary chair in one corner. However, as he attempts to pull it towards his desk, he falters. He is distracted by a particular sound: the far-off yelp of a dog. When he glances through his cabin side scuttle he catches a glimpse of everyday harbour life . . . seamen, fishermen, officials, gendarmes, families, lovers, strollers all amble and gesticulate as they discuss the harbour's sounds and sights. He notes that his ship, HMS *Basilisk*, is a focus of interest. Locals seem unabashed as they gaze across and point. They chat about her, about her twin funnel arrangement, her step-shaped hull with the pennant number

H11, and about the destroyer's distinctive aura of threat. They debate the reasons for her presence. They talk about other ships too, and the events that influence the life of Saint-Jean-de-Luz and her small harbour.

In a sudden movement, the lieutenant tries to ward off an insect blustering towards his cabin. With irritation he swipes at it but misses; the insect swerves then disappears. He mutters an oath and looks outside again at the swirls of heat haze above the roads and buildings and at the water's surface, quickened by dazzles of reflected sunlight. The intensity of the heat can seem insufferable at times, although he realizes that a sea breeze should offer relief eventually. He continues to gaze through the porthole and as he does so he notices a man in military uniform walk up to a young woman seated on a harbour bench. The military man salutes. The young woman's reaction is one of surprise. A friendly nod, however, indicates that she knows the man. She hesitates, then stands up and shyly steps towards him. A conversation begins and after some moments she throws back her head in a gesture of spontaneous laughter. Perhaps, muses the lieutenant, the two are lovers. The impromptu scene intrigues him, but he realizes that time presses; he should hurry. He grasps the chair again and this time drags it firmly towards his desk.

He places the chair in position but he feels somewhat forlorn as he remains standing. He would prefer to be outside enjoying the sun and the open air, but he needs a relative haven, somewhere to concentrate, with less chance of disturbance. He has reports to write up, the deck and the ship's logs to check, and he hopes, as well, to make time to pen a letter or two home. His gaze alternates between desk and chair as if reluctant to commence. He has to decide on his priorities. As the ship's second lieutenant he appreciates that he should catch up on paperwork to do with the ship's non-intervention patrols around the Spanish coast. Additionally, he has to write a special report following the *Basilisk*'s involvement in last month's coronation naval review at Spithead. He wavers for some moments while he deliberates. Should he tackle the Spithead report first? Perhaps he should. The captain wants to see this report in draft form before a final copy is produced. As he cogitates, the lieutenant recalls the background; how the ship was stationed at Gibraltar under a different captain, Commander DeWinton, before the Spithead review. Her crew had cheered when their ship was selected for the coronation review; they were glad to be part of an historic event, and were happy about the prospect of home leave.

HMS *Basilisk* had set off for home waters early in May. Like the other hundred or more ships involved, she had to be newly painted and specially prepared for the review. The event, on 20 May, 1937, was hailed as an outstanding success although, as can be the case with momentous occasions, its conclusion had led to an air of anticlimax. There had been

A.W.F. Sutton at Christ's Hospital School

2. A.W.F. Sutton as cadet at HMS *Erebus*, 1930.

Christ's Hospital School circa 1929. A.W.F. Sutton (2nd left) (*badge on shoulder indicates naval cadet*)

4. View of HMS *Repulse's* guns

5. HMS *Repulse* in the Azores, en route to the West Indies

6. HMS *Repulse's* brass-funnelled picket boat

ib-lieutenants' course at Greenwich. (*A.W.F. Sutton centre row, far left*)

adets at HMS *Erebus*, August 1931. (*A.W.F. Sutton top row, far right*)

10. "Making smoke"

11. 4.7-inch guns firing at 40 degr elevation

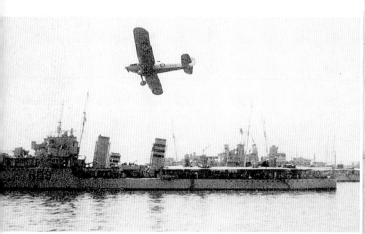

12. Lowering a whaler to pick up torpedoes

13. Smoke float

14. Aircraft practising dummy
attacks on destroyers

15. Lieutenant
A.W.F. Sutton
c 1935

16. HMS *Basilisk* at Port Said, 1936

17. HMS *Basilisk*

18. HMS *Basilisk*'s wardroom

19. HMS *Basilisk*

Captain of Italian destroyer boards HMS *Basilisk*, February 1937

HMS *Basilisk*, 1937

20. Perparations to welcome the Duke of Seville on board HMS *Basilisk*, February 1937

21. HMS *Hood* at the fleet review, 20 May, 1937

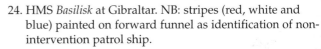

23. Royal yacht *Victoria and Albert* passes HMS *Basilisk*, 20 May, 1937

24. HMS *Basilisk* at Gibraltar. NB: stripes (red, white and blue) painted on forward funnel as identification of non-intervention patrol ship.

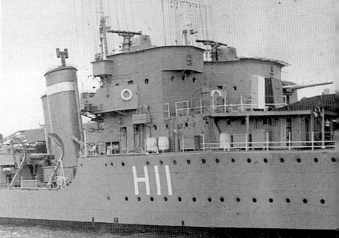

26. Queen Elizabeth, King George VI and Princess Elizabeth at the review of the fleet at Spithead, 20 May, 1937

27. Fleet Air Arm flypast at the fleet review, 20 May 1937

28 & 29. Fleet Air Arm flypast at fleet review, 20 May 1937.

30. Miss M. Cazeaux as Franco Nurse, 1937

31. Above: Miss M. Cazeaux (*front left*) - Lieuten A.W.F. Sutton (*front centre*) summer 1937

32. Left: Lieutenant A.W.F. Sutton writing the de log, HMS *Basilisk*, 1937

33. Below: The inner harbour at La Pallice, France

34. HMS *Boreas* approaches HMS *Basilisk* in order to pass mail by line, 1937

35. Merchantman in northern Spanish waters, 1937

36. Ships stand off near Bilbao, northern Spain

37. Aerial view of Littlehampton, 1938

38. No. 32 Naval Observers' Course, January-June 1938

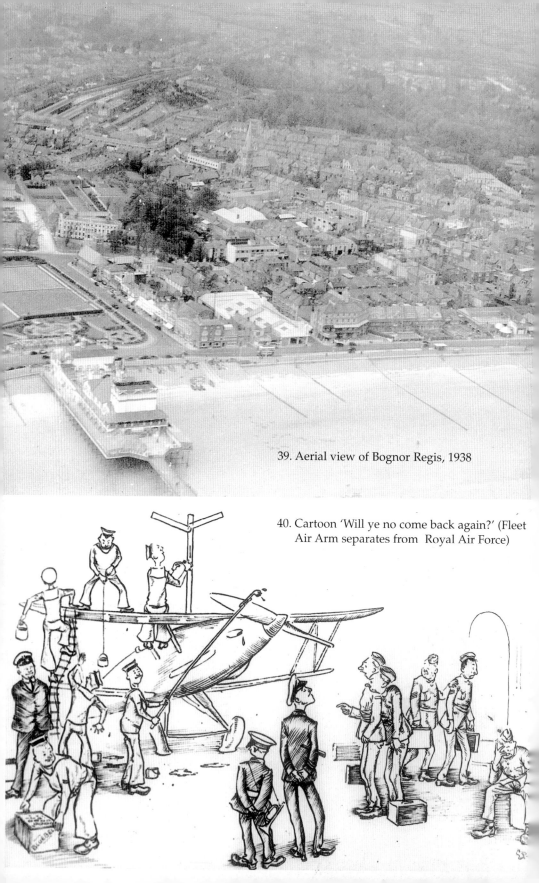

39. Aerial view of Bognor Regis, 1938

40. Cartoon 'Will ye no come back again?' (Fleet
Air Arm separates from Royal Air Force)

41. Swordfish aircraft launches from HMS *Glorious*, 1938

42. Swordfish aircraft after landing on HMS *Glorious*, 1938

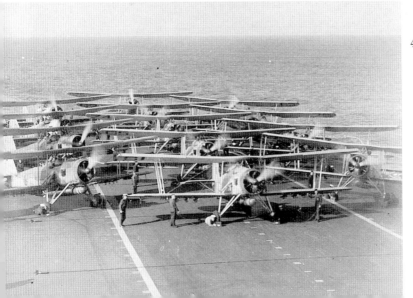

43. Swordfish aircraft ranged on deck of HMS *Glorious*, 1938

44. Osprey float plane after crash-landing (pilot - Lieutenant C. Horsfall)

45. Damaged Osprey (left) - Swordfish fitted with floats (right)

46. 823 Sqn overfly HMS *Glorious*

47. Pilots and observers watch aircraft operate ahead of the fleet on passage from Greece to Alexandria, 1938

48. HMS *Glorious*, 1938

49. HMS *Glorious*, 1938

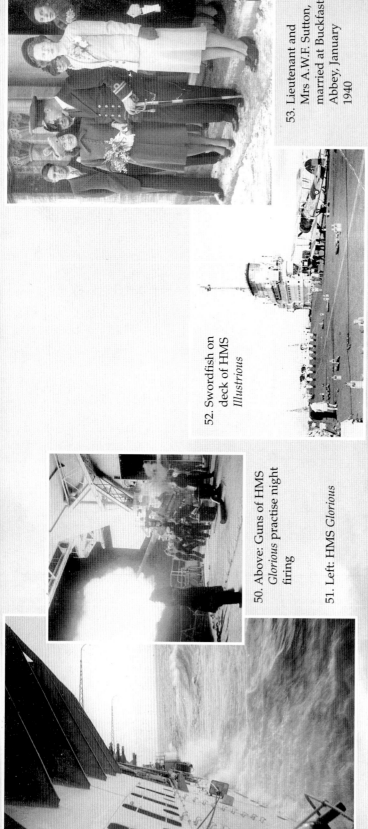

50. Above: Guns of HMS *Glorious* practise night firing

51. Left: HMS *Glorious*

52. Swordfish on deck of HMS *Illustrious*

53. Lieutenant and Mrs A.W.F. Sutton, married at Buckfast Abbey, January 1940

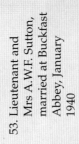

54. Combined Mediterranean and Home

a curiously downbeat atmosphere when the ships had dispersed to resume their normal duties. In the case of the *Basilisk* this had meant a return to non-intervention patrol duties, although she would no longer be based at Gibraltar. In future she would patrol the northern Spanish coasts in a rotational cycle with other ships; the Admiralty had directed her and other Royal Navy destroyers to police the Spanish coasts as part of an international effort to limit the spread of the civil war that erupted across Spain in July last year. At that time, the British government had relied on a policy of non-intervention, the politicians hopeful that the struggle might peter out for lack of arms and ammunition. The ship would spend ten or so days at sea before sailing for replenishment at the port of La Pallice, near La Rochelle on the west coast of France. After replenishment, the ship would reposition at the small harbour at Saint-Jean-de-Luz until ordered to recommence patrol duties. The period at Saint-Jean-de-Luz usually meant a few days of enjoyable leisure time for the crew of a dozen or so officers and around 120 men.

As the lieutenant stands by his desk he seems relaxed. However, he becomes tenser and his frown deepens when he considers another, more personal, aspect. The *Basilisk* is now under the command of a new captain, Commander Dangerfield. Lieutenant Sutton had enjoyed the set-up at Gibraltar and had liked Commander DeWinton; the two had got on well. He feels worried, though, about the new man; he hopes sincerely that the name will not turn out to be regrettably apposite. But he knows he should not dwell on such matters; he must concentrate on his paperwork instead. At length he sits down fretfully. He stares gloomily at his desktop. He picks up his pen then impatiently, mechanically, taps the nib against the desktop. He rubs his brow as if urging inspiration. A descriptive and interesting report, said the captain, platitudes to be avoided. That is easy for the captain to ask. The lieutenant glances at the photograph on his desktop and his serious expression softens to a smile. In the centre of the picture a young woman seems coy as she returns his smile. She is, he thinks, uncommonly handsome. She reminds him of happy days of leave during the Spithead period. He sighs; perhaps the relationship was not destined to blossom; perhaps it cannot be seen as long term. Perhaps, perhaps . . . but that smile: so tentative and teasing, at once confident and reserved. His smile lingers as he notices her dress. He gazes with admiration at the classic style, the puffed sleeves, the soft frill around the neck. The long design may cover her legs but he gives a nod of delight as he observes how these are curled elegantly on top of his picnic rug. By her arm a picnic basket is laden with fare.

But he must proceed with his report. He checks the photographs he took at Spithead and glances at the assorted press cuttings he managed to set aside. 'The King Reviews His Navy's Might,' declares one head-line. As he studies the sub-heading, he reads with fascination: '20 May 1937. In ideal weather, King George VI, accompanied by Queen Elizabeth and Princess Elizabeth, reviewed at Spithead the greatest assembly of shipping, naval and mercantile, ever gathered. After the guns of more than one hundred warships had thundered a salute, His Majesty, on board the royal yacht *Victoria and Albert*, passed through eight lines of vessels covering 24 square miles.'

As he thinks about this, Lieutenant Sutton gives a quiet gasp of astonishment. '. . . the greatest assembly . . . *ever gathered* . . .' He holds his pen firmly while he contemplates the significance of such a state-ment. He moves his head slowly from side to side, a gesture of respectful appreciation, before he reads on:

'Officers had exchanged their work-a-day uniform for gold lace full dress, cocked hats and swords, while the ships' companies were groomed as only British bluejackets can be. At 1.30 p.m. the review area was closed to all except official craft. At 3 o'clock all eyes and all glasses were trained on the narrow entrance of Portsmouth Harbour. Twenty minutes later the Trinity House yacht *Patricia* emerged, and behind her the fine form of the royal yacht *Victoria and Albert*. For several minutes there was silence, broken only by the waves lapping against the sides of the ships, the fluttering of flags, and the crying of gulls. Then the royal salute thundered out from more than one hundred vessels as each ship fired the prescribed twenty-one rounds.'

He remembers the din created by that royal salute. In his mind he pictures the smoke generated by the guns, the seemingly endless rows of ships, the distant crowds on the shore, the atmosphere perceptibly tense. He glances at an adjacent photograph and sighs nostalgically as he continues to read:

'The royal yacht traversed the van of line A at 3.30 p.m., and across the water could be heard the ringing cheers of ships' companies followed by what seemed to be echoes but which were in fact new vocal salvoes from ships further down the line. The *Victoria and Albert* set off initially on a north-westerly course through lines D and E. The king's review then continued for some one and a half hours until, at around five o'clock, the royal yacht returned to her anchorage. For over half an hour there was something like a 'stand easy', but at 5.40 p.m. the sky was filled with the noise of many wings when one hundred and eight aircraft of the Fleet Air Arm flew over the *Victoria and Albert*, the aeroplanes dipping in salute. Late last night came a magnificent spectacle when, against a dark sea, all assembled ships blazed into outlines of glittering light, swept the sky with their searchlights and sent up great bouquets of star shells, rockets and roman candles. Throughout the day enthusiastic crowds totalling nearly a million people lined the shores of the Solent.'

He glances up, lost in thought – a million people. Eventually he looks down again, forcing himself to concentrate as he rechecks the article to seek confirmation of certain facts: '. . . initially on a north-westerly course through lines D and E'. This concurs with the details and with the timing he needs for his report: HMS *Basilisk* was positioned in line E next to HMS *Kempenfield* to the east and HMS *Boreas* to the west. That will be the start point of his report. His expression alters as he becomes focused; he grips his pen resolutely and begins.

For some while his mind remains fixed on the specifics of his report but at length, as he nears the end of the draft, he looks up. He puts down his pen and rummages for a particular photograph. He remembers that his box-Brownie camera was at hand when the royal yacht passed by the *Basilisk*. When he finds the picture and studies the images, he chuckles quietly to himself. He realizes that he should have been stiffly at attention as the royal yacht passed, his right hand in formal salute. Perhaps he will not show this picture to Commander Dangerfield. He stares at the photograph for some seconds. He recalls the cheers from the *Basilisk* and the surrounding vessels, the graceful form of the Trinity House yacht as she swept ahead of the *Victoria and Albert*, the succession of liners trailing behind, and the diminutive figures, barely visible, as they waved from the royal yacht. The atmosphere becomes clear in his mind as he stares at his personal, if unofficial, photograph and at others in the newspaper. As he rechecks the newspaper reports, he spots the words of Leslie M. Oyler, the writer whose sentiments seemed to epitomize the attitudes of the period – a period when the nation was proud of its navy, of its heritage, and of its empire. He reads the poem:

EMPIRE DAY

Our empire, like a mighty chain
Grows longer yet and yet again
It circles many seas and lands
Is grasped by many eager hands

But still at home its clasp is set
And Britain's sons will not forget
That every link bought with a price
Is forged with love and sacrifice

Brave souls on land as well as sea
Have kept our country fine and free
So let us work and work with might
To keep our chains of empire bright.

Chains of empire? Eager hands? Are these apt descriptions, or is Oyler reflecting romantic and outdated concepts? As the lieutenant thinks of the volatile world scene, the opposing forces of fascism and communism, the rise of extremist leaders – Hitler, Mussolini, Stalin, Franco – and the relentless rearmament of Germany, he speculates on whether the chains of the British Empire are about to be severed for ever. He wonders whether the British are facing up to international realities and if not, what are the implications for Spain and the growing Spanish tragedy? Is the response from Britain seen as rational and honest? Does the might of the British Empire, that empire apparently grasped by so many eager hands, hold the solution to Spain's conundrums?

He realizes that such an idea is flawed. At the start of the Spanish Civil War last year, when the French had suggested a policy of non-intervention, the proposal was accepted eagerly by Britain and by other nations. Non-intervention was seen as a pragmatic response to intractable difficulties, a convenient way to side-step complex issues. With memories of the Great War still in politicians' minds, the main concern was to confine the war to Spain; to prevent it, as a matter of priority, from spreading to France and elsewhere. Thus the formal acceptance last August of a non-intervention agreement by twenty-seven nations was hailed as a fair solution to a troublesome problem, a problem for which Britain and other nations had been woefully ill-prepared.

The non-intervention agreement, however, was swiftly revealed as spurious. The lieutenant recollects last year's hopes when the non-intervention committee was set up in London on 9 September, but such hopes had proved groundless. In the words of the German representative, Joachim von Ribbentrop, the non-intervention committee might be more aptly named 'the intervention committee'. But it is Germany, ponders the lieutenant, along with Italy and the Soviet Union, that most openly and ruthlessly flout the agreements. When the *Luftwaffe*'s Condor Legions attacked Guernica in northern Spain just a few weeks ago on the 26 April, their action was surely the grossest, most extreme form of intervention. The Germans had tried to disclaim responsibility but reports had leaked out and the world had learned the truth about a cruel and calculated action. The initial foray was heralded by a lone Heinkel 111 bomber which, like some teasing, pernicious harbinger had appeared suddenly, dropped its load, then disappeared. As local people emerged from shelters to help the injured, it seemed to be the signal for a full squadron to fly over, prompting a stampede of people into the fields. At that point squadrons of Heinkel 51 fighter-bombers began to strafe the fleeing men, women and children, even the nuns from the hospital and the livestock. The major part of the attack, however, was yet to come. By early evening, when Junkers 52s had completed their two and a half hours of systematic carpet bombing, when cows, sheep and fighting bulls ran crazily between burnt-out and burning buildings, when blackened humans staggered blindly between flames, smoke, dust, when others used bare hands to scrabble at rubble to rescue friends and relatives, eyewitnesses described the scenes in terms of hell and the apocalypse. The world would learn that the people of Guernica had been the innocent victims of a calculated experiment in *blitzkrieg*.

The ruthlessness displayed at Guernica, the flagrant disregard for the non-intervention committee, had appalled the world and had underlined the frailty of international politics. Other insidious implications had emerged, for example how the non-intervention arrangements worked to the advantage of the right wing Nationalist forces but against the interests of the fragile but legitimate left-wing Republican government. And as the Germans and the Italians continued to support Franco's Nationalists, so the Soviet Union felt obliged to reinforce the Republican camp. In public, Stalin claimed that the Soviet Union was neutral, but in the seas around Spain, Lieutenant Sutton and his fellow officers could see examples of a rather different policy.

The lieutenant recalls that in the autumn of last year, when Soviet-backed anti-fascist International Brigades began to amass at a secret location in Paris before moving to their base at Albacete in Spain, Stalin said: 'The liberation of Spain from the yoke of fascist reactionaries is not the private concern of Spaniards alone but the common cause of progressive humanity.' The activities of the International Brigades, however, were marked by idealism and by a tendency to simplify the conflict as a clear-cut struggle between left and right. They remained indifferent to the murky undercurrents and complexities of the situation, to the three main axes of conflict – left-right, centralist-regionalist, authoritarian-libertarian – and to the confusion of cross-sections, factions, sub-factions, fascists, communists, Carlists, monarchists, Catholics, non-Catholics, anarchists, syndicalists, Falangists, anti-Stalin communists, Basque separatists, Catalan separatists, further groups and anti-groups, civil wars within the civil war.

The lieutenant realizes that frictions within Spain have built up over many years, especially following the Spanish-American war of thirty-nine years ago, a war which had led to Spain's loss of Cuba, Puerto Rico and the Philippines, and which effectively had spelled the downfall of the Spanish Empire. Subsequent problems that should have been confronted were not, and spiralled out of control as a consequence. This led to the present-day obscenities with Spaniard seeking revenge against Spaniard, with brother set against brother, father against son. Violence breeds further violence, individual identities are submerged within an aura of mysticism and superstition, fear and mistrust fester unchecked, acts of unspeakable, murderous barbarity are repeated routinely – peasant women tied to chairs, humiliated, beaten, doused in paraffin and torched while the men are forced to watch as a preface to their own torture and death. Almost daily there are examples of Ernest Hemingway's 'carnival of treachery and repeated rottenness': a retired military officer shot dead for shouting 'long live Spain!'; innocent, gentle nuns absconded, beaten, humbled, raped; a church fired because the perpetrator knew of the priest's Nationalist sympathies (the priest was his brother); domestic pets held by the neck, their terrified shrieks ignored by masked men who beat their front legs to useless, tangled pulps; *Guardia Civil* policemen, their screams surging above those of their offspring, the men compelled to watch as their children's eyes are gouged out – screams that will terrify, and haunt them for the remainder of their lives, screams mingled with the screams of the perpetrators, of the children, of the priests burned alive or skewered on meat hooks, of the eternal censure of a thousand lips, of the gods of compassion, conscience, reason crying: 'Stop!'

'Sir!' The lieutenant looks up suddenly as he hears a voice and someone rapping at his cabin door. 'Excuse me, sir.' The seaman steward calmly pushes open the cabin door. 'Sorry to interrupt, sir, I know you're busy, but I wondered . . . I thought you might like a cup of coffee. We've got some of this rather good French stuff . . . just been supplied to the wardroom, sir.'

'Thank you.' The lieutenant glances at his watch. 'You're right – a break – just the thing.'

'Would you like the coffee here, sir, or in the wardroom?'

The lieutenant waves one hand airily. 'Make it the wardroom. Change of scene and all that.'

'Yes, sir. Five minutes be all right?'

'Five minutes will be perfectly all right. By the way, thank you for the good job . . .' the lieutenant nods towards the clothes chest under his bunk. The seaman steward grins. 'I'll get that coffee organised, sir.' He hurries off towards the galley.

With one hand the lieutenant mops his brow; the high temperature is not, perhaps, the only cause of his sense of agitation. He reflects on the considerable advantage of working within the relative safety of an armed warship. He ponders the hazards faced by the naval patrols, the potential repercussions at international level. These require support at the highest echelons of the Government and of the non-intervention committee, even though the minds of British elements appear firmly focused on the need not be seen taking sides, the need to avoid the spread of the conflict. The chairman of the non-intervention committee, Lord Plymouth, is known for his ability to proceed with agonizing slowness. The Soviet Union's ambassador to London has said of him: 'In this large, imposing and well-groomed body dwells a small, slow moving and timid mind. Nature and education have made Lord Plymouth an ideal personification of English political mediocrity, nourished by traditions of the past and by well-worn sentiments. As chairman of the committee, Plymouth presents an entirely helpless and often comical figure.'

Is this, wonders the lieutenant, the growing perception of Britain and her empire? Are Leslie M. Oyler's sentiments as outdated as the splendours of the coronation review, the rows of ships, the flypasts, the cheers, the fireworks, the 21-gun salutes at Spithead? Do the nations of the world, far from grasping the British Empire with eager hands, now sneer at the decline of an archaic institution?

The lieutenant sighs: Britain's *Basilisk*: the empire in microcosm. He reflects on HMS *Basilisk*, her overall length of 323 ft, her displacement of 1,360 tons, her four 4.7 in guns, her eight 21 in torpedo tubes, her twin anti-aircraft guns, her two turbines capable of propelling the ship at 35 knots for the efficient conduct of non-intervention patrols. In three years' time HMS *Basilisk* will be attacked by Nazi Stukas, the rescuing role of her crew tragically reversed as the ship is committed to the bottom of the Straits of Dover during the evacuation at Dunkirk. The reports and logs Lieutenant Sutton now completes will go down with the ship. The *Basilisk* will become another casualty of fascism, of obsolete perceptions, of lack of vision. By then a former First Lord of the Admiralty by the name of Churchill will have told Prime Minister Neville Chamberlain that he had a choice between dishonour and war but that by choosing dishonour, the result would be war. And when that war comes, when Churchill replaces the discredited Chamberlain, the incoming prime minister will deliver dire warnings of a new dark age. The Germans will have developed and fine-tuned *blitzkrieg* techniques learned at Guernica and Spain's civil war, Britain's empire, Spithead's glories will be eclipsed under the shadow of world war. And the ordinary folk Lieutenant Sutton now observes in a quiet harbour on the southern coast of France will have become embroiled in a conflict escalated to a scale which, at this moment, they would regard with bewildered and horrified disbelief.

CHAPTER TWELVE

Harbour Life

Discreetly sited beneath HMS *Basilisk's* eight 21 inch torpedo tubes is the ship's wardroom. To outside observers the destroyer may present a warlike exterior, but viewed from the inside the wardroom's scene is rather less forbidding. Although not lavishly luxurious, the room is nonetheless functionally comfortable, with carefully placed cushions to grace armchairs and a single sofa of typical 1930s design. Circular tables of similar character have been positioned next to chairs beside a heater set against a bulkhead. The tables have been freshly polished and laid out with the stipulated number of ashtrays: two per table. The sofa and chairs, loose-covered to allow the wardroom attendants access to clean or replace them easily, have been manufactured with material of approved naval standard. This reflects the tastes of the period – zigzagged lines, interwoven dots, vertical dashes in series as if to indulge some fabric-maker's version of the Morse code. Identical material has been used for small curtains fastened to rails above each porthole, (side-scuttle in naval parlance), and now neatly tied back. For a homely touch, a few pictures have been hung in a somewhat haphazard fashion between the portholes. At one end of the wardroom a dining area of sufficient size for the ship's dozen or so officers has been set aside. The dining table itself has been laid in preparation for the next meal.

Positioned along a passageway from Lieutenant Sutton's cabin, the wardroom is a convenient distance for him, although having made the journey he discovers that even minor exertions seem to emphasize the heat of the day. He mops his brow fretfully as he enters the room. He appreciates, at least, the cleanness of the handkerchief provided by his seaman steward and he appreciates, too, the familiar ambience of 'home' when he enters. It is deserted; other officers have left the ship to make use of a day's shore leave in the environs of Saint-Jean-de-Luz. His own opportunity for shore leave will come later in the day when he is relieved as duty officer. For now, though, he remains conscious of the oppressive heat as he glances in turn at each of the room's portholes to ensure that the port-lights are fully open to encourage a through-draft.

He observes with approval the lustre of the recently polished brass tundishes below the portholes, and the securing screws of the port-lights and dead-lights. Before proceeding to sea, his duties as second lieutenant will include confirming port-light security. He will check reports that all port-lights have been hinged across and screwed in place. In heavy weather, dead-lights above the portholes will be pivoted down as an additional safeguard.

The lieutenant now spies the coffee left by the seaman steward on a side table laid out with newspapers, magazines, and journals. He picks up his cup and strides across the wardroom to inspect the polished brass at close quarters. He examines the brass with a critical eye, then glances out of a porthole to observe the goings-on around the harbour. The scene is similar to that from his cabin, with numbers of people ambling and pointing, the *Basilisk* still a focus of interest. However, the air of bonhomie and relaxation is, he thinks, curiously misleading. The tensions and terrors of Spain, just a handful of miles away beyond the border, cannot be far from the minds of most folk. The two scenarios, French and Spanish, provide a sorry contrast. He sips his coffee as he dwells on this. He picks up the wavering notes of an accordion player, a nostalgic-sounding melody – so strongly reminiscent of France – breathing across the harbour like some seductive opiate. The accordionist remains hidden; perhaps the player is reticent, too carried away with the raptures of the music. Less reticent, though, are two *gendarmes*, their uniforms smartly distinctive as they patrol the harbour area. As the lieutenant gazes at them, he ponders the French consciousness of the dangers that could spill across the border. Last year, the French government appeared disorganized, almost panic stricken, as they mooted the policy of non-intervention. The French authorities, muses the lieutenant, have faced dilemmas at every level, international and local. The authorities in Saint-Jean-de-Luz, for example, will be concerned about troubles stirred up by the presence of foreign seamen around town, the attendant and predictable alcohol misuse, the propositioning of local women.

This last point, recalls the lieutenant, was emphasized just recently when a seaman in his division had approached him for advice. The seaman was worried about an unfortunate (if intriguing) experience with a harbour prostitute. He was embarrassed when he related how he 'stumbled across the prostitute in a poorly lit doorway'. She seemed to recognize the Royal Navy uniform and switched easily to English. 'You pay me now or later, sailor boy?'

The woman, he said, had her back to him in a teasing, tempting manner. She half-turned towards him when she spoke. There was a further exchange, after which she led him along an alleyway then up some stairs to a small room, dingy but spotlessly clean. The bed was of iron and brass, the brass highly polished to appeal to the naval mind. In one corner he glimpsed a wash-stand. He saw a few cheap ornaments around the room, some cheap prints on the walls.

At this stage, the lieutenant coughed politely. 'Perhaps you'd prefer to omit further details?'

The seaman had blushed at this and stared awkwardly at the floor. He felt confused; this was his first experience of such matters. He was too embarrassed to talk to his work-mates but surely he should be able to share confidences with his divisional officer.

'It's up to you,' said the lieutenant.

The seaman hesitated a little longer. Eventually, though, he decided that he wished to continue. He was anxious about repercussions; he felt it best to confide in his divisional officer. 'If you don't mind, sir, I'd like . . .'

'It's your decision, but carry on if you wish.'

The seaman nodded as he said: 'Well, sir, after going to this upstairs room, like, the woman closed the door.' He paused again. The lieutenant waited for a moment before prompting him: 'Well?'

'She asked me if I liked wine.'

'Wine? And your reply?'

'I said: "Yes." ' The seaman floundered; the lieutenant waited. The seaman went on: 'She asked: "I get you some wine?" . . . I said: "Yes, please". She said: "Make yourself at 'ome."'

There was another pause. 'Then what happened?'

'She disappeared, sir, behind a door hidden at the back of the room.'

The seaman glanced at the lieutenant. This time, though, the lieutenant remained silent. The seaman then began to talk fluently. He recalled that he had sat down and waited for the woman to return, how he observed the layout of the room, the faded decoration, the dim lighting. He said that when the woman re-entered the room, he saw that she had changed her street clothing for a flimsy *peignoir* gown. She held a wine bottle and two glasses. She walked slowly towards him; he studied her profile while she moved. She carefully laid down the bottle and the glasses. Her hair was now loosened and fell down her back. She held the edges of the *peignoir* gown casually with one hand. He could tell that she was naked underneath.

'No 'urry, sailor. Drink some wine.' She poured some wine and handed him a glass. He stared at the bottle and the glass; by this stage of the evening he had consumed plenty of alcohol already. He swallowed some wine anyway. The taste, he found, was tolerable though sharp, acidic. Now she moved in front of him and knelt down. She still clutched her gown with one hand. With her other hand she reached out for a glass of wine. He noticed her slender arms, the elegant line of her neck, the urgent swell of her breasts. She sipped her wine then turned to replace the glass. Her gown fell open a little.

'I sit on your knee, sailor?'

'Yes . . . please do.' He had felt ridiculously British.

'You're a 'andsome sailor.'

'You're a pretty girl.'

'You like us – us bad girls?' She felt for one of his hands and placed it on top of her gown. He was aroused; he wanted to move his hand beneath the gown but he was affected by a sudden wave of nausea, then another. She sensed this but misinterpreted it: 'I'm too 'eavy for you?'

'No. That's not the problem.'

She stood up anyway, and she moved towards the bed. 'It's a nice bed. Nice and soft.' She folded back the bedclothes diligently then turned to look at him. She let the gown slip from her shoulders. She sat down and swung her legs under the bedclothes in a desirable mix of reservation and neglect. The room's dim lighting cast a shadow on the wall. The end-rails of the bed began to wobble and frolic before him. He stood up to move towards the bed but he was gripped by a further wave of nausea.

At this stage of his account, with the lieutenant now intrigued, the young seaman faltered again. He gazed helplessly at the lieutenant as another uncomfortable silence developed. At length, the lieutenant asked: 'Did you . . . um . . . make it to the bed?'

'That's the bugger of it, sir. Up to that point I remember everything clear as a bell, like. But then . . .'

'So what *do* you remember?'

'The next thing I knew, I woke up in the street.'

The lieutenant struggled to hide his reaction, a mix of astonishment and hilarity. 'The street? You exchanged a nice soft bed for the street?'

'Yes, sir. I couldn't 'elp it, sir. The street – with an 'eadache.'

'A headache?'

'Yes, sir.'

The lieutenant, aware of the need to restrain his personal feelings, adopted a studiously sober expression. 'Was there anything else?' he asked.

'Yes, sir. All me money was missing, sir.'

At this the lieutenant groaned. 'So what did you do next?'

'I came back to the ship, sir. Nothing else I could do, like.'

The lieutenant drummed his fingers quietly, impatiently. 'The wine could have been drugged, I suppose. Have you had a medical check-up?'

'No, sir. But I don't think the wine was drugged, sir. She seemed – oh, I dunno – a decent sort at heart. I think I'd just 'ad too much to drink, like.'

'That wouldn't have helped,' sighed the lieutenant. 'But I suppose you'd better have a check-up. We'll arrange for the medics to have a look at you. They'll have to make sure you haven't picked up anything . . . how should I put this? . . . contagious. And I'll have a quiet word with the captain about the money. See if we can help out with a loan until pay-day.'

'Thank you, sir. And, sir . . . if you wouldn't mind . . .' the young seaman's expression was a mixture of hopelessness and helplessness.

'Don't worry. I'll be as discreet as possible.'

But when the lieutenant had discussed the matter in confidence with the captain, Commander Dangerfield had been distinctly unsympathetic. 'We can't go around baling out every Tom, Dick, and Harry who happens to get himself into trouble with harbour prostitutes.'

'He's only a young lad, sir. Shouldn't we try to assist?'

But the captain was of the old school: hard rules to be applied. The best he could offer was an undertaking to think about the matter. The lieutenant felt aggrieved by this. He had the suspicion that some antipathy between him and the captain may have influenced the decision unfairly. Perhaps the lieutenant could raise the matter another time, but he feared that this might serve just to irritate the captain further. A productive outcome seemed unlikely.

And now, as he reruns the events in his mind, he has a growing sense of disgruntlement. He cannot avoid the fact that he remains unhappy about the captain, about having to deal with him. He does not like the fellow and he suspects the feeling is mutual. There is, however, little to be done about it. The lieutenant knows he would be foolish to brood. He should think about more positive things, for instance the life of the outside world. He continues to observe through the wardroom porthole as he sips his coffee. He hears the ongoing melodies of the accordionist. He notices the two *gendarmes* walk out of sight. The atmosphere seems to change with the symbolic disappearance of authority. He looks away, gazing instead at the familiarity of the naval scene, the polished brass, the Morse code chairs, the haphazard pictures, the layout of the wardroom. He glances at the selection of reading matter on the side table and decides to follow the *gendarmes*' example: he will move on. He will try to forget about the captain, concentrating instead on broader perspectives, a bigger world. He will choose some reading matter, a comfortable armchair and enjoy his cup of coffee in an atmosphere of peace and quiet.

As he walks to the side table to select some reading material, his eyes are drawn to a magazine, to the bold headlines: 'Wallis Weds Duke'. He remains standing and, without lifting the magazine, leafs quickly through the pages. He stops at the relevant section. With a sense of fascination, he begins to read about the tribulations of a woman at the

summit of the social spectrum. At the summit, doubtless, but is that, he
wonders, a desirable route to the joy of life? Is she as tormented as some
at lesser levels, some who regard the top as untouchable? The harbour
prostitute? The seaman on his division? He angles his head as he
deliberates. He glances again at the article:

3 June 1937. In the romantic setting of a chateau in a valley near
Tours, Wallis Simpson today married the former King Edward VIII,
and became the Duchess of Windsor. Although hundreds of French
sightseers had arrived in Tours, the ceremonies themselves were
simple with few witnesses. The first ceremony, conducted by the
Mayor of Monts, was to comply with French civil law. The salon at
the Chateau de Cande was decorated with two large vases of pink
carnations and red peonies; the bride and groom sat in armchairs
before a table covered with fawn-coloured velvet embroidered
with gold. The mayor said that he represented a nation 'which has
always been sensitive to the charm of chivalrous unselfishness and
bold gestures prompted by the dictates of the heart.'

Chivalrous unselfishness? Bold gestures? The lieutenant contemplates a
one-time king who has put self before duty, displayed misplaced loyalties, created a constitutional crisis. Someone who has betrayed trusts and
let down his country. As time passes, as dreadful, unpalatable truths
seep out, the former King Edward VIII will be ignominiously dubbed the
'traitor king'. He will be described as 'a silly man of bad judgement, of
vanity, incredibly indiscreet, someone who believed in the likelihood of
a German victory when nobody had a right to believe in such a victory,
and worst of all who talked about it in places where nobody had a right
to talk about it'.
    The lieutenant reads on:

Fifteen minutes later, in the music room of the chateau, the couple
were married under the rites of the Church of England by the vicar
of St Bride's, Doncaster. The room had been hastily converted to a
chapel and the Duke and Duchess knelt in front of an old oak chest
which served as an altar. Later, after a buffet wedding breakfast,
the newly married couple left for their honeymoon in Austria. The
Duke issued a statement which said: 'After the trying times we
have been through we now look forward to a happy and useful
private life' . . .

Trying times? Happy? Useful? The lieutenant shakes his head un-
sympathetically. He thumbs through the pages of the magazine. He

scans an article about the Spithead coronation review, about the retirement of Prime Minister Stanley Baldwin (honest Stan) at the end of last month. The new prime minister, Neville Chamberlain, has a style of leadership predicted to be: 'less relaxed than his phlegmatic predecessor'. Chamberlain is seen as a 'more austere figure, keen on administrative efficiency'. The lieutenant frowns at the thought of such a man. He flicks forward to a different section, which recaps a feature from an earlier edition:

Coronation of George VI. The Unlikely Monarch

The BBC made its first television outside broadcast when, on 12 May 1937, with all the pomp and ceremony of time-honoured tradition, King George VI and Queen Elizabeth were crowned at Westminster Abbey. They were watched by people who had travelled from the furthest parts of the empire. It was twenty-six years since the coronation of the king's father, and London had a tremendous air of excitement for days. At 10.30 a.m. a golden coach drawn by eight horses left Buckingham Palace for the Abbey. It was a splendid sight with four postilions and six footmen plus eight grooms and four men of the guard walking alongside. The king was in robes of deep red and snow-white ermine with the Cap of Maintenance on his head. The queen's procession was led by the Herald Extraordinary, his uniform a dazzle of red. Flanked by two bishops, the queen looked relaxed in a gown of satin embroidered with the emblems of the British Isles and Dominions. An eight foot train of purple velvet . . .

The lieutenant ponders such pageantry. As a naval officer he appreciates traditions and ceremonies. The coronation and the subsequent naval review at Spithead had boosted national morale, indulged the British appetite for royal events and the baubles of wealth and empire. Surely Britain has earned some relief after a decade of troubles – abdication, general strike, developing international tensions. Criticism could be seen as churlish, but is there a danger that the pomp and ceremonial will conceal uncomfortable truths, lure the nation's eye away from outside realities? The lieutenant muses on the world's rapidly changing attitudes, the trend towards internationally minded outlooks. Will the outside world appreciate Great Britain's royal machinations, her emphasis on empire and custom? Will other nations respect and esteem her royal personalities? Perhaps they will be seen as figureheads, members of a dull, dysfunctional family, individuals who have achieved their position by right of birth instead of qualities of personal merit.

The lieutenant flicks forward again. He hesitates when he spots a picture of the Spanish Nationalist leader, General Franco. He stares at the face; the face stares back. The general appears calm but beneath that placid exterior, does Franco's trim moustache, his purposeful pose, his cold, dark glare, betray the horrors his nation now endure? Or is there a cynical indifference, a cruel determination to persist regardless of consequences? The lieutenant considers whether the British are prudent, perhaps, to settle for dull and dysfunctional over deranged and dangerous.

He glances at the article next to the photograph. *Caudillo* Franco is depicted as a dour, un-*Duce*-like figure with an icy presence, a core of steely obstinacy. During the fateful days of April 1931 when the Spanish polls revealed an anti-monarchist landslide, the article reminds readers that the King, Alfonso XIII, made desperate attempts to retain his crown. However, when the head of the civil guard announced that his men would no longer support the monarch, and when memories of the French revolution were revived and the King was forced into exile, there was a gradual and unenthusiastic acceptance of Franco's destiny. A sense of inevitability about the nation's slide towards civil war began to spread.

The article points out that when the Second Spanish Republic was declared on 14 April 1931, Franco was a little-known general in charge of the army officer cadet college near Madrid. He watched with horror as celebrations of the new republic turned into acts of lawlessness and violent anarchy. He declared: 'Things cannot go on like this. I'm going to take some cadets to Madrid in lorries and restore order.' Typical of his vacillating, however, Franco changed his mind the next day: 'One has to be realistic. The important thing is to see how the republic behaves.' Although a convinced monarchist, he then wrote a letter of allegiance to the republic. The article highlights other features of the enigmatic Franco: his lack of a coherent political philosophy, his treacherous ambition, his focus on his own career, his intellectual paucity. The British ambassador in Madrid, Sir Samuel Hoare, grumbled about Franco's 'imperturbable complacency . . . like a doctor with a big family practice and a good bedside manner'. Now aged 45, Franco is a short individual who has become distinctly plump, with a high-pitched, almost priestly, voice. He comes from a nautical background (his father was a naval paymaster) and he is known for his personal courage. He is, however, feared as a martinet with a singular lack of imagination and humanity. His Asturian wife, Carmen, is noted for her piety. She believes that with the heavy burden of his responsibilities, Franco has reached spiritual maturity.

In three years' time a meeting between Franco and Hitler will be arranged. To his anguish, the German *Führer* will be kept waiting for over an hour. He will then try in vain to extract concessions from Franco. After the meeting, Hitler will remark that he would never again wish to endure such a frustrating experience; that he would prefer instead to have several teeth pulled out; that when he mentioned Spain's debt to Germany for aid during the civil war, Franco made him feel 'almost like a Jew trading in the holiest possessions of mankind'.

The lieutenant now turns to another section of his magazine. He spots the headlines: 'Spanish Republican Bombers Hit German Battleship.' He is about to read the fate of the German pocket battleship *Deutschland* when his seaman steward appears in the wardroom entrance. 'Everything okay, sir?' He gestures towards the coffee cup: 'Meant to be good stuff, sir – French. Can I offer you a refill?'

'No thanks,' Lieutenant Sutton nods in gratitude. 'Though it *is* good coffee.'

The seaman steward grins. 'Is there anything else, sir?'

'Thank you, but no.'

'Just give me a shout, sir, if you need anything. I'll be next door in the pantry. Stock check before we go to sea tomorrow.'

'Of course. Good fellow. I'll do a tour of inspection around the ship soon. The tides are about to turn so I'll check things out on the bridge.' The lieutenant falters. 'If you wouldn't mind, there is one thing.'

'Sir?'

'The coffee's splendid, but in this heat . . . a glass of water, perhaps?'

'No problem, sir, I'll get that organized right away. By the way, you should have company before too long. I've just bumped into Midshipman Fanning. I think he's heading for the wardroom.'

'Okay, that's fine,' says the lieutenant, aware that on smaller-crewed ships such as the *Basilisk*, midshipmen are permitted to make use of the wardroom. He returns to his magazine: 'When Spanish Republican bombers left Ibiza in the Balearics to strike at the *Deutschland* on 29 May 1937, a bomb penetrated crew quarters killing twenty-three German seamen. On hearing the news, *Herr* Hitler flew from Munich to Berlin for an emergency conference. A statement was issued later: "This criminal attack compels the German government to take measures which it will at once communicate to the non-intervention committee."'

That, thinks the lieutenant, is a bit thick, is it not? What about the criminal attacks on Guernica? The intervention of the Heinkels and Junkers? Does *Herr* Hitler wish to issue a statement about the strafing and carpet-bombing?

'Ah . . . second lieutenant!' cries Midshipman Fanning as he enters the wardroom. 'The steward mentioned you were here. Mind if I join you, sir?'

The lieutenant bows his head in assent. As they enter into conversation, the two officers decide to sit down. The lieutenant moves towards his favoured Morse code armchair. He will be glad of the young midshipman's congenial companionship. He realizes, too, that the midshipman seems in a state of excitement, that he is impatiently eager to impart some news.

CHAPTER THIRTEEN

Discussions
with a Midshipman

'So,' says Lieutenant Sutton to Midshipman Fanning, 'you've been sampling the delights of Saint-Jean-de-Luz? I trust you haven't been doing things I wouldn't have done?'

'Indeed not, second lieutenant,' says the midshipman. 'That is . . . probably not.' He attempts to conceal his excitement. 'To be honest, my trip was rather uneventful to begin with. A walk around the main square, a bit of shopping – postcards and such. Then I investigated the bathing beach area.'

The lieutenant gazes at the other. He is aware of the midshipman's restlessness, his anxiety to announce news of unusual and (presumably) startling interest. He realizes, however, that the young man should not be hurried: the cause of his excitement will be revealed in his own good time. He notes that, despite his agitation, the midshipman remains a flawless example of an off-duty naval officer. The smart double-breasted suit, polished shoes, suavely-groomed hair, public-school image – all are clearly beyond reproach. The lieutenant feels an inner nod of approval. 'And what about the famous fish port?' he asks. 'Did you explore around there?'

'In fact I did. I met up with the engineering officer, Lieutenant Richards – "Chiefie". We wandered round the fish port for a bit, then we decided to visit a street café, one with loads of bustle and character. It was most enjoyable. The locals chattered away nineteen to the dozen. They seemed glad to see us. No one appeared to understand much but we managed to get by. There was a particular atmosphere,' he becomes reflective, 'quite romantic, I suppose. The sun glinting through the trees . . . an accordionist's music in the background . . . the happy chirruping of the birds. Life felt good. Actually . . .' He falters. 'We . . . um . . . had a stroke of luck. I was going to tell you that—'

'Hello Mister Fanning, sir,' the seaman steward appears in the wardroom entrance. 'Can I get you something, sir? The coffee's good – French, you know.'

'French coffee? In the wardroom?' The midshipman half-turns. 'Wonders will never cease. But a coffee will be most welcome, thank you.'

'Leave it to me, sir.' The steward disappears.

'You were going to tell me?' says the lieutenant.

'Oh yes,' the midshipman coughs politely. 'We had quite a stroke of good luck. It all started when—'

'Sorry, sir, excuse me,' the seaman steward reappears. 'White coffee or black, sir?'

'White, please.'

'No problem, sir. I shall lay the tray accordingly.'

The midshipman gazes into the distance. The lieutenant smiles but says nothing. An awkward silence seeps into the room but is broken by the seaman steward's further appearance: 'I should have asked, sir, if you like strong coffee.'

'Yes please.'

'And by the way, sir, I've just had a message. I've been told to pop along to the captain's cabin right away. It'll take a few minutes, then I'll make a fresh brew when I get back.'

'Okay. No hurry. Thank you.' Another uncomfortable silence follows, with the midshipman put off, perhaps, by the interruptions.

'I've been writing reports,' says the lieutenant eventually, not wishing to appear over-eager to hear the other's news. 'And I've been dealing with logs. Then I came here to read the wardroom's gossip columns.'

'Did you read that report on the airship disaster?'

'Airship disaster?'

'The *Hindenburg* affair.'

'That happened a while ago now, didn't it?'

'About a month ago.' The midshipman lets out a low whistle of astonishment. 'Incredible thing. Just imagine those poor passengers. First, a protracted trans-Atlantic flight with head-winds, thunderstorms, delays. And when the airfield at New Jersey eventually came into sight, the landing area was unusable – obscured by storms. That great machine had to rumble around for an hour, circling, waiting for the right moment. Thunderstorms cracked around the framework, turbulence rocked the passengers. Imagine the alarm while they waited. Consider the sense of relief when the captain finally announced his intention to moor. And then, just as her mooring lines were dropped, a flash from the rear gondola.' He stares at the lieutenant.

'So did they discover the cause of the explosion?'

'I don't believe they did. There's rumour that static electricity built up during the storm, that the machine's hydrogen gas was ignited and that led to . . . bang!'

'Thirty-three souls lost?'

'Thirty-three souls,' says the midshipman. 'Rum business, this flying, if you ask me. Strictly for the birds.'

'I used to enjoy a bit of flying when I was a young lad,' says the lieutenant. 'I would save up my pocket money to pay for joy-rides. Have you ever had a flight in an aeroplane yourself?'

The midshipman shakes his head. 'I may have been tempted from time to time, but no, not yet.'

'You should try it sometime. Look for a good opportunity.'

'Perhaps. Then again, perhaps not. Though I suppose the future lies with air travel – not to mention the more sinister use of aircraft. Think of Guernica.'

'And think of that saga at the start of the Spanish Civil War.'

'What do you mean?'

'Major Hugh Pollard, Captain Cecil Bebb and company? Did you not read about their bizarre adventure?'

'I don't believe so.'

The lieutenant waves one hand in the direction of the side table. 'Details are in one of those magazines over there.'

'Sounds intriguing. Tell me what happened.'

'What you might call a Canary Island crusade.'

'Crusade? I thought they held cruises to the Canary Islands.'

'Perhaps Pollard, Bebb and Co were conned with similar thoughts.'

'Conned by whom?'

'By the Spanish coup plotters.'

'Coup plotters?'

The lieutenant leans forward. 'When the Spanish coup was being plotted last year, General Franco was based in the Canary Islands. However, he was needed to take command of the Spanish Army of Africa. The coup planners had to arrange for him to be taken clandestinely to Morocco. Unfortunately for them, no reliable civil aircraft could be found in Spanish territory.'

'So what did they do about it?'

'A secret meeting was organized in London. After the meeting, a retired British army major, Hugh Pollard, was approached and asked if he could fly to Africa the next day with two girls, to which he replied, "Depends upon the girls." Pollard, though, was persuaded to take part in a thrilling adventure and in turn he persuaded a young ex-RAF pilot, Captain Cecil Bebb. Neither of them knew the real reason behind what was described as a wizard wheeze – most exciting, most suitable for dashing RAF types.'

'What were they told?'

'That some official in the Canary Islands had to be flown to a secret destination in Spanish Morocco to start an insurrection there.'

'Pollard and Bebb agreed?'

'They evidently considered it a "lovely challenge". To them it sounded like the plot of a thriller novel – an expensive frolic of the idle rich, one of amateur daring. When Major Pollard's daughter and her friend (two beautiful blondes) boarded the aeroplane chartered for the flight – a de Havilland Dragon Rapide – the impression was meant to be that of wealthy folk having a good time.'

'So what happened to them?' asks the midshipman.

'In mid-July the de Havilland Rapide flew from Croydon Airport to Las Palmas, Gran Canaria. When it reached Las Palmas, Captain Bebb waited there while the others went by boat to Tenerife. Everything was kept hush-hush and the due password . . .' The lieutenant stands up and goes to the side table where he thumbs through the pages of a magazine. 'Here it is. The details are still sketchy, but evidently Major Pollard was contacted by agents who asked him for the agreed password – *Galicia saluda a Francia* – then told him to lie low until contacted. The scene is summed up in a letter written by Pollard's daughter. She wrote to a friend: "Dear April, I am having a mild flirtation with the pilot who is a redhead . . . At midnight we had to sail from Las Palmas to Tenerife since Pop has business there . . . This is Spanish territory and they are very unsettled in Spain at the moment."'

The lieutenant returns to his seat. 'Franco needed an excuse to leave Tenerife without raising suspicion and by luck or misdeed – nobody is sure which – he was given good cause. A fellow officer had died in Gran Canaria and Franco cabled the War Ministry in Madrid for permission to travel to Las Palmas to attend the funeral. Permission was granted, and he used the island ferry to travel at midnight from Tenerife to Las Palmas. Major Pollard and the girls were on board too. Miss Pollard wrote about "grim-faced civil guards patrolling the decks and armed men in the corridors". The next day, while Captain Bebb waited anxiously at the airstrip, he eventually saw "a scruffy tugboat come into view around the headland. Soldiers waded out to carry passengers in military uniform ashore. One of them turned out to be Franco."'

'What was Bebb's reaction?'

'He learnt, at last, the truth about his mission.'

'He must have felt a little weak at the knees. What did he do next?'

'He must have felt stuck between a rock and something even harder. A couple of days later he flew Franco to Tetuan in Morocco and he told how, as the Dragon Rapide approached Tetuan, he was given a smoke signal for clearance to land. He then taxied across to where soldiers of the Foreign Legion were drawn up on parade to welcome the very important passenger. Before long, everyone had to dive for cover when a Republican Dakota made a low pass to drop bombs. The bombs, however, landed wide. Franco wanted Bebb to retaliate, to load bombs onto the Dragon Rapide and to attack Madrid. However, Bebb managed to talk his way out of that. Eventually he was sworn to secrecy and allowed to return to Britain.'

'Sworn to secrecy?'

'Perhaps the girls were less discreet. Various details seemed to have leaked out.'

'And that peculiar episode was the cloak and dagger start of the Spanish Civil War?'

'Cloak and dagger . . . excitement . . . romance . . . danger, all rolled into one.' The lieutenant glances at his magazine. 'And talking of excitement, romance, danger, there's something else here.'

'Something about us perhaps?'

'Us?'

'You know – affairs naval.'

'As a matter of fact there is. Something that should be close to your heart.'

'About beautiful girls then?'

'About non-intervention patrols.'

'Even better than beautiful girls!'

'This will fascinate you so much, Mister Fanning, that you'll be bound to forget all about beautiful girls.'

'Fascinating indeed.'

'This is about the *Seven Seas Spray* incident that occurred a couple of months ago.'

'A couple of months ago? I seem to remember a couple of months ago I was . . . oh, never mind!'

'The *Seven Seas Spray* had a narrow escape,' says the lieutenant. 'She was one of the British merchantmen trying to reach Republican-held ports and we know that these vessels are in danger of attack from Franco's warships.'

'As many as forty cargo ships have been sunk, I believe.'

'So we've been told. And twice that number have had their cargoes confiscated. As a consequence the non-intervention committee have been pressed to seek a solution. By last April there was a compromise plan whereby Germany and Italy would patrol Republican-held territory in the Mediterranean and we, as you know, were sent here to supervise the Basque coast blockaded by Franco. We know, too, about the desperate plight of the Basques and about the public sympathy in Britain which has encouraged British freighters to take risks.'

'British freighters have been further encouraged,' the midshipman rubs together his thumb and forefinger in a financial gesture, 'by the large profits to be made.'

'Then there have been the arguments in the British press and in parliament about the humiliation when our vessels are stopped and searched by Franco's forces – unofficial forces of a rebel clique. To get around the problem, the government wanted to veto the movements of all merchant ships attempting to run the blockade. The ineffectiveness of this plan was shown up by the persistence of merchantmen like the *Seven Seas Spray*.'

'The *Seven Seas Spray*, I seem to remember, was in the news after an especially daring voyage. Weren't there celebrations when she managed to reach Bilbao harbour safely?'

'The populace were no doubt in grateful admiration of the show of ingenuity and cunning, not to mention the considerable amount of luck. The event was a good example of the situations we'll have to confront on our naval patrols. The experience was described by the captain's nineteen-year-old daughter.'

'The captain's daughter on the voyage?'

The lieutenant nods. 'And she was greatly touched by the events. She was moved, too, by what was going on in Bilbao. The town presented her with a gold brooch as a mark of gratitude. She tells her own story. Perhaps I should read it aloud?'

'Please do,' says the midshipman.

'She wrote: "We left Swansea in March 1937 to unload coal at Savona in Italy. While unloading, we were told that the ship had been chartered by the Basque government and that we had to sail at once. *En route*, we stopped at Gibraltar before setting course for Bilbao. When we were nearly there, my father received a message that his ship had to obey naval instructions and that he was to proceed to Saint-Jean-de-Luz." The lieutenant waves one hand towards the harbour area. "At Saint-Jean-de-Luz we waited for a few days until a Basque representative approached us in considerable secrecy. Anxious discussions were held, and eventually the Basque representative persuaded my father to take the risk of running the blockade. My father informed the senior naval officer about this, after which we left Saint-Jean-de-Luz late at night, slipping out of harbour in a darkened ship. We experienced frightening moments during the night but we reached Bilbao early the next morning to be greeted by the hooting sirens of the fishing fleet. The people of Bilbao then treated us like VIPs. As we sailed down the long, narrow river there were people in every window on both banks, cheering, waving sheets, shouting "God bless you" and making the sign of the cross. I never felt so humble. The poor people had only four days' food left. Children used to gather at the foot of the ship's gangway begging for scraps." '

'A sobering scene.'

'Even more sobering,' says the lieutenant, 'must have been her experience when, at the end of April, she witnessed the aftermath of the nearby Guernica tragedy. She said it was "soul destroying to see the refugees coming away, some pushing wheelbarrows or handcarts, perhaps with a donkey or a pony. It looked as if there were only three buildings still standing. The whole place seemed to have been evacuated. There wasn't a soul about." '

'The Guernica episode told us much about the German leadership. They even tried to deny responsibility.'

'That taught us even more about their attitudes, not to mention their ruthless approach to life.'

'The Germans must think us very naïve.'

'They must scorn the weakness of our leaders, the ineffectiveness of the international organizations – the League of Nations, the non-intervention committee, the naïve activities of the International Brigades in Spain.'

'One has to feel sorry for them I suppose.'

'The Germans?'

'Hardly, although in a way . . .'

'One wonders why.'

'Why?' says the midshipman.

'Why individuals should become involved with these International Brigades.'

'Mixed up is probably the right term.'

'Mixed up and misled . . . there's a feature here—' the lieutenant waves his magazine, '—and it involves young people who you might consider to be on our own side.'

'Which country?'

'America.'

'The gullibility of some Americans is astounding.'

'He describes how he was transferred to the American volunteers' training camp at Tarazona and how, after a few weeks of instruction on the use of rifle and machine gun, the volunteers were considered fit for active duty. They were destined for front-line service even though they'd fired just five live rounds each because of an ammunition shortage. They were ordered to head for the Aragon fronts. He wrote this to his mother: "You see, Mom, there are things that must be done in life which are more than just living. In Spain there are thousands of mothers like yourself who never had a fair shake in life. They got together and elected a government that really gave meaning to their life but a bunch of bullies decided to crush this wonderful thing. That's why I went to Spain, Mom, to help these poor people to win this battle, then one day it would be easier for you and for the mothers of the future. Don't let anyone mislead you by telling you that all this had something to do with communism. The Hitlers and the Mussolinis of this world are killing Spanish people who don't know the difference between communism or rheumatism. And it's not for setting up some communist government either. The only thing the communists did here was to show people how to fight and how to win what is rightfully theirs."'

The lieutenant lowers his magazine. The two officers listen to the sounds flowing into the room – harbour activities, distant chatter, a military band just starting up, the raucous cries of gulls. The officers hear the seaman steward as he clatters in the next-door pantry. At length the midshipman asks: 'Does the article say what happened to this fellow?'

'He was posted missing, believed killed. In the confusion of war it can be hard to trace individuals.'

'You have to admire their pluck.'

'The families must rue the day they became involved, especially when volunteers become disillusioned.'

'It's pathetic, really,' says the midshipman.

'Political naïvety and misleading propaganda lure young volunteers from all walks of life. There's a tale here about a young English ex-public schoolboy who joined a particular brigade because he thought it represented "liberal republican organizations". However, as he went through the organization's training regime, he discovered different truths. The brigade was communist-run and he began to feel bitterly unsympathetic towards its dogma. It was too late by then, of course. He lamented that he would "spend the rest of my life walking up to that ridge a few hundred yards away and that will be the end of me".'

'Was he correct?'

'I'm afraid he was. His parents spoke about the tragedy of a pointless sacrifice.'

'They must have realized that the false propaganda—'

'Here we are, gentlemen,' the seaman steward re-enters the wardroom with a carefully laid tray. 'Sorry about the delay. This should be a fine brew. It's good coffee, sir – French, you know. Did I mention that before?'

'I think you did. And by the way, is the captain in his cabin?'

'He's on the warpath, sir.'

'That's all we need.'

'I think I'd better hurry along, sir.'

'Thanks for the coffee.'

As the steward departs, the midshipman stands up and walks towards a porthole. 'Look at this,' he says pointing outside. 'See that military band over there. They'll drown the efforts of the accordionist.'

'Perhaps the accordionist has given up.'

'That's unfortunate. His music reminds me . . .' the midshipman falters.

'Yes?'

The midshipman glances at the second lieutenant. 'It's nothing much. I was just going to tell you something.'

'You have a secret to reveal, Midshipman Fanning?'

'I was going to tell you about this girl I met.'

'A beautiful girl?'

'A beautiful girl – most attractive – French, you know,' he grins. 'Someone I met at the café and someone who, with a bit of luck, I might be seeing again soon.'

'Well, well, Mister Fanning. Perhaps you'll marry a French girl next.'

'Or Spanish.'

'Spanish?'

'There are a few Spanish girls around town. Mainly from rich families; types who could afford to escape the troubles of their own country.'

'Would you like to marry a Spanish *señorita*?'

'I think I might, yes,' the midshipman angles his head as he deliberates. 'In fact,' he goes on, 'I think I might even like it quite a lot.' He glances at his colleague. 'How about you, second lieutenant? Would you marry a Spanish girl?'

'I must confess I haven't given it much thought. But now you come to mention it – well, yes. A Spanish *señorita* or a French *mademoiselle*. Why not?'

'Why not indeed.' At this the officers both break into hearty laughter, although they might be astounded to learn how a mere matter of weeks will go by before this mirth rebounds on them.

CHAPTER FOURTEEN

Inspection Reflections

As he steps out of the wardroom, Lieutenant Sutton makes for a ladder to take him up to an area by HMS *Basilisk*'s aft-facing 4.7 inch guns. He briefly inspects this area before following the ship's upper deck past depth-charge throwers and 21 inch torpedo launchers. He aims to reach the bridge via a watertight door just forward of the ship's forward funnel. Beyond this door is a lobby with a central ladder that leads directly to the bridge. He climbs the ladder and as he reaches the top step, he casts an experienced eye at the bridge set-up. He observes the special telephones at the back of the bridge, the conduits of pipelines threaded along bulkheads, the 20 inch signal lamps port and starboard, the voice-pipes to the engine and boiler rooms and the wheelhouse. At the front of the bridge is a compass platform situated above the bullet-proofed wheelhouse. The *Basilisk*'s bridge, unlike those of larger ships, is open to the elements although canvas screens have been rigged up just now to provide temporary protection from the sun.

The lieutenant sees at a glance that the bridge set-up appears in order. He nods acknowledgement to the two seamen who come to attention crisply as they spot him. He notes the particular aura of the bridge and for a moment he recalls with secret satisfaction his early days in the Royal Navy, his initiation into naval life on HMS *Repulse*. His experience over the years has led to an ability to view with easy familiarity the ship's operational heart, the powerhouse to control the fate of vessel and crew. He says: 'Carry on, please,' to the seamen: one man resumes his brass-cleaning duties while the other, a leading seaman, joins him to walk towards the front of the bridge. They look towards the forecastle to view the top section of the 4.7 inch gun immediately below them. They also observe a separate gun of similar calibre which, to ensure barrel clearance, is positioned beneath and ahead of the first. As the men inspect the guns they check, too, the security of adjoining canvas screens rigged to provide some cover for the guns and a section of the forecastle.

The two men discuss tides and other relevant details for some minutes, after which the lieutenant instructs the leading seaman to fetch the ship's copies of local French tide tables and Admiralty tidal charts. The latter hastens from the area and during his absence the lieutenant observes the activity around the Saint-Jean-de-Luz harbour. He sees how some folk still point towards HMS *Basilisk*, discussing her presence. He notes, too, that the *gendarmes* have reappeared although they seem unmindful of the *Basilisk* as, along with others, they enjoy the pleasant interlude provided by the military band. He watches the band for some moments. The music reminds him of marine bands on larger ships. Then he glances around the forward part of the bridge, at the cabinets, chart tables, and surrounding bulwarks. He observes the satisfactory gleam of a section of brass rail. He makes a favourable comment to the seaman, who continues with his brass-polishing. The lieutenant contemplates the functional need. The polished rails will act as more than mere ornaments when they are grasped by grateful hands in rough weather. This was illustrated graphically when the ship made her recent passage to Saint-Jean-de-Luz.

At the start of non-intervention patrol duties, as the *Basilisk* returned from the Spithead review and as she traversed the central region of the Bay of Biscay, storm-force winds had hit her on the beam. She began to yaw from side to side, the violence of her movements reflecting the velocity of the wind. As she held her south-easterly course across the bay, her yawing became increasingly wild and her steering gear had difficulty retaining directional control. To those on duty on the bridge it seemed on occasions that she rolled over so far she might never come back. The minds of the crew began to drift instinctively to thoughts about the ship's construction. Men speculated on the quality of workmanship. They pondered her gestation and her growth seven years ago from a metal ant-heap that swarmed with dockyard workers. As they wondered about the skills of the ship's Clydebank builders, they offered quiet prayers, begging reassurance that the welders and fitters who fashioned her hull plate by plate, the naval architects whose designs lay at her core, the shipwrights who stowed her anchors and cables, the carpenters and plumbers who installed her cabins, messes, wheelhouse, charthouse had all done a job thorough enough to withstand the present stresses and strains. There were inner sighs of relief when the ship emerged from the bottom of the swell. The crew realized that the *Basilisk* was sturdily built after all. Their prayers had been answered; the ship was sufficiently robust to survive the next wave.

And when the next wave came, when spray drenched the forecastle and bridge in sheets, smacked against oilskins and sou'westers before rushing and gurgling along the bridge scuppers, the look-outs and officers of the watch were half-blinded and had to grip stanchions and rails to avoid injury. When they squinted aft, those on the bridge could see ferocious white furrows carved across the sea and the thrashing screws hurling up distinctive plumes as if a water main had burst. The crew members listened to the creaks and groans from the straining superstructure, the shrieks and whistles of the wind, the hollow drone of the ventilation fans drawing air to the interior, the insistent high-pitched whine of the turbines. As the *Basilisk* lurched and vibrated, as she juddered and shuddered across the bay, the crew had to brace their stomach muscles and knees to meet her motion. Items left unsecured in cabins and messes tumbled to the deck. And while the ship battled the elements, while the crew fought their private anxieties, eventually their tired minds would try to blot out present tensions. They would think instead of better times, of evenings by a fireside, of the body of a pin-up girl, of sleep in a warm, still, bed. But the storm, as if sent by Poseidon himself, turned out to be as relentless as most in that region – storms to torment seafarers presumptuous enough to challenge the Bay of Biscay and her infamous waters. The suffering had to be endured for hours, endless hours. Ultimately, though, Poseidon had relented and then, at last, his forbearance meant that men could enjoy hot cocoa and soup brought up to the bridge to help calm their frayed nerves.

As he recollects some of the tensest moments of the crossing, the lieutenant has mixed feelings. He recalls the personal soul-searchings, the mind's deeper questions, the sense of quiet gratitude, the stern discipline. But such occasions, he thinks, justify the easier atmosphere of days in harbour. And today, therefore, with most of the crew off duty, men have earned their shore leave before the ship sets sail again. Still musing the age-old conundrums of a mariner's life, he steps towards the after section of the bridge and gazes upwards to inspect the main mast. He looks down again, and moves to one side. He leans against a bulwark to check the area abaft the ship's twin funnels. He visually checks the effectiveness of further canvas awnings rigged to protect the aft 4.7 inch guns and the quarter-deck area. The ship's sick bay is located beneath the guns, along with the officers' galley and cabins, the wardroom and the captain's cabin. He wonders if the captain is still on the warpath, perhaps fuming within the solitude of his cabin. He becomes aware of another seaman clattering clumsily up the ladder steps to the bridge. A communications rating, earphones on head, requests permission to carry out test messages.

'Go ahead,' says the lieutenant.

After a while he hears: 'Fire control from bridge, do you read?'

The lieutenant can just make out the crackled reply through the rating's earphones: 'Bridge from fire control, loud and clear.'

'Bridge testing – one, two, three, four, five.'

'Bridge from fire control, you're still loud and clear.'

The lieutenant tries to disregard the dull communications procedures. He concentrates instead on visual checks astern, the security of the motor boats held by davits either side of the funnels, the state of the funnels themselves. He turns to the bridge ladder as he hears further clattering on the steps. He sees the leading seaman returning, as instructed, with the tidal charts. He gestures with one hand towards the chart table at the front of the bridge. The leading seaman lays down the charts and together they lean forward to discuss and interpret the tables. French tide tables offer information in a different format from that in the Admiralty charts. Data has been compiled from French hydrographic surveys and tide and height differences are given for *vives eaux* (spring tides) and *mortes eaux* (neap tides). Additionally, the French have a system whereby tidal coefficients for a particular day have been pre-calculated. These coefficients can be applied to determine high- and low-water times and the rate of tidal flow. The two men now discuss the possibility of double tides, which could occur in the vicinity of amphidromic systems with, perhaps, two high waters or two low waters in each tidal cycle caused by shallow water effects. They know, however, that such conditions normally occur at specific places (for example, with low waters at Portland where it is known locally as the Gulder, and at the Hook of Holland where it is known as the Agger) and that the harbour of Saint-Jean-de-Luz is unlikely to be affected today.

At length, having routinely checked the tide tables and considered how berthing hawsers may have to be readjusted, the two men move away from the chart table and walk to another area of the bridge, continuing a friendly conversation. They were both members of the ship's complement at the time of the *Basilisk*'s commission in Gibraltar. As they reminisce about their mutual experiences, they recollect that the leading seaman was among the crew detailed to man the ship's motor boat for Lieutenant Sutton (in his capacity as the ship's intelligence officer) to go ashore at Almeria in southern Spain at the start of the civil war last year. The *Basilisk* was at the time moored a short distance from Almeria and the captain, Commander DeWinton, had instructed his intelligence officer to investigate the sound of gunfire from the town. He had swallowed nervously before responding: 'Who me, sir?'

'Yes you, sir.'

'What, there, sir?' The intelligence officer had pointed solemnly at the town where the gunfire was becoming more than just occasional.

'Yes, there, sir,' said the captain. 'Go ashore, Mister Sutton, and find out what's happening.'

The intelligence officer had decided that discretion was the better part of valour; that his best plan, for safety's sake, would be to don full naval uniform. He trusted that by making himself an officer of conspicuously British bearing, the townsfolk would be less likely to see him as a possible opponent, a potential target for the odd pot-shot. He went to his cabin and put on his white uniform while his best white shoes were hurriedly re-checked by his seaman steward. He attached epaulettes to each shoulder and placed a naval pith helmet on his head. He strapped a ceremonial naval sword around his waist, wondering as he did so about its effectiveness as a weapon of defence. Eventually, as he inspected himself in a mirror, he reminded himself of the captain's words: 'Go ashore, Mister Sutton, and find out what's happening.' He saluted the pristine image, then left his cabin to check the ship's pilot's guide. He needed to confirm details about the British consul, where he could be contacted. This process, however, was interrupted by a warning cry from the bridge look-out: 'Motor launch approaches on the starboard bow!'

'Shall I wait?' the intelligence officer asked the captain.

'Yes, you can wait,' said the captain.

And when the motor launch was secured to the side of the *Basilisk*, when the visitor stepped aboard, the caller turned out to be none other than the British consul who, with similar thoughts about dissident pot-shots, had dressed himself in full consular uniform. Profusions of gold tumbled from his shoulders, white feathers fluttered in his topee hat. 'The town's garrison has risen,' he said. 'Townsfolk have stormed the garrison and the soldiers have been overwhelmed.' He lowered his voice: 'Their fate is unknown.'

'Unknown?'

The consul shrugged. He pointed heavenwards with one hand, with the other he drew a single finger across his throat. 'Who knows?'

Now it was the captain's turn to swallow nervously. 'Exactly which side,' he croaked, 'did the garrison support?'

The consul shrugged again. Allegiances were confused at this early stage of the war. He believed, however, that the garrison's soldiers were Franco's men. 'The picture, as I understand it,' he went on, 'is that the soldiers are right-wing supporters, the townsfolk left-wing. But there is, shall we say, considerable confusion.'

'So what, exactly, would you like the Royal Navy to do about it?' asked the captain.

'There are some British interests in the town, mainly to do with waterworks and other utilities. I wondered if you could consider helping them to protect themselves?'

After further discussions it was decided that the town's *Alcalde* would be invited to visit the *Basilisk* to confer with the captain. The consul then left in his motor launch, which returned after an interval with the *Alcalde* in company with an assortment of uninvited and rough-looking individuals. The *Alcalde*'s morning coat and chain of office gave a good impression, but the appearance of his attendants was less appealing. With guns slung across their shoulders and knives thrust in their belts, they turned out to be a mixed group of heavily armed anarchists, syndicalists and communists, the likes of which had not been seen before on the decks of HMS *Basilisk*. Nevertheless, it soon became clear to the captain and to his intelligence officer that these were the people who ran the town. The *Alcalde*, it seemed, was just their mouthpiece. Furthermore, he was a very frightened man.

At length it was agreed that a group of officers from the *Basilisk* could go ashore that afternoon. The *Alcalde* and his men would arrange for two open-topped touring cars to transport them to one of the sites of British interests. They then departed. The officers decided to follow the example of their intelligence officer: all donned their best white uniforms with pith helmets and ceremonial swords. Eventually, when they were taken ashore, they were greeted by an unexpected and eccentric-looking reception party. A number of Al Capone lookalikes lounged in the vicinity as they waited alongside the open-topped touring cars. If the Royal Navy officers were startled, they wondered, too, whether to feel glad or sorry to be welcomed by these henchmen, still heavily armed and now, additionally, heavily grinning. The bemused officers glanced at each other as they stepped into the cars before being driven through the streets of Almeria. When crowds of onlookers began to acknowledge them with clenched fist salutes, the officers decided to respond with formal Royal Navy salutes.

As the cars drove out of town towards a hilly area to the north, the officers became gradually more relaxed. Soon they began to appreciate the fine views. The road twisted past a steep gorge with brushwood and occasional pine trees clinging to the hillside. At the bottom, a brook ran in white water through rocks and boulders down to the main stream fed by the *Rio Andarax*. In one spot, however, just to one side of the brook, the officers saw a sight that shocked them. A huddle of people in earnest debate could be glimpsed standing above a number of corpses, human and animal. The *Alcalde*'s men, though, hardly seemed concerned as the car continued to swish along the road at speed. There was little other traffic on the narrow road, in places barely wide enough for two cars to pass. The sun was in their eyes when eventually they rounded a corner to reach an enclave of good-quality housing. As the cars drove into the enclave, the British manager of the waterworks hastened from his home to meet them. 'Thank God!' he cried. 'Thank God you've come!'

'Thank you,' said the officers, stepping out of their cars. 'Thank you very much. That's most kind of you to say so.'

'No, no,' exclaimed the manager. 'You don't understand. We were visited this morning by a gang of ruffians. They've threatened to blow up all our houses.'

'Blow them up?'

'Yes, blow them up.'

'They can't do that.'

'Why not?'

'Because we're British, that's why not. We won't allow it to happen.'

'That's very nice of you.'

'Not at all. Any time.'

'Would you like some tea?'

'That's very nice of you.'

'Not at all. Please come in.'

And when the *Basilisk*'s officers had entered the manager's home, they enjoyed pleasant cups of tea while they talked about their best course of action. After a while the intelligence officer had suggested that one of the *Alcalde*'s henchmen should be asked to join the discussions. A man who could speak reasonable English was summoned and it was explained to him that the warship in the harbour was a British ship. Did he understand that?

'Yes, meester.'

It was further explained that the house where he was presently enjoying a cup of tea was British-owned property. Did he understand that?

'Yes, meester.'

'The warship has powerful guns,' explained the intelligence officer. Eventually he judged that the *Alcalde*'s man had understood the point. The man then left to deliver the message. The officers, meanwhile, continued to enjoy leisurely cups of tea. At length, Union Jack flags were handed out in order that British-owned properties could be clearly marked. The officers then decided that they should return to their ship.

The return journey, however, was more problematic. Word from the *Alcalde*'s man must have spread and the officers felt distinctly vulnerable in their open-topped touring cars. In place of exuberant closed-fist salutes, the onlookers watched in sullen and threatening silence. The officers' anxiety was hardly eased by the escorts of gunmen who leaned out of the cars to wave their rifles at the belligerent crowds. On reaching the waterfront, the officers were relieved to spot the *Basilisk*'s motor boat ready and waiting to whisk them back to the ship without delay.

'I remember seeing the cars drive up, sir,' says the leading seaman.

'The officers all looked a bit peevish, I should say.'

'We probably felt a little subdued.'

'I think so, sir.'

'Although I don't suppose that lasted for long.'

'Sir?'

'You'll remember, I'm sure, the gunfight along the waterfront later in the day.'

'Like a bleedin' battlefield, it was.'

'We watched through binoculars from the bridge,' says the lieutenant. 'Until, that is, the bullets began to whistle close to our heads.'

'Didn't the odd bullet start to ping off the ship's side?'

'The captain had to order everyone to go below decks.'

'I remember it, sir. We had to run below double quick, like.'

'It seems odd looking back. We were a fully armed warship yet the captain had to send his crew running for cover. But I suppose a neutral ship is bound to be awkwardly placed in situations like that.'

'Were we really neutral?'

'That's a good question, and we still face the dilemma.'

'Sir?'

'Well our government's sympathies seem to lie with the Republicans who, after all, represent the legitimately elected government of Spain. However, Royal Navy ships are not supposed to take anything other than a strictly neutral stance. This can be problematic at times, especially when forced to witness events like those at Almeria. Even worse were those at Malaga a few months later.'

'Didn't some duke come on board?'

'We were visited by none other than Colonel the Duke of Seville.'

'I forget, sir, who was he?'

'He was one of Franco's men, the colonel in charge of the attack on the Republicans in Malaga.'

'Why did he come on board the *Basilisk* then?'

'He requested the visit. His forces had overwhelmed the Republican opposition and I suppose he wanted to meet the captain of a British ship to make himself known as the new civil governor. As a neutral ship we could hardly refuse.'

'The colonel seemed to take over Malaga without much difficulty.'

'He and his men were backed by large numbers of Italian forces, and the Italian Air Force used *guerra celere* tactics – the Italian version of *blitzkrieg* – to smash the Republican efforts. The *Basilisk* was ordered to stick to the non-intervention policy – to remain in the background. But a German battleship, the *Admiral Graf Spee*, showed no such restraint when they provided back-up to the Nationalist ships bombarding the town.'

'The Republican warships didn't seem to make much of a show.'

'The Republican warships didn't even leave their port in Cartagena.' The lieutenant shakes his head. 'Frankly, the whole Republican effort was a shambles and they didn't stand a chance. When the Duke of Seville visited us in February, you'll recall how we piped him aboard with due pomp and ceremony. The picture onshore, however, was altogether different – appallingly so. Franco's men showed no mercy and we heard harrowing reports of Republican militiamen waiting to be put up against a wall, the soldiers apathetic in the shock of defeat. Thousands were shot in revenge killings. On the outskirts of the town, as smoke drifted upwards from houses wrecked by Nationalist shells, fleeing civilians and exhausted militiamen tried to find refuge along the coastal road to Almeria. Refugees assumed it would be a place of relative safety but regretfully it proved to be the exact opposite. In dreadful and brutal acts of reprisal, the refugees, already desperate from hunger and exhaustion, were shelled from the sea, bombed from the air and machine-gunned.'

'Not a very nice picture, sir.'

'It was the most—' the lieutenant is interrupted by the sound of raised voices below decks. The leading seaman glances at him with quizzical eyes.

'Isn't that the captain's voice, sir?'

'I think it is.'

'Between you and me, sir, I've heard he's on the warpath.'

'I've heard the same rumour,' says the lieutenant darkly. 'I think I'd better go down to investigate.' He nods a terse farewell to the leading seaman and heads for the bridge ladder. As he tramps gloomily down the steps he contemplates how best to cope with a captain who is apparently on the warpath. This situation is one he could well do without, but he understands the need to avert ill-feeling. The crew have to be on top form for tomorrow's commitments. Tomorrow HMS *Basilisk* will leave harbour at the start of her sea patrol duties.

CHAPTER FIFTEEN

On Patrol

The silhouette of Saint-Jean-de-Luz shrinks into the distance as HMS *Basilisk* is steered on a course west by north-west away from the town's harbour. As she leaves port for the commencement of non-intervention patrol duties, she passes diverse vessels: fishing smacks, sailing dinghies, ketches, a steamer with hand-waving passengers. From his position on the bridge Lieutenant Sutton grasps a handrail as he leans outboard to view the *Basilisk*'s wake and to check clearance from other vessels. He observes the ship's progress and, along with other officers, he supervises the crew to ensure the men follow the seamanship routines with practised efficiency. Those on the bridge maintain a prudent lookout. The captain uses binoculars, others rely on keen eyesight to monitor the ship's passage along the Gulf of Capbreton. Some crewmen, however, sneak occasional glances back towards the town. Perhaps, ruminates the lieutenant, these men seek far-off figures waving from the shoreline; perhaps there are feelings of private regret as the *Basilisk* holds her course. He senses secret farewells when far-off figures fade into the distance and eventually, when separated lovers become engulfed by morning mists, crewmen concentrate on closer distractions: hand-waves for the steamer's passengers, watchful eyes on the sailing dinghies and the ketches, the fishing vessels heading purposefully towards harbour, the local fishermen eager to unload their early-morning hauls and impatient to be rid of the gulls hovering above the nets.

The captain, when satisfied that the *Basilisk*'s wake will not interfere with other vessels, calls for an increase in speed. The engine room staff react; the whine from the ship's twin turbines rises as power from the 34,000 shaft horsepower is unleashed. Soon the wake piles up, the bow churns white furrows in the sea, crewmen feel their legs respond instinctively to meet the ship's new motion. Men look ahead in order to appreciate the developing breeze, nature's remedy for torpor induced by lethargic spells in harbour, the day's growing heat, the special charms of southern France. Those on the bridge continue to scan ahead although they glance down occasionally to check the sea for adjacent hazards. Others watch the hull carve tidy trenches before the waters collapse into a chaos of froth. Lookouts on the bridge squint experienced eyes against the wind and early sun. The crew listen to the lazy clang of halyards escalate to agitated chatter.

'Check the charts please, Mister Sutton.'

'Yes, sir.' The second lieutenant steps forward to the chart table. He is the *Basilisk*'s navigation officer, one of a number of roles allocated to the second lieutenant of a small ship (others include boarding officer, intelligence officer and torpedo officer). Soon, beyond the Cape of Figuer, the helmsman in his wheelhouse will be ordered to alter course to a more westerly direction. The *Basilisk* will be steered past San Sebastian towards the Cape of Machichaco; beyond lies the estuary leading to Bilbao's harbour. For the patrol, the *Basilisk*'s captain has been instructed to concentrate surveillance duties along the coastline of 40 or so nautical miles between Bilbao and Santander. The lieutenant studies the charts for the ship's immediate area and advises the captain that the *Basilisk*'s present course is good. He then rummages through the relevant publications, conscious that the *Basilisk* could be given Admiralty orders to extend patrol beyond Santander. It will be prudent, he thinks, to re-acquaint himself with the maritime particulars for northern Spanish waters as far as Corunna. In the process of checking the condition and currency of the marine charts, he spots a version of the coverage for Cape Ortegal and district. He examines this chart, noting the coast's south-westerly directional change towards Corunna. He recollects how the port acted as a stepping-stone for a historic and heroic Spanish conflict of another era.

These waters may be feared for their volatile nature, but they are known, too, for their legendary links. He reflects on this and recalls how, in the days of the Armada, a violent storm had scattered the Spanish fleet. He pictures the scene. The grand galleons of King Philip II had stopped for victual replenishment and for war councils at Corunna and, following the storms, an emergency council was held at Corunna's town hall. Those at the meeting decided to advise the King to abandon his plans to attack England but by mid-July 1588 there was a change of heart: the Spanish Armada would try again. So it was that on 21 July 1588, 130 Spanish ships with a complement of some 30,000 men set sail to attack the English fleet. Those on board where confident of the justice of their cause, of the inevitability of a God-given victory against English wickedness, of the need to deliver a mortal blow against Tudor England and the heretic Protestant Queen Elizabeth I.

It was nine days before the Spanish men of war were glimpsed by English eyes, but at dawn on a Saturday morning, watchers on Cornish cliffs were awed by the size and splendour of enemy galleons. Lieutenant Sutton recalls history's depiction of the scene. Views of the Spanish Armada were hampered by banks of mist and by successions of squally showers, but Tudor technology swung swiftly into action; tar-soaked brushwood was set aflame as a signal of urgency. Within minutes a pin-prick of light to the east confirmed that the alarm had been spotted and was being sent down the line to the English fleet at Plymouth.

And when the signal was received at Plymouth, the leading English ships began the tricky and laborious procedure of warping out of harbour with the ebb tide. The commanders ashore could do nothing until their ships had cleared port with the tide, and those hours gave Sir Francis Drake the opportunity to finish his game of bowls on Plymouth Hoe. As dawn broke the next morning, the 1,000 ton Spanish flagship *San Martin* was ordered by Captain-General of the Ocean Sea Don Alonso Perez de Guzman el Bueno, Twelfth *Señor* and Fifth Marquis of San Lucar de Barrameda, Ninth Count of Niebla and Seventh Duke of Medina Sidonia, to hoist the signal for the Armada to take up battle formation. Vice-Admiral Drake and Lord Admiral Charles Howard knew that their fleet, by then formed up in Plymouth Sound, was all that stood between England and catastrophic defeat.

Howard soon gave his orders. From the ranks of the English emerged an 80 ton barque, appropriately named the *Disdain*, which dashed within hailing distance of the enemy to fire a derisory and token shot into the foe's midst. This was followed by Howard's galleons storming across the Spanish rear, there to employ tactics which were so revolutionary in terms of mobility, audacity and flexibility that the enemy's resilience was rapidly undermined. The benefits of this flexible mentality, muses Sutton, are felt by the Royal Navy to this day. He remembers how, after the first opening shots and in the confused and bloody hours that followed, two Spanish ships, the *Rosario* and the *San Salvador*, were lost. And when the fight eventually ceased by evening, the Armada's shocked leaders knew they would have to spend at least a day reassessing and regrouping before the next fight off Portland Bill. This took place on 2 August 1588, with a further skirmish off the Isle of Wight on 4 August.

By 10 August, two days after the final confrontation at Gravelines, a brisk gale had sped a chastened but still formidable Spanish fleet due north towards Scotland and the Northern Isles. A 600 ton English royal galleon, the *Victory*, exemplified the scene. As her captain, Sir John Hawkins, surveyed the scarred carcass of his ship, he speculated on her ability to remain afloat. He gazed with alarm at the state of her gaudily painted upperworks, now stained with gunsmoke. He saw how the royal standard at her mainmast and the flags of *St George* at her fore and mizzen tops were in tatters as they flapped in the breeze. He noted that the ship's rigging showed signs of makeshift repair, that the bowsprit and main mizzen were shot-splintered and that the ship's longboat was missing. Although still seaworthy, the 34-gun *Victory* was in no condition to re-engage the enemy: her shot-lockers were completely empty. In his postscript to a report to the Queen's Secretary of State, Hawkins wrote about the need for 'an infinite quantity of powder and shot to be provided to combat the greatest and strongest combination that ever gathered in Christendom'. But the autumn gales blew early that year, ensuring the continuation of 'the singeing of the King of Spain's beard'. Fortune did not favour the Spaniards and as their ships were driven north, dozens were wrecked along the storm-torn Scottish coasts.

Lieutenant Sutton imagines the naval merrymaking, the excited chatter in taverns up and down the country as the news spread: victory for England . . . the dreaded Spaniards defeated . . . God save Queen Elizabeth! The Queen herself was hunting in Epping Forest when she heard of the Armada's retreat from Gravelines and, according to tradition, in a burst of joyous exultation she galloped her horse up the stairway of a nearby hunting lodge. On 18 August 1588 she sailed down the Thames to Tilbury, where her troops were assembled and where she delivered a speech famed for its brevity and cogency: 'I am amongst you as you see, at this time, not for my recreation and disport, but being resolved, in the midst of heat of battle, to live or die amongst you all, and to lay down for my God and for my kingdom and for my people, my honour and my blood, even in the dust. I know I have the body of a weak and feeble woman, but I have the heart and stomach of a king, and of a king of England too, and think foul scorn that Parma, or Spain, or any prince of Europe should dare to invade the borders of my realm . . .' The lieutenant pictures the 54-year-old 'virgin queen', her dark and watchful eyes beneath a Tudor bonnet that veiled her fiery-coloured hair. Perhaps the shake of her slender fingers betrayed the fervour of a woman struggling to cope within a man's world ('I would not open windows into men's souls'). This was a passion of dedication, he muses, a spirit of service which was grievously absent in the royal machinations of more recent times.

The Queen may have breathed easier, Englishmen may have rejoiced and Tudor liquor flowed, though cooler heads began to acknowledge that victory was due as much to the forces of nature as to the forces of Her Majesty. 'I sent my fleet against men,' King Philip would say, 'not against the wind and the waves.' And just as storm-force winds had sealed the Spanish Armada's fate, so are today's seafarers no less vulnerable to the ravages of wind and wave.

'Check our course again please, Mister Sutton.'

The lieutenant stares a little anxiously at his charts before responding: 'This course is still satisfactory, captain.'

'Thank you Mister Sutton.' The captain seems brusque as he acknowledges. The lieutenant, as he continues to study his navigational charts, contemplates the captain's unpredictable temperament. Following yesterday's difficulty, and in view of the considerable amount of tact needed to smooth the senior officer's ruffled feathers, he had hoped to see the captain in an improved state of mind today. He should be happier with his ship at sea and gainfully employed; periods in harbour are notorious for creating trouble for captains. With the day still young and the *Basilisk* about to go on patrol, the lieutenant trusts the captain's spirits may yet improve. But with a spontaneous shrug of his shoulders Sutton contemplates that long periods of inactive patrol can also lead to problems.

The captain, once the ship is established in the patrol zone, will order a reduction of speed to an economical cruising level and the crew will revert to a four-hourly watch system. Those on lookout will search for vessels headed towards northern Spanish coasts and the *Basilisk*'s crew will help enforce maritime laws agreed by international treaty. Of particular significance is the international agreement that a ship within 3 nautical miles of a coastline is subject to national rules; beyond 3 nautical miles the seas are regarded as open. If a ship displaying a British flag is seen to approach the 3 mile zone, the *Basilisk*'s boarding crew will be alerted. Lieutenant Sutton will take charge of the motor cutter, and he and an armed party will be taken to the merchantman to warn the ship's master about Franco's trigger-happy warships stationed within national waters.

'The border town of Hendaye,' he calls, 'is coming up on the port bow, sir. Beyond the next promontory, a port turn of twenty-five degrees will take us towards San Sebastian.'

'Thank you, Mister Sutton,' said the Captain. 'We'll aim to stay within three to five nautical miles from the coastline.'

'Yes, sir.'

The lieutenant sees an ancient-looking rigger ahead but her course and type make her an unlikely candidate for interception by the Royal Navy. With large areas of sea plied by many varied craft, the naval patrols can face dilemmas. Merchantmen are duty bound to display the non-intervention pennant and nationality flags, but some ships seem keen to remain inconspicuous. This is especially true of those spurred by financial incentive. Two months ago when the *Seven Seas Spray* ran the Nationalist blockade, her night journey was one of exceptional daring; most merchant masters would be unwilling to navigate such hostile coastal waters at night. However, with the attitude of ships' masters softened by the prospect of financial reward, the lieutenant wonders if they might sometimes try to deceive naval patrols with camouflage. It was well known that, in past days, sailing ships on long voyages would fit wooden guns and paint themselves to look like frigates in order to mislead enemy warships. Today such measures could be applied in reverse. Merchantmen loaded with arms and ammunition, for example, could disguise themselves as innocent trawlers. The lieutenant speculates on the duplicity and how sea captains might seek to emulate the resourcefulness of the legendary Captain Dance. The latter was in company with three other merchant sailing ships in the Indian Ocean when they were surprised by an enemy squadron. Captain Dance, however, made a show so effective that the enemy sheered off, thinking them too strong to be attacked.

And modern-day merchantmen might contemplate the concealment techniques, if not the final assault, of the so-called mystery ships of the Great War. These vessels, camouflaged to look like merchantmen, aimed to lure warships, especially U-boats, into making an attack until, at the last second, they would drop their screens, reveal their guns and open fire. Then as now, the problem of blockade meant a serious interference with wartime sea communications with consequent loss of vital supplies. Furthermore, there were harrowing tales of rescue scenes, of British women and children half-clothed, wet and cold, being hauled aboard salvage vessels. The Royal Navy had to find a solution urgently; the mystery-ship concept was mooted. The need for exceptional cunning was realized at an early stage – enemy spies were a constant problem, and U-boat commanders were well-informed and wary. There were other hazards, many with parallel significance for today's non-intervention patrols. For example, two ships seldom appear exactly the same: an experienced sea eye will detect minor differences, even between sister ships – the rigging, perhaps, or the arrangement of the boats or of the awning stanchions.

The lieutenant remembers how, in spite of these difficulties, the courage and tenacity of the mystery-ship crews soon proved effective, often dramatic. The experience of one captain, Lieutenant Commander Gordon Campbell, was a case in point. Disguised as the master of a fake merchant trawler, the SS *Farnborough*, he was operating in the southern Irish Sea in the spring of 1916. The *Farnborough* was steaming north in misty conditions with a visibility of barely 2 nautical miles. It was early evening when a large ship of foreign build was seen to loom out of the mist. It turned out to be the Dutch steamer *Soerakarta*. Suddenly a submarine suddenly broke surface nearby and hoisted a signal to both vessels. What followed was reported by a member of the *Soerakarta*'s crew to a Dutch newspaper:

We were ordered to stop by a German submarine. Our captain obeyed the order and the German told us to come to the U-boat with the ship's papers. We had no choice but to obey. However, scarcely was our boat let down to convey these papers when something extraordinary occurred. It was still foggy and we saw in the obscurity a grey ship emerge. Sails on the mysterious ship were pushed aside suddenly and at the same time some guns vomited a hellish fire. The German submarine had caught sight of the masked ship probably sooner than we, for it had launched a torpedo. But the torpedo went wide and before long the terrible fire that flew around, some near us, hit the submarine. In a very short time the submarine sank in the deep.

The thought of such hellish fire against a non-intervention ship of today is hard to imagine. Or is it? That ancient rigger as she steams placidly on the *Basilisk*'s starboard bow would make ideal cover for. . . .

'Turn port twenty-five degrees.' The *Basilisk*'s captain speaks to the officer of the watch who then bends towards a voice-pipe to bark orders to the wheel-house. The helmsman responds; the crew feel the heel of the ship as she alters course and they see the coastline change to a south-westerly direction towards San Sebastian. Lieutenant Sutton checks his charts once more. Beyond San Sebastion will be the coastal towns of Zarautz, Ondarroa, Lekeitio and Bermeo, the latter tucked around a small bay beyond Guernica's estuary. After this is the Cape of Machichaco and 40 or so nautical miles beyond is the Cape of Mayor, overlooking the harbour at Santander. The lieutenant is hopeful that clear visibility will allow him to put the two major landmarks, the Capes of Machichaco and Mayor, to good use as navigational aids. The *Basilisk*'s present speed is maintained for a period, but as Cape Machichaco appears on the port beam, the captain orders a reduction to an economical cruising speed of around 15 knots.

At length, when the *Basilisk* settles into her patrol routine, the captain leaves the bridge and the crew's four-watch system is brought into operation. Lieutenant Sutton realizes that today will probably bring the non-intervention patrols' customary pattern: extended spells of boredom punctuated by occasional bursts of frenetic activity. When watch duty takes him to the bridge, the lieutenant has to make conscious efforts to remain diligently observant. He uses glasses to scan the horizon although he sees few ships; most merchantmen regard the Santander–Bilbao coastal area as unduly hazardous. In time, when he feels the patrol's tedium beginning to affect his alertness, he has stratagems to keep his mind agile. He will consider the fickle seas: the ship's tranquillity one day, her metamorphosis the next. He will picture the ship as she lunges at mountainous waves . . . the bow rising up until it seems the whole vessel must become airborne . . . the waves passing astern . . . the bow plummeting. In his mind's eye he will see the bow hitting the water with a cannon-like crack that causes keel plates to shudder and men to think that the ship must come apart with the impact.

He will think of other scenes too: his navigational duties, his numerous and varied tasks. As the boarding officer he has ensured that his team has been briefed, that drills have been practised including the carriage of firearms and search techniques when a merchantman has been arrested. As the ship's torpedo officer he has supervised exercises to keep his men proficient. From time to time this will involve the firing of drill-round torpedoes at dummy targets: men will observe the 'tin fish' launched from the ship's side, watch the device dive down to some 10 to 20 ft, learn to recognize tell-tale bubbles on the sea's surface.

Just now, however, the crew find their lives ruled by predictable patterns: off-duty . . . on-duty . . . routines on the bridge, in messes, engine rooms, communications sections. On-duty rotas are drawn up: lookout pickets, training sessions, maintenance schedules, deck scrubbing, torpedo-tube greasing. While on-duty personnel are kept occupied, off-duty men play cards, chat in messes, organise *dhobi* firms, write letters home. At least once per patrol the *Basilisk* will receive a delivery of mail from another ship (usually HMS *Boreas*) and the two vessels will steam on parallel headings while ratings carry out the precarious process of firing a line to create a physical link. Eventually, when the mail has been passed and when the *Boreas* has turned away, the *Basilisk* will return to her original course and her patrol pattern will resume: searches, routines, interminable days without significant action.

But then something happens.

Basilisk's Boarding Party

The *Basilisk*'s Tannoy system pipes an order: 'Man the port seaboat – boarding party to your stations.' In an instant the lethargy of patrol is cast off; men register the meaning and jump to. Lieutenant Sutton, who is off duty at the time, hastens to the bridge, where he is joined by the captain. The officer of the watch now briefs both men. A British-registered merchantman was observed steaming towards Bilbao. The *Basilisk* intervened and ordered the vessel to stop. The vessel obeyed, now further instructions are awaited. The captain gazes at the merchantman through his glasses as he assesses the situation. 'You'd better take a boarding party, Mister Sutton,' he says eventually. 'That fellow looks like trouble.'

As the pre-boarding routines are followed, davits for the 25 ft motor cutter are brought into operation, firearms are drawn, boarding dress is donned: whites for the seamen, naval cap, white uniform and white shoes for the boarding officer. Before long the motor cutter is launched, the coxswain and crew and the six-man boarding party take their positions on board. When instructed, the coxswain steers away from the *Basilisk*'s hull. The cutter's wake builds up when he advances the vessel's throttles and heads towards the merchantman. The coxswain aims for a pilot ladder and the cutter slows again before being secured to the side of the merchantman. Two armed seamen now climb the pilot ladder ahead of the boarding officer.

When he reaches the top step of the ladder, the boarding officer observes the details of the ship. The men of the boarding party sense the merchantman's unusual aura, the contrast to the atmosphere on board a Royal Naval ship. This is a British ship with British officers, yet the vessel lacks the shipshape rigours of the military scene. Coils of rope, canvas awnings, sea chests, odd casks cover the decks in a seemingly haphazard manner. The merchantman's second mate stands by the pilot ladder ready to receive his visitors. 'What-o, lads,' calls a voice from the other side of the deck, but the second mate swivels on his heels to scowl at a young deckhand. Duly chastened, the deckhand glances down. The second mate, a square-jawed individual with eyes that peer from beneath bushy eyebrows, nods a greeting to the boarding officer. 'This way, please, lieutenant. The master's in his cabin.'

'Thank you.'

As he follows, the boarding officer assesses his surroundings. He notes the brisk manner of the second mate, the determined set of jaw that suggests a man of action, someone accustomed to command. The lift of his shoulders as he walks, the turn of his head as he glances instinctively at the sky, mark an experienced seagoing man. Conversation is minimal as the boarding party follow him to the master's cabin. Here, they find the master pacing to and fro, impatient to proceed. 'Come in, come in,' he cries. The *Basilisk*'s armed seamen remain by the open cabin door as the boarding officer enters. The master dismisses his second mate before saying; 'Sit down, lieutenant, sit down. Can I offer you something? Rum, whisky? Tea, coffee?'

'Thank you, but no.'

There's a pause. 'What can I do for you then?'

'I should like to inspect your ship's papers, please.'

'Indeed.' The master is prepared: he hands across his bill of lading, the crew manifest, cargo manifest, customs documents, insurance documents. He remains calm and tries to chat casually with the lieutenant, who eventually asks: 'Can you confirm your port of departure and your final destination, please?'

The master vacillates; he shifts uncomfortably in his chair. He states his port of departure, then mumbles something about 'northern Spain'.

'Whereabouts exactly?'

Another pause.

'Well?'

'Bilbao.'

'You realize the risks?'

The master remains silent.

'Royal Navy patrols are aware of Spanish warships in the vicinity of Bilbao,' continues the lieutenant. 'The Spaniards are a trigger-happy lot.' The master grins and by way of reply pulls open a desk drawer. He points down. The lieutenant half-stands and leans across. What he sees makes him gasp: gold bracelets, pearl necklaces, diamond clusters, rubies, emeralds, brilliant crystals, watches, abundant hordes of treasure – all glint an alluring welcome.

'If the price is right . . .' the master's grin broadens.

'I'm not empowered to stop you,' says the lieutenant, 'but it's my duty to warn you of the hazards. These Spanish warships are positioned inside the three-mile zone and they're ready to pounce.'

The master shrugs. 'They wouldn't dare do much.'

'What makes you so sure?'

'Your presence for one thing.'

'I can assure you that Franco's men are ruthless. We've heard bad reports.'

'Franco's men represent an illegal regime.'

Now it is the lieutenant's turn to shrug. 'That's true, but if a warship decides to open fire . . .'

'It's a risk I'm prepared to take, lieutenant,' says the master with a frown. Further discussions follow, but the master remains adamant. Even the lieutenant's parting shot – 'Don't complain about a lack of warning' – appears to have little impact. Having decided that the master will not be dissuaded, the Lieutenant leads his boarding party back to the cutter, thence to the *Basilisk*, where he reports to the captain.

'Well, Mister Sutton?' the captain is impatient.

'He's bound for Bilbao, sir. I've warned him –I've told him about the Spanish warships, but he's determined to proceed. He thinks we'll be able to offer him some sort of protection.'

'Then he's deluding himself.' The captain orders a message to be sent to the senior naval officer at Saint-Jean-de-Luz, and he uses glasses to watch the merchantman resume her course towards Bilbao. A return message from Saint-Jean-de-Luz confirms that the *Basilisk*'s relief destroyer will depart shortly and that other Royal Naval warships in the area will be alerted.

An interval of some hours follows but by early evening, trouble is first signalled by a lookout on the *Basilisk*: 'Two ships sighted on the port bow!'

The officers hasten to the bridge to observe events off the port bow. Soon the British merchantman reappears, this time on a northerly heading and in convoy with a Spanish warship. The crew gaze through glasses to identify the Spaniard. Eventually, it is recognized as the cruiser *Canarius*. The Spanish warship indicates that she has arrested the merchantman and that she intends to escort her out to sea for a fate as yet undetermined. The *Basilisk*'s captain confers briefly with his officers and states his intention to intervene. He yells orders; these are relayed into voice pipes; the helmsman reacts, the *Basilisk* is manoeuvred to create a buffer between the *Canarius* and the merchantman. The Spaniard now signals a series of protestations: the *Canarius* is within her rights; she acts within the aegis of international maritime law; the British destroyer's actions are illegal.

The *Basilisk*'s captain responds by directing the Spaniard's attention to a distant speck on the horizon. Before long, as the speck enlarges and another British destroyer appears on the scene, officers on the *Basilisk* monitor the *Canarius'*s reaction. The Spaniard's protestations, however, persist. The *Basilisk'*s captain therefore directs the other's attention to a further speck on the horizon. This time, as the 31,100 ton Queen Elizabeth class battleship HMS *Barham*, with her twin-mounted guns of 15 inch calibre, and her twelve single-mounted guns of 6 inch calibre, begins to loom, the protestations peter out. The Spaniard slinks quietly out of sight. HMS *Barham* passes greetings to her fellow warships, then sends a politely apologetic signal: as she has other important commitments, she regrets that she must depart the scene forthwith. While the battleship steams majestically out of sight, the *Basilisk*, now at the end of her period of patrol duty, hands over to her relief destroyer. She then heads north for refuelling and replenishment at the port of La Pallice before steaming south again for Saint-Jean-de-Luz.

There will be cheers of self-congratulation on board the British ships. The tactics worked . . . the Spaniard was defeated . . . God save King George! With excited chatter above and below decks, an abundance of merry-making in the messes, the Royal Navy men will replicate the age-old naval celebrations. For the *Basilisk'*s crew, enthusiastic about a return to the seaside town buried within the sand dunes of France, there will be more than one reason to celebrate. With the eagerness of the innocent, the *Basilisk'*s second lieutenant enters into the spirit of the festivities. However, he can have no inkling of the timeless torpedo shortly to be launched across the bows of his life. For he, that vulnerable soul, is about to face forces every bit as cogent as those confronted by the Seventh Duke of Medina Sadona, every bit as devious as the ruses of the Great War mystery ships, and for which every bit of his naval training is bound to prove completely – absurdly – all at sea.

CHAPTER SEVENTEEN

Cupid's Cocktail Party

HENDAYE, SOUTHERN FRANCE.

As they edge towards the door, the two lieutenants attempt to peer inside the room. Their progress is slow, even slower when they are forced to a halt by people blocking the door – tiresome types who insist on hanging around a doorway while still in earnest conversation. The lieutenants stand on tiptoe and crane their necks as they try to glimpse the scene inside the room. Even for heroic naval officers the atmosphere seems a little intimidating; those in the room seem exotic folk, almost foreign – which, of course, many of them are. 'Excuse me . . . would you mind . . . ?' the navy men attempt further progress. Each knows the other has scant enthusiasm for this affair. They even regard their presence here as some kind of penance.

'When we reach Saint-Jean-de-Luz,' the captain had said as the *Basilisk* steamed south from La Pallice, 'two officers from this ship have been invited to attend a cocktail party hosted by Sir Henry Chilton, the British ambassador in Madrid, now decamped to Hendaye.' The captain glanced around the wardroom. 'Do I have two volunteers?'

Silence. The captain's expression developed into a frown. He glowered at the assembled officers: 'Any volunteers, please gentlemen?'

Still silence, eventually broken by the captain saying: 'Lieutenants Sutton and Richards? I'm sure you'll both be glad to offer your services.'

'If you say so, captain, but—'

'Come now gentlemen, no "buts". I'm sure you'll both thoroughly enjoy yourselves.'

'Well, sir, not—'

'Just think about it: you'll be representing the Royal Navy. Is that not an honour and a privilege?'

'Yes, sir, but—'

'Good. I'm glad you see it that way.'

'The only thing is—'

'We'll take it as settled then gentlemen.'

'Yes, sir.'

And now the two lieutenants are stuck. To make matters worse, they feel like aliens as they watch groups of pressing, hand waving, jaw-wagging people. The variety of accents is baffling – French, Spanish, Italian, Swedish, American and, of course, British. Not much sign of the Germans, though; *persona non grata* probably. 'Excuse me . . . would you mind . . . ?' The two lieutenants persist in their efforts to ease through the crowds. Lieutenant Sutton glances back at his fellow officer: 'Cheer up, Chiefie,' he says, 'we'll make it one day.'

'Don't be so sure, old boy.'

'May I pass, please? Gangway!' But the appeals fall on deaf ears. So many people talking and gesticulating, but not so many listening, though.

The lieutenants make a small amount of progress. They spot a steward who clutches a drinks tray. The drinks, at least, look inviting although the steward, poor fellow, appears anxious. The lieutenants will ease his burden; they'll gladly relieve him of a couple of drinks. But now more people have decided to dally. 'May I get by, please? Thank you . . . excuse me.' At last! They manage to squeeze past the dawdlers in the doorway and find a little more leeway inside the room itself. They head for the steward and his drinks tray. 'May we . . . ?'

'*Oui, monsieur. Merci . . .*'

The lieutenants take their drinks then look around the room; so many people, so many faces, so many strangers. But who is that? Lieutenant Sutton glimpses an attractive-looking young woman. She slips from view when he is nudged in the general crush. He glances at Lieutenant Richards: 'Did you see . . . ?'

'See what?'

'Never mind, Chiefie. If you care to go port,' he nods one way, 'I'll go starboard. Divide and conquer?'

'All right – why not?'

HMS *Basilisk*'s second lieutenant decides he will have to muster his naval prowess. He will exercise his skills at mixing; he will find a likely-looking group, attach himself, make genteel conversation, keep his eyes and ears open. With any luck he may come across that attractive-looking young woman again. He may be unenthusiastic about the proceedings; the ambassador's cocktail party may be no substitute for the delights of Saint-Jean-de-Luz, but that's just too bad. He'll put his best foot forward and try to make the most of the situation.

'Eight generals!' As he eases between groups, the lieutenant falters when he overhears a man's voice. At least the voice speaks in English; perhaps he should take advantage of this group.

'I thought it was nine,' cries a female voice. 'And all of them shot.'

'All of them?'

The lieutenant clears his throat briefly before interjecting: 'And if Stalin treats his generals like that, just think how he might behave when it comes to colonels!' Two members of the group, a man and a woman, pick up the remark; they look a little shocked as they turn towards him.

'Why, yes . . .' says the woman.

'Please forgive the outburst,' says the lieutenant now looking shame-faced, 'but I couldn't help overhearing your remarks.'

'That's perfectly all right,' says the man politely. He and the woman take the lieutenant's interruption as an excuse to ease away from the main group. They step to one side. The man introduces the woman, a diplomat's wife, then himself.

'And I don't think we've had the pleasure . . . ?'

'Alan Sutton.' The lieutenant bows his head slightly.

'Delighted.'

'Do you live in Hendaye?' asks the man.

'No. I'm in the Royal Navy.'

'Ah! A navy man. An admiral, no doubt. Very commendable. May I ask which ship?'

'The *Basilisk*. She's in harbour at Saint-Jean-de-Luz for a few days. And I'm a lieutenant actually.'

'Oh, yes, very good. And the *Basilisk*, I think I am correct in saying, is one of His Majesty's finest destroyers. I saw her sister ship when I was in Saint-Jean-de-Luz the other day.'

'But you were talking just now of . . .' The lieutenant hesitates.

'Stalin, as you rightly guessed.'

'On top of all this trouble in Spain,' says the diplomat's wife. 'Wasn't it just so awful . . . I mean, General Tchaikovsky, or whatever his name is . . . was . . .'

'Marshal Tukhachevsky.'

'That's the fellow. Well, one never quite knows what goes on inside the Soviet mind, in their secretive society, but we all thought he was supposed to be a good man – a military genius even. What are we supposed to make of it all?' she shakes her head. 'I don't understand what the world's coming to.'

'On the last May Day parade,' says the man, 'he was standing next to Stalin. Soviet faces, as we know, are disinclined to break into beaming smiles, but as far as one could tell everything looked fine and dandy.'

'So much for Stalin's friendship,' says the lieutenant.

'I mean . . .' the diplomat's wife gestures with one hand as she struggles to find appropriate words, '. . . it's hardly believable . . . one minute side by side in apparent peace and harmony. And then before he knows it, the poor marshal is arrested – wounded in the process – and taken to that disgraceful Stalin on a stretcher.'

'And Stalin, of course,' says the man, 'showed no mercy. He contrived that . . . what was it?'

'Stalin claimed that the Red Army was plotting a coup,' says the lieutenant. 'He accused the top brass of passing secrets to the Germans. *Pravda*, I seem to remember, came up with some choice expressions.'

'Something about "poisonous pygmies,"' says the man. 'And something else about "the reptile of fascist espionage has many heads but we will cut off every head and paralyse and sever every testicle."'

'Excuse me.' the diplomat's wife coughs delicately into her clenched fist.

'I think you meant tentacle,' says the lieutenant in a quiet tone.

'Thank you, lieutenant,' says the diplomat's wife.

'Oh did I?' says the man. 'I'm frightfully sorry. You're probably right. That means I must—' but he is interrupted when a passer-by slips and bumps against him. The drinks of both men spill onto the floor.

The passer-by totters, wipes his mouth with one sleeve, then says, 'Whoops-a-daisy.' His voice is high-pitched. 'Silly me.' He catches the lieutenant's eye and grins. He notes the Lieutetant's smart civilian suit, his polished shoes. He draws heavily on a cigarette before blowing gales into the atmosphere. His grin thickens and with one hand he tries to salute: 'Another navy man, I should say? You can spot 'em a mile off! Jolly Jack Tar and all that. Where's your parrot? Ha ha. Lost? Must be the black patch over his eye. Ha ha.'

The lieutenant feels anger well up inside him. Bloody fellow; how dare he speak like that? There's no question: a rebuke is called for. He tries to summons his sternest form of naval reprimand but suddenly he catches another glimpse of that attractive young woman. His anger begins to melt away; he tries to mouth a reply but words fail him. Anyway, what does he care about this drunken idiot? If only that young woman would come closer. He can see her more clearly now, but she disappears again.

The passer-by cackles with exuberant laughter before, with a languid wave of one hand, he resumes his journey. The diplomat's wife glances at the lieutenant. She is about to make a remark but something causes her to falter: she appears struck by the expression on his face.

'I think,' says their companion as he studies his now empty glass, 'it is my duty to find us all another drink. Same again for everybody?'

'I'll stick to this one for now, thank you,' says the diplomat's wife.

'Well, if you wouldn't mind,' says the lieutenant with a sigh, 'it'll be the same again for me, please.' As their companion disappears, the diplomat's wife sneaks another glance at the lieutenant. She remains intrigued by his expression. She decides to ease the atmosphere. 'I'm sorry about what happened there,' she says in a sympathetic tone.

'Oh it was nothing . . . just one of those things.'

'Absolutely. Some people appear to get carried away at these affairs, don't they? But are you sure you're all right?'

'Thank you, yes, I'm perfectly all right.' His eyes soften. 'Well actually, no . . .' He hesitates. 'To be honest . . . I'm not so sure that I am.'

'Not so sure?'

'Well it's just that . . .' he flounders. 'I was wondering . . .'

'Wondering?'

'I was just wondering about . . . do you mind me asking . . . but who is that young woman?'

'Which young woman?'

'Over there – by the window.'

Discreetly she searches the room, then her face brightens. Her expression becomes one of sudden recognition: 'Why I do believe you mean Mary Cazeaux de Grange.'

'Cazeaux de Grange?'

'Yes, she's a member of an aristocratic family – Cazeaux, Marquis de Grange, of the *Ancien Régime*. They were lucky to escape the troubles in Spain: her father made it just a day before Bilbao fell. Now the family live in France; they've rented a villa near here. She was educated in England – Benenden School, I believe – so she speaks perfect English. But perhaps in time, when the troubles are over, they'll return to their home in Spain.'

'She is very beautiful.'

The diplomat's wife steps back a fraction. The lieutenant swallows. She stares at him. The sounds in the room seem to dissolve. He looks away in embarrassment; in the distance he watches a flock of birds break from the trees. She searches for a nearby table to put down her glass. He clears his throat and speaks softly: 'I . . .' he falters. 'Sometimes it's hard t-to . . .' his tongue feels twisted and his stammer elicits a sigh from her.

She remains quiet but her mouth begins to curl into a gentle smile. 'Why lieutenant,' she says drawing out her words in exaggerated fashion. 'Am I to imagine there is someone you would like to meet?'

His gaze drops to his glass then meets hers again shyly. 'Do you think . . . ?'

'Think what?

'Think that you could . . . arrange something?'

'Arrange something?'

'A meeting?'

'Well, well, lieutenant.' She raises her eyebrows and her smile broadens. 'That's a bold request if ever I've heard one.'

'I'm sorry,' he murmurs.

She studies her fingernails for a moment then one hand travels absently to her earlobe. 'Perhaps . . .' She smiles wistfully.

'When?'

'Details, details . . .'

'But—'

She tosses her head: 'Is this to be a naval campaign?'

'The best laid plans . . .' he hesitates. Who is he to argue? He sips from his glass trying to look unruffled.

She raises an innocent hand: 'I suppose I might be able to manage something.' An awkward silence ensues and the sound of her voice startles him when she next speaks: 'Perhaps a dinner party could be arranged.'

Two spots of red begin to glow on his cheeks. 'There's one snag,' he says.

She seems to debate for a moment before asking: 'You're making conditions?'

He glances again at the young woman by the window – her charismatic smile, her elegant cocktail dress, her mysteriously seductive gaze, her delicate-looking skin. 'It's just that my naval routine—'

'Routine? Life's important events to be dictated by routine?' Her eyes find his and seem to linger. He tries to decipher their meaning.

'It's nice of you,' he blurts out.

'Nice?' she puts one hand close to her mouth to conceal a giggle. She tilts her head to one side. 'I suppose you're not the first dashing young gentleman to swoop in and sweep away our girls and I don't suppose you'll be the last.'

He tries to grin but his mouth forms a line instead.

'The *Basilisk* did you say?' She has become business-like. He nods obediently. 'And this ship is due to remain in harbour for a few days?'

'Yes.'

'Leave it to me then, lieutenant,' she smiles. 'Somehow or other, I'll make sure you get a message.' Now the diplomat's wife mutters that she wishes to 'powder her nose' and with a backward glance she glides off to another part of the room.

'Here you are, old boy.' The man returns and holds out the lieutenant's drink. He searches for the diplomat's wife: 'Has she gone?'

'She said something about powdering her nose.'

'Women!' he raises his eyes heavenwards. 'Always seem to find the need to powder their damn noses. Well, maybe we should take it as a hint. Perhaps we should move on – mix with other groups.' He winks.

'It's been a pleasure to meet you, old chap.'
  'The pleasure was entirely mine.'
  'Maybe bump into you later.'
  'Of course.'
  They each go their own way. In the case of one of them at least, tumultuous emotions now begin to bubble up – the kind that accompany those tentative, invisible bonds when a man and a woman first sense the quiver of a Cupidian shaft. The lieutenant's toes may start to tingle, he may feel as though he is treading on air. Oh, lieutenant, lieutenant! And you have yet to meet the author of your joy? You may be resolute, tenacious, single-minded. You are a man of determination, dash and valour, and over the years these may prove indispensable merits for the state of wedded bliss. But take solemn note: you will need them for other reasons too. My friend, the naval duties you are about to confront will require qualities of a nature and of such scale that even if the word 'Herculean' sounds a little overdone, nonetheless the description will be, in the opinion of most, entirely apposite.

PART THREE

Italian Job

CHAPTER EIGHTEEN

Maiden's Prayers

NOVEMBER, 1940

His smile is wistful as he gazes at the photographs held lightly in his hand. Lieutenant Alan William Frank Sutton studies the photographs carefully, without haste – even though he yearns to reread the accompanying letter from his wife. He decides, however, to delay his third reappraisal of the letter – or is it his fourth? – in order to relish the prospect. He sits with others in the wardroom of HMS *Illustrious* and when, now and again, he glances up he notes how conversations die out as officers become absorbed with far-off worlds introduced along with the ship's latest delivery of mail. When they nod their heads, smile, chuckle, occasionally frown, they give unwitting glimpses of private lives. The wardroom's special ambience is enhanced for Lieutenant Sutton as he savours occasional and pleasurable wafts of scent from the hastily opened envelope now lying in his lap.

He scrutinizes the photographs again. He has seen them before, but in the last letter to his wife he asked her to send extra copies. He sighs nostalgically when he considers the passage of time: nearly one year has elapsed since the photographs were taken on the day of his marriage to Miss Mary Margaret Cazeaux de Grange, now Mrs Peggy Sutton. On their first wedding anniversary on 24 January 1941 he will try to arrange leave, although wartime commitments make this unpredictable. The date, in any case, seems a long way off just now. He peers at the pictures, at the family groups gathered on the steps of Buckfast Abbey in Devon. Smatterings of snow on the steps reveal that it is midwinter. His bride may have been snatched from the sunnier climes of France and Spain but her smile still defies the frostiness of the Devonshire winter scene. He notes the proud way in which she clutches her bouquet, how she seems unconcerned that, with the constraints of wartime, no hint of white has been permitted to touch the colour of her wedding dress.

He studies the images of his young wife – her attractive hat of fur, her dress buttoned to the neck – and he notes, too, the pictures of himself as bridegroom. He stands by her side in his naval lieutenant's uniform, with his right hand offering her support as, with his other, he grasps his naval sword. He was an observer in the Fleet Air Arm by then, his new status indicated by a small 'A' (to denote aircrew) placed within the loop of his naval badge of rank. On his left side stands his stalwart mother, whose attire of warm hat, thick gloves, sensibly sturdy shoes, clearly announce her determination to defy the winter temperatures. If her expression is anxious, that is understandable: she it was who had responsibility for the organization of her son's wedding and that, poor woman, at short notice and without the support of her husband. Also anxious-looking is the sombre face of the bride's mother, whose long coat with its ample collar of fur seems designed to test the most Arctic of conditions. The bride's father, stricken with pneumonia, is absent.

The circumstances leading up to that January wedding day were, he recalls, hectic. The dinner party arranged by the diplomat's wife at Hendaye had turned out to be a marked success. There had been laughter and cordial conversation, after which he had been flattered by Miss Cazeaux's consent to a further meeting; it seemed that the quiver of Cupid was felt by both. There were, however, problems. His naval routine caused frustrations and Miss Cazeaux's Catholic and high-born background meant, on occasions, the need for a chaperone. And when he was embedded on patrol on the *Basilisk*, stuck with her tiresome captain, the drag of time seemed interminable. The more he wished time away, the more slowly it passed although when, at last, the ship returned to Saint-Jean-de-Luz, life assumed the aura of some form of seventh heaven. He still treasures the photographs of Miss Cazeaux when, along with her brother Luis and other young friends, she was invited to visit the *Basilisk*. Evident from the expressions on their faces is the happiness of those sun-tanned and relaxed-looking young men and women as they chatted and smoked, laughed and bantered while they lazed in deckchairs on the ship's quarterdeck. Careful examination of some of the photographs reveals another factor: the *Basilisk*'s second lieutenant clearly had eyes for just one person.

However, by the end of 1937 that seventh heaven had come to an end. In accordance with his career structure, the 25-year-old Lieutenant Sutton was required to choose a specialist arm. For a variety of reasons, including the attraction of an enhanced salary in the form of flying pay and, additionally, memories of his enthusiasm for aviation as a young-ster, he decided to apply for the up-and-coming Fleet Air Arm. As a sea navigator he wished to pursue his interest in navigation; he therefore volunteered to train as a navigator/observer as opposed to a pilot. But his application, when accepted, led to mixed feelings: sadness at having to abandon the delights of Saint-Jean-de-Luz; relief at the opportunity to escape the unfortunate atmosphere on the *Basilisk* and his poor relations with the captain.

So it was that, in January 1938, he was posted to the School of Naval Co-operation of the Air Force. He joined No. 32 Naval Observers' Course; his fellow students included seven officers from the Royal Navy and two from the RAF. The school, based at Ford, near Arundel in Sussex, was under the control of RAF Coastal Command. The grass airfield at Ford, last used by the military in the First World War, had been recommissioned as part of the RAF's expansion plans in the late 1930s. In addition to the naval school, the aerodrome was used by a small company, owned by the legendary Alan Cobham, that specialized in the novel art of flight refuelling.

The naval school, discreetly placed at one end of the airfield, taught students the skills of navigation, reconnaissance and fleet auxiliary work. In addition to technical instruction, the students learned that the Fleet Air Arm was treated with suspicion, even scepticism, by members of the naval hierarchy. Certain officers wished, it seemed, to replicate the attitudes of the First World War, when traditionalists were known to complain that the presence of aircraft on manoeuvres tended to spoil the event. Those eager to fly often had to learn at their own expense. A case in point was Sub-Lieutenant F. E. T. Hewlett, whose tribulations caused wry amusement within the Fleet Air Arm. He was taught to fly by his enthusiastic, if eccentric, mother, who insisted that she wore clogs and smoked her pipe during flight lessons. Perhaps such events did little to ease the sense of disdain felt by admirals and captains towards the Fleet Air Arm, some of whom saw the Swordfish and other aircraft as mere extensions of a ship's visual scouting capability; the use of aircraft as powerful forces with separate strike potential did not seem to enter their thinking. Although these outlooks would modify with the outbreak of war, nonetheless certain intransigent types could not appreciate the potential of carrier-borne aircraft.

Such, then, was the prevailing attitude within the Royal Navy when Lieutenant Sutton qualified as a Fleet Air Arm observer after his six-month course at Ford. He was posted in June 1938 to HMS *Glorious*, an aircraft carrier based in the Mediterranean theatre.

Meanwhile, Miss Cazeaux had spent time as one of Franco's Nationalist nurses before moving to England for a year-long course at the St James Secretarial College. She and the lieutenant, although in regular touch, were conscious that it was frowned upon to marry too soon in the relationships of those days. They did not, therefore, become officially engaged. However, with Britain's declaration of war against Germany in September 1939, viewpoints began to alter and early in the New Year of 1940 she received a letter from the lieutenant which sent her pulse racing and caused butterflies to run riot in her tummy. He asked for her hand in marriage. Then came a telegram in which he urged her to meet him as soon as possible. She duly travelled to London where she telephoned Mrs Sutton to ask the whereabouts of her elder son. Mrs Sutton replied that she did not know and put down the receiver. Miss Cazeaux tried again. This time Mrs Sutton was persuaded not to replace the receiver. Miss Cazeaux asked her to agree to be introduced and Mrs Sutton duly agreed, and together with her parents, she travelled to Torquay. A meeting was arranged and a wedding date of the 24 January 1940 was set. Mrs Sutton then had just a matter of days to put in place the wedding arrangements: registry office formalities at Newton Abbot, a Catholic wedding service at Buckfast Abbey, a reception at the Imperial Hotel, Torquay.

The lieutenant continues to study his photographs as memories run vividly through his mind. One picture of the new Mrs Sutton displays the overcoat he was begged to place across her shoulders; he imagines her shivering with cold, eager to move on, as she and her groom posed beside a waiting car. When, at last, the photographer had finished, the couple were driven to the Imperial Hotel at Torquay where more pictures were taken inside the hotel. As he observes those images now – some of groups, some of his bride on her own – he sees how radiant her smile is. She stands nobly in a private drawing room, the room's elegance exemplified by tall windows, polished furniture, chairs covered in exquisite material that bears scant resemblance, he thinks, to the Morse code variety of naval wardrooms. She grasps her wedding bouquet with both hands and clearly appreciates the warm glow produced by the room's open-hearth fire.

After the enchantment of that day, the newly-weds hired a car for their brief honeymoon. They then headed for Littlehampton in Sussex and their first home of wedded bliss. However, with naval commitments, frequent moves and regular intervals with her husband away on duty, Mrs Sutton soon learned the harsh realities of service life. He was posted to No. 819 Squadron, Fleet Air Arm, which was formed at the beginning of 1940 and equipped with Fairey Swordfish aircraft. Sited near the naval observers' school, the squadron was based temporarily at Ford but earmarked for the Royal Navy's newest aircraft carrier, HMS *Illustrious*, due to be commissioned in April 1940. Two other Fleet Air Arm squadrons were assigned to the *Illustrious*: a second Swordfish squadron (No. 815), and one equipped with Fulmar and Skua fighter aircraft (No. 806). As personnel began their work-up to operational standards, spells of separation from their wives were inevitable when training schedules took crews to various parts of the country. There were frequent visits to the west coast of Scotland, where aircrews made use of pre-planned targets in a Wigtownshire Bay to familiarize themselves with the quirks of the Swordfish biplane and its capabilities as a torpedo-bomber.

Popularly known as the 'Stringbag', the Swordfish was crewed, in normal circumstances, by three men – a pilot, an observer, and a telegraphist air gunner (TAG). For long-range sorties a 93 gallon auxiliary fuel tank could be strapped into the centre cockpit, thus displacing the observer and his bulky Bigsworth chart board to the cramped rear cockpit. In this case, the TAG would be excluded and the observer had to carry out extra duties. Additionally, the observer had to contend with the danger of becoming soaked in high-octane aviation fuel when the aircraft took off, climbed, or manoeuvred. This unenviable position was worsened in combat conditions when the Stringbag's fabric-covered cockpit was at risk of being pierced and set alight by anti-aircraft shells, commonly known as 'flaming onions'.

With all three of the Stringbag's cockpits exposed to the elements, the aircraft's obsolete image was hardly enhanced by the appearance of the aircrew: leather flying helmets, silk-lined gloves, leather gauntlets, woollen balaclavas over flying helmets, woollen scarves, layer upon layer of thick clothing to combat the intense cold. Once, when an American exchange officer was being shown around the *Illustrious*, his escorting officer pointed towards a line-up of Stringbags at one end of the flight deck. The American seemed aghast at the sight. 'Where the hell do they come from?' he asked.

'Fairey's.'

'That figures,' said the American.

But the Swordfish, despite an impression of flimsy obsolescence, had qualities of ruggedness and reliability which made her well-suited to the rigours of carrier operations. With a wing span of 45 ft 6 in, a length of just over 36 ft, a height of 12 ft 10 in, it was a large machine. Powered by a single 690 horsepower Bristol Pegasus 111M.3 engine or a 750 horse-power Pegasus XXX engine to drive her three-bladed airscrew, the aircraft had a maximum speed of 139 mph, cruised (theoretically) at 104–109 mph at 5,000 ft, and took seven minutes to climb to 5,000 ft. It had a service ceiling of 15,000 ft, a range (without the auxiliary fuel tank) of 350 nautical miles, and was armed with one fixed, synchronized Browning machine gun forward and one Lewis or Vickers K gun aft. There was provision for one 18 inch, 1610 lb torpedo, or one 1,500 lb mine to be carried below the fuselage. Alternatively it could be fitted with combinations of 250 and 500 lb bombs or three Mark VII depth-charges.

A later version of the Swordfish, the Mark II, could carry rocket projectiles. For carrier operations the aircraft's wings could be folded manually, thus reducing her span to 17 ft 3 in.

In addition to these features, the Swordfish had a number of remarkable and unexpected attributes. These included a manoeuvrability which was described by one experienced pilot thus:

> You could pull a Swordfish off the deck and put her in a climbing turn at 55 knots. The aircraft would manoeuvre in the vertical plane as easily as straight and level. Even when diving from 10,000 ft the airspeed indicator never rose much above 200 knots. The controls were not frozen rigid by the force of the slipstream and it was possible to hold the dive to within 200 ft of the water. The Swordfish could be ditched safely and even the machine's lack of speed could be turned to advantage against fighters. A steep turn at sea level towards the attacker just before he came within range, and the difference in speed plus the small turning circle made it impossible for the fighter to bring its guns to bear for more than a few seconds. The approach to the carrier deck could be made at a staggeringly slow speed, yet response to the controls remained firm and insistent. Consider what these qualities meant on a dark night when the carrier's deck was pitching the height of a house.

If such an accolade suggested a long lineage, this was misleading: the machine's origins were comparatively recent. Lieutenant Sutton was aware that the forerunner of the Swordfish, the Fairey TSR I, first took to the air at Fairey's Great West Aerodrome just seven and a half years ago on 21 March 1933. Produced as a private venture, the TSR I possessed features similar to the Swordfish although with detailed differences, for instance a shorter fuselage, a fin and rudder of higher aspect ratio, and, originally, a spatted undercarriage. The two-bladed airscrew was driven by a Siddeley Tiger engine, although the Bristol Pegasus was used in later trials. The initial flight tests were promising, but when the aircraft was lost in an accident on 11 September 1933, the pilot escaping by parachute, the machine was replaced by the TSR II. The latter became the Swordfish prototype (K 4190) and was modified in a number of respects, for example an extra bay was incorporated in the fuselage and the tail assembly was redesigned. The TSR II first flew on 17 April 1934; seven months later, on 10 November, the twin-float seaplane conversion made its first flight at Hamble. Subsequent catapult-launching trials took place aboard the ship of the lieutenant's first commission, HMS *Repulse*. Further flight tests were conducted at Martlesham in East Suffolk, after which the Air Ministry decided to adopt the TSR II and to name it the Swordfish. In April 1935 Fairey received an initial contract for eighty-six Swordfish. Others followed and by early 1940, when Fairey handed over Swordfish production to Blackburn Ltd, the parent company had delivered 692 Swordfish aircraft.

As he recalls these events, Lieutenant Sutton reflects, too, on the Fleet Air Arm's reliance on the Swordfish and her potential. This was impressed on him at the naval observer's school, although on leaving the school his first experiences as a naval observer revealed how, in the wider navy, the Fleet Air Arm faced unfortunate, unnecessary obstacles. These became evident at an early stage of his posting to HMS *Glorious*. The foolish attitudes, regrettably rife within the Royal Navy, were demonstrated by certain non-aircrew officers, men who were ignorant about aircraft and uninterested in the development of their use. Some of the old-school types tended to resent Fleet Air Arm officers, even refusing to talk to them, considering that they had diluted the status of officer. The sorry state of affairs led to many wasted opportunities and the situation was hardly improved when the *Glorious*, like the *Basilisk*, was taken over by a controversial, cantankerous captain whose presence created a deplorable, unhappy atmosphere on board.

Matters did not improve when the *Glorious* was reassigned for war service. Based at Alexandria for peacetime duties, the ship was ordered at the outbreak of war to steam south through the Suez Canal to her new base at Aden. When established there she was tasked with patrolling the seas around the Horn of Africa. Royal Navy ships had Admiralty orders to intercept and attack German raiders that menaced the British focal points of trade in the Indian Ocean. However, the captain of the *Glorious*, Captain Hughes, had perverse ideas about the use of the aircraft on his ship. Furthermore, he was inclined to squabble with his senior Fleet Air Arm officers. The carrier's capabilities were squandered as a result and the morale of the ship's crew deteriorated. The lieutenant ponders that if such was the attitude of the captain of an aircraft carrier, little wonder there were problems within the navy at large. An urgent rethink of attitudes was required if the Fleet Air Arm squadrons, including the thirteen operational Swordfish squadrons established by the start of the war, were to be used effectively as an offensive force.

But the Fleet Air Arm, which had expanded rapidly after its separation from the RAF in May 1939, was hardly used to best effect when, in the opening months of the war, the squadrons were employed chiefly in convoy-escort and fleet-protection duties. However, the pressures of war seemed to provide a much-needed catalyst and the lieutenant reflects that some seven months ago, when Swordfish squadrons became involved in the Norwegian campaign, Fleet Air Arm aircraft for the first time contributed directly to offensive operations. On 13 April 1940, in a naval engagement at Ofot Fiord during the second Battle of Narvik, a catapult-launched Swordfish from HMS *Warspite* acted as spotter aircraft for the guns of the *Warspite* and other vessels. The skilful actions and the courage of the Swordfish crew (the machine was piloted by Pilot Officer F. C. Rice) led to the destruction of seven enemy destroyers, one of which was attacked directly by the Swordfish. The crew then went on to bomb and sink U-64, the first enemy submarine to be destroyed in the war by a Fleet Air Arm aircraft. The following month Swordfish squadrons began to bomb enemy-held Channel ports and to lay mines under the direction of RAF Coastal Command. It seemed that at last the Fleet Air Arm's potential was being employed appropriately.

As he muses on this, the lieutenant recollects that it was at the time of the Norwegian campaign that the urgently needed *Illustrious* was being completed by her constructors at Barrow. By the late spring of 1940, when the carrier was ready to receive her three squadrons, they were ordered to fly north to join the ship on completion of her steaming trials off Scotland. The Admiralty instructed the *Illustrious* to sail to Bermuda – an area close to the USA and not normally plagued by U-boats – for her work-up. The lieutenant's memories of that tropical paradise remain poignant: suddenly distant were images of the retreat from Dunkirk of 337,131 Allied troops, of the sinking of the *Basilisk*, of the impending Battle of Britain, of blitz and blackout back at home. He remembers, too, his sense of relief at being posted, at last, to a happy ship commanded by a respected captain. Captain Denis Boyd was an informal, popular man whose background in aviation, and energy in pressing for naval aviation to be handed back to the navy, was much admired. His right-hand man, Commander J. I. 'Streamline' Robertson, was another well-respected individual with a strong belief in naval aviation. Although the training schedule was intense, nevertheless the captain, no doubt conscious of the rigours his crew would face before long, wisely ensured that the ship's company had a clear day or two to relax ashore at weekends. The *Illustrious* would anchor in Hamilton Bay and the men would be allowed shore leave to swim in warm temperatures, bask in sunshine, admire beautiful girls.

However, two events during the work-up brought men sharply back to reality. They were a reminder, too, of the feisty nature of the Swordfish.

The first occurred when aircraft returned to the *Illustrious* following flight exercises. Pilots were faced with insufficient head-wind and although all the Swordfish, with their slow landing speed, recovered without mishap, the ship's Skua fighters were less fortunate: several of them crashed on landing. The lieutenant remembers the crews' sense of helplessness and the subsequent chaos – including the mayhem caused when one of the fighters landed on the seventeenth fairway of the Belmont golf course, a narrow strip of sandy grass hedged on either side by luxurious palm trees.

Thankfully there were no serious injuries or loss of life, but sadly that was not the case in the second incident. This involved combat exercises between a single Swordfish aircraft and a Skua fighter, the crews having been briefed to work out the best defensive tactics for the Swordfish when attacked by a fighter. Both aircraft ended up at low level after practice runs – something the Skua pilot seemed to have forgotten when he turned in for his final attack. The Swordfish pilot reacted as before: a wrench of his aircraft into a violent stall turn towards his opponent, then a dive down to very low level. The Skua pilot's response was equally vigorous but unfortunately, in the excitement of the chase, matters began to go wrong. Perhaps the Skua pilot forgot to check his altimeter; maybe he was misled by the translucent lure of the Caribbean waters. Whatever the cause, he was seen by the Swordfish pilot suddenly to flick into an inverted spin before plunging into the sea. Horrified, the crew of the Swordfish immediately alerted the *Illustrious*. Rescue vessels hastened to the scene but despite a careful search nothing was discovered apart from the Skua's tail wheel. The body of the pilot, a young father whose wife had just had her first baby, was never found.

There was a subdued atmosphere on the *Illustrious* following this tragedy, an atmosphere that lingered for the remainder of the ship's time in Bermuda. However, on completion of her work-up and when she set sail for the Mediterranean, crews managed to console themselves in one way at least: the best method of defence for the Swordfish had been proved: imaginative use of the machine's uncanny manoeuvrability would save the lives of Fleet Air Arm crews in the future. Conversely, its tactics would cause confusion for enemy pilots in the years ahead.

'Alfie!' Lieutenant Sutton glances up at the approach of his pilot, Lieutenant 'Tiffy' Torrens-Spence. 'Found you at last!'

'Hello, Tiffy.' Lieutenant Sutton twists around in his chair. 'Something up?'

'Just that . . .' Tiffy hesitates as he catches sight of his observer's wedding-day photographs. 'Good heavens, man . . . fine pictures of you in your heyday, I presume?'

'Evocative memories sent by mail.'

'You made a handsome couple.'

'Indeed . . .' Alfie falters. His mood seems wistful. 'You've been looking for me? Everything all right?'

'Pictures of a different kind have just turned up: the RAF's latest reconnaissance photos. By fair means or foul the captain has managed to get hold of them.'

'Fair means or foul?'

'The RAF lads, for reasons best known to themselves, seem reluctant to impart information to the humble Fleet Air Arm. Apparently they regard their photo reconnaissance pictures as their own property – not to be shared with the likes of us.'

'My God! Is it the Royal Navy or the Italians that these RAF fellows support?'

'Probably neither. Something to do with inter-service rivalries, old boy.'

'For God's sake!' Alfie shakes his head. 'So what do these pictures show?'

'That Italian ships have begun to mass in Taranto harbour.'

Alfie lets out a low whistle of astonishment. 'Can we take it, then, that Operation Judgement will proceed as planned?'

Torrens-Spence glances nervously around the room. Even within the confines of the wardroom certain confidences – including the code-name for Royal Naval plans to attack the Italian fleet at anchor in Taranto harbour – should be respected. 'Yes,' he nods discreetly.

'When it was postponed last month . . .' Alfie's voice fades away.

'What about it?'

'Well, Trafalgar Day and all that.'

'Bloody silly idea to choose these anniversary dates, if you ask me. Anyway, what with that fire in the hangar, one thing and another, they had no option but to postpone.'

'So November the eleventh it is then.'

Torrens-Spence nods again. 'It's the optimum date, so we're told. There should be plenty of moonlight.'

'We'll need that,' says Alfie. 'And in case the RAF decide to reclaim their lousy photographs, I'd better make haste – inspect them pronto.'

'You'll find them in the ready room.'

'There's another thing, though,' Alfie hesitates. He waves the letter from his wife. 'It's hard to know . . .'

'It's got to be done, Alfie. You must write to her. You must write back straight away.'

'It's just that . . .'

'Well?'

'What if it's the . . . you know . . . the last?'

The tall pilot, an Ulsterman, gazes at his observer. Their anxious eyes meet briefly. Lieutenant Torrens-Spence looks away, embarrassed by his observer's discomfiture, the stumble of his words. An awkward silence persists but the observer seems determined; he needs, somehow, to seek solace. But how? He yearns for impossible answers to impossible questions. Should he pray? He could try, though he lacks religious conviction. He is tortured by photographic flashbacks – images of Hendaye, of groups (handsome individuals) on the *Basilisk's* quarterdeck, of Buckfast Abbey, of his beautiful bride. He glances uneasily around the wardroom until, perhaps by chance but perhaps not, he conjures a solution. Now his inner turmoil calms; his sense of resolve quickens; comprehension floods through his head. The prayers will be offered by her.

CHAPTER NINETEEN

Goofers' Gallery

The so-called 'goofers' gallery' placed within the island of an aircraft carrier's deck allows people to observe what is going on outside – flight deck operations, weather conditions, the ship's general progress. Lieutenant Sutton decides to walk via this gallery before he makes for the aircrew ready room to inspect the RAF's latest reconnaissance photographs. He has a sense of awe when he first reaches the gallery and when, suddenly, he glimpses the wakes piled astern the assembled might of the Mediterranean Fleet. Four battleships – HMS *Valiant*, HMS *Malaya*, HMS *Ramillies* and HMS *Warspite*, the latter acting as flagship for ABC (the fleet's abbreviation for their commander-in-chief, Admiral Sir Andrew Browne Cunningham) – provide the fleet with impressive firepower. They cruise in company with their protégé, the aircraft carrier *Illustrious*, as do a number of cruisers and destroyers, although some of these have been sent ahead of the main body in order to search for Italian surface vessels. Admiral Cunningham suspects that the Italian fleet might yet sally forth to present him with a major engagement. Such an opportunity would suit him well: he is renowned for his traditional views and for his antipathy towards the Fleet Air Arm. The captain of the *Illustrious*, Captain Boyd, recently expressed fears that the admiral seemed to regard carriers and their aircraft as 'second rate to the rest of the fleet'.

In truth, though, the admiral has been delighted with the performance of the *Illustrious* to date. Until her arrival in August, his Mediterranean Fleet had relied for protection on HMS *Eagle*, a First World War battleship converted to an aircraft carrier, which had outrun her proper length of life. Following Italy's declaration of war on 10 June 1940, Italian aircraft would create havoc every time the *Eagle* put to sea. The Italian *Regia Aeronautica*, with a fleet of some 5,400 aircraft, would attack the carrier with machines such as the tri-motor Savoia-Marchetti

SM79 Sparviero heavy bomber, or the Cantieri Cant Z506B torpedo bomber, or the Breda 88 aircraft with twin Piaggio engines, two 7.7 mm cannon and three 12.7 mm machine-guns. As the *Eagle* was not equipped with radar, swarms of these Italian machines would arrive without warning and the old carrier's four anti-aircraft guns of 4 inch calibre would struggle to beat them off. Until the arrival of the *Illustrious*, the *Eagle*, despite valiant efforts, would seem almost over-whelmed by the opposition.

The *Illustrious*, following her work-up in Bermuda, had been sent to the relative safety of Scapa Flow while the Battle of Britain started to unfold. When she received her subsequent orders, they were unequiv-ocal and urgent: in company with a large number of ships, she was to set sail as soon as possible for the Mediterranean. In navy parlance, her departure from Scapa on 22 August 1940 had involved a 'pierhead jump': a last-minute rush to get aboard. (Two members of aircrew later related how they had gone fishing with their wives for the day and a young Scots lad, leaning over a stone wall, had asked politely: 'Are you in the navy, sir? Because I think you're wanted on the phone.') The captain was amongst those who, in the scramble to reach the ship in time, had to leave without seeing his wife. When the *Illustrious* set course for the Mediterranean and her new base at Alexandria, her presence there was regarded as crucial. With her sixteen 4.5 inch dual-purpose guns, her 2 lb multiple pom-poms, her radar equipment, her eight-gun fighters and her speed of 31 knots achieved through three-shaft geared turbines of 110,000 shaft horsepower, she would give HMS *Eagle* the support she needed so badly.

The operation to reinforce the Mediterranean Fleet, code-named Operation Hats, involved the Royal Navy in complex planning. The *Illustrious* reached Gibraltar safely, but by the time she left there on 30 August 1940 in company with the *Valiant*, the *Calcutta*, and the *Coventry*, the Axis spies in Gibraltar had done their job: the British force was spotted quickly by the Italians. Bombers flew regular sorties against the *Illustrious* whose Fulmar fighters mounted air patrols to engage the enemy. A number of Italian machines were shot down, including three bombers within sight of the fleet on 2 September 1940. When the British neared Italian territory, the enemy's air attacks came in relentless waves. Nonetheless, in large part thanks to her radar, the *Illustrious* safely negotiated the Pantellaria Straits *en route* to Malta before she passed to the south of the island. Despite the limitations of the new-fangled radar equipment, the 40–50 miles of early warning proved key to her defence. Anti-aircraft crews were alerted in sufficient time; Fulmar fighters were given effective direction to intercept enemy bombers. Although the *Regia Nautica* remained determined to give the *Illustrious* aggravation, it was clear to both sides that her arrival in the theatre had shifted the region's balance of power. While she proceeded for the second half of her journey along the Mediterranean, the Italians began to comprehend that Benito Mussolini's arrogant boasts about *mare nostrum* – our sea – and his indifferent attitudes to the rights of other countries with Mediterranean coastlines were being challenged at last.

And now, while he gazes at the steady movement of the *Illustrious* as she steams due west towards Taranto, Lieutenant Sutton reflects on the ship's potent capabilities. With an overall length of 753.5 ft, she is nearly 100 ft longer than the *Eagle* yet, at around 23,000 tons, the standard displacement of both ships is similar. With a freeboard height of 43 ft between the waterline and the flight deck, the *Illustrious*'s profile is less conspicuous than other carriers (the *Ark Royal*, for instance, has a freeboard height of over 60 ft). Her flight deck armour is 3 in thick over the hangar and 4.5 in thick on its sides, with breaks restricted to the area of the fore and aft hangar lifts. Further protection comes from the armoured shutters inside the hangar which, in the event of fire, divide the area into three sections. The hangar has ample headroom – 16 ft – and the capacity to hold thirty-six aircraft.

One pilot, after landing on the *Illustrious* in his Swordfish, recorded his first impressions thus:

> As we were struck down on the lift to the hangar deck I looked through the folded wings of nearly forty aircraft. The machines were stacked together very tightly according to some preconceived plan so they could all be stowed down below. On the bulkheads brightly coloured markings indicated fuel points, connections for high pressure air or oil, water, electric power, all vividly painted in clearly defined colours so there could be no mistake. Overhead, metal fire-screen curtains were rolled and stowed, ready to be dropped in an emergency to separate the hangar into compartments. The deckhead was a series of overhead stowages with spare aircraft engines, airscrews, long-range tanks – all manner of objects. The whole of the deckhead bristled with little sprinklers a few inches apart so that at the turn of a switch the fire curtains would fall and the entire hangar would be sprayed with jets of salt water.

The pilot joined several of his colleagues before the men went up to the flight-deck: 'We were astonished at the amount of space available. The flight-deck had not looked particularly large from our cockpits a few moments earlier, but flight-decks never do look very large from the air. We were joined by Captain Denis Boyd who surprised us because of the informal way he greeted us and welcomed us aboard. He was a famous man with a great reputation.'

The aircrew were taken to their cabins, usually shared by three or four men, although officers of sufficient seniority (including Lieutenant Sutton) were allocated single-berth cabins. After they had settled in, they were briefed on the practicalities of life on board the carrier. Fresh water was a particular difficulty. With the *Illustrious*'s complement of around 1,400, the ship's four evaporators would sometimes fail to match demand. If water became short, the priority was for the ship's three boilers and in deference to the Royal Navy's insistence on high standards of cleanliness and hygiene, the crew would wash and shave in salt water. The distilled water produced by the evaporators was tasteless, although the *Illustrious* was ahead of other ships in one way at least: a recreation room was provided with a civilian NAAFI manager who sold soft drinks. The accommodation for the officers was cramped, but matters were even worse for those below the rank of petty officer. Ratings lived cheek by jowl with colleagues and there was little room for modesty or privacy. Hammocks were still used in the lower decks, a reminder to Lieutenant Sutton of his days on the *Repulse*. The lower mess deck had no side scuttles and on hot nights conditions became almost insufferable. When not on watch duty, junior ratings would spend most of their time in their messes or in the recreation room where they could play cards or board games. The *Illustrious* still followed the naval tradition of grog and at 1100 each day the mixture of one-third rum, two-thirds water was anticipated keenly, although some men preferred to leave their issue until they came off watch.

Food was basic, though the men realized that they probably fared better than the civilian population at home. Food was prepared centrally before collection by the duty cook from each mess. To the chagrin of old hands, this system thwarted the naval tradition of the 1 lb cake – a concoction which included 1 lb of every available ingredient (evidently, after a tot of two-and-one grog almost anything could be eaten). Mealtimes for ratings were modest events, but less so for petty officers and above, who were served their food by stewards. As in most ships, messes were at the centre of social life for all ranks. Midshipmen on the *Illustrious* were permitted to use the officers' wardroom but they were deemed too young to be served spirits (a rule nevertheless circumvented by the determined).

In operational matters, the situation in the Mediterranean grew increasingly complicated. The British, with bases in Gibraltar, Malta, Cyprus and Egypt, represented the major Allied power in the area but British resources had become progressively overstretched since the fall of France. The Royal Navy was committed to convoy escort duties to

Malta and Greece, while the Italians ferried arms, supplies and troops into North Africa through the Straits of Messina, past Malta and on to Tripoli and Benghazi. The Italian fleet lacked an aircraft carrier and any form of radar, but the 'eyes of the fleet' were provided by the thousands of aircraft of the *Regia Aeronautica* with bases in Sicily, Sardinia and the Dodecanese, and a seaplane station at Taranto. There had been frequent skirmishes between British and Italian forces, and although the efforts of the British submarines and aircraft based at Malta had been sterling, nevertheless the enemy convoys had managed to get through with little damage or loss. There were other problems: the Italians had dug themselves in at Sidi Barrani in Egypt, their forces had made progress in Greece despite the initial successes of the Hellenic army, and ships of the Vichy French regime presented difficulties.

To resolve these problems, Admiral Cunningham considered that his best tactic would be to lure the Italians into a major fleet engagement. However, in spite of their powerful fleet of six battleships, seven heavy cruisers, fourteen light cruisers, 122 destroyers and torpedo boats and 119 submarines, the Italians had proved evasive. The Italian battleships included the Littorio class, ships of 35,000 tons capable of over 30 knots which were impressively armed: nine 15 inch guns, twelve 6 inch, four 4.7 inch, twelve 3.5 inch, twenty 37 mm and thirty-two 20 mm. Why, then, were the Italians so reluctant to employ their firepower? Lieutenant Sutton and his colleagues were briefed that generic troubles lay at the heart of the matter. The Italian standard of training was poor, as was the study of naval warfare by their officers. The older officers had aristocratic outlooks; they looked down on their younger colleagues who had joined the navy during the period of Mussolini. The gap between officers and men was even greater than that of the pre-war Royal Navy; the Italian officers described their ratings as 'peasants'. They lacked, as Nelson would have put it, the 'sense of all being of one company'. Although the Italian navy excelled in the use of small specialist forces such as two-man human torpedoes, they had not dealt with large-scale conflict since the Balkan wars of thirty years ago, and had not engaged in significant fleet action since the creation of modern Italy in the nineteenth century.

Lieutenant Sutton muses that some five weeks ago, at the end of September, the keenness of the Italians to evade a major engagement was illustrated by a particular incident. Admiral Cunningham had received intelligence reports that five Italian warships had put to sea; he ordered the *Illustrious* to set off in fast pursuit in company with battleships. Lieutenant Sutton and his pilot, Lieutenant Lee, were among the Fleet Air Arm crews instructed to fly a co-ordinated search in a fan-shaped pattern some 100 nautical miles ahead of the fleet. At first there was little sign of activity, but at length they started to observe lines on the surface of the sea marked by occasional items of debris. Lieutenant Sutton took bearings while his pilot turned to follow these lines. The pilot flew 150 nautical miles ahead of the main fleet until, gradually emerging from the Mediterranean mists, he could identify the five Italian battleships in company with destroyers and cruisers. The Swordfish crew reported urgently and Lieutenant Sutton could recall his sense of excitement when sending the priority Morse signal: 0 – 0 – 0. This signal, transmitted when enemy ships had been sighted and strictly on no other occasion, caused the immediate closedown of all other radio traffic. An expectant hush dominated the airwaves while radio operators anticipated the next transmission: details of the enemy's position. While Lieutenant Sutton passed on this information, his pilot continued to shadow the enemy. Before long, when they saw the Italian's sterns go down and wakes pile up, a further message was required. Lieutenant Sutton signalled that he saw no sign of the enemy ships turning to confront the British fleet; instead, the enemy had increased speed and altered course towards Taranto.

As he considers how the Italians had avoided the feared fleet engagement, Lieutenant Sutton recalls another aspect of this incident which created considerable consternation. He and his pilot, having decided to follow the enemy to the limit of their Swordfish's fuel endurance, allowed for slender reserves in their fuel calculations. When the pilot turned to head back towards the *Illustrious*, and when adverse winds began to reduce their ground speed, these reserves proved inadequate. The crew were forced to lighten their aircraft by every available means. Depth charges were jettisoned, deciphering equipment was discarded, even Lieutenant Sutton's valued Bigsworth navigational board was tossed away unceremoniously. When the *Illustrious* finally came into sight, and despite the reduction of aircraft weight by all means possible, the pilot had insufficient fuel to make a normal pre-landing circuit. The Swordfish by this stage had been airborne for four and a half hours, the theoretical limit of flight time to tanks dry. The pilot therefore decided to make his approach for landing directly to the carrier's deck, and he kept height in hand to remain within gliding distance in case his engine suddenly cut out. While they continued down, no doubt with fingers and toes firmly crossed, perhaps the crew reminded each other of pithy entries from the Fleet Air Arm songbook:

They say in the air force the landing's okay
If the pilot gets out and walks away.
But in the Fleet Air Arm the prospects are grim
If the landing's piss poor and the pilot can't swim.

And sung to the tune of 'My Bonny Lies Over the Ocean':

> *The Swordfish fly over the ocean*
> *The Swordfish fly over the sea*
> *If it were not for King George's Swordfish*
> *Were the 'ell would the Fleet Air Arm be?*

For the final stages of the approach, the deck landing control officer waved yellow bats to guide the aircraft. That officer's signals, though, became progressively more frenetic until, realizing the futility of further orders to 'go round again', he decided to dive for cover at the last second. Fortunately, the strong fixed undercarriage of the Swordfish survived the heavy landing, the hook picked up one of the carrier's four arrestor wires and all turned out well in the end. All, that is, apart from one point of detail: the small amount of petrol that remained in the carburettors drained back into the tank when the tail went down. As the pilot taxied his Swordfish forward to the hangar lift, his engine cut out.

Perhaps this incident, Lieutenant Sutton now muses, helped to persuade Admiral Cunningham that his planned major fleet engagement was unlikely to occur and that he would have to consider alternative tactics. The admiral knew that once the Italian fleet had reached the safety of Taranto with its harbour neatly tucked inside the heel of Italy, the ships would find everything a naval base could require. There was sheltered anchorage with an outer harbour *(Mare Grande)* and an inner harbour *(Mare Piccolo)*, gun emplacements, extensive systems of defence. An Italian fleet ensconced in Taranto was a constant threat to British shipping, especially to the convoys destined for Malta. A surface attack against the heavily-defended harbour would result in the almost certain annihilation of the attacking ships. Admiral Cunningham therefore had to face the reality of his least-favoured option: the use of aircraft. While he would prefer the attack to be undertaken by land-based aircraft, he nevertheless had respect for the opinions of his fleet's rear-admiral of carriers, Rear-Admiral Lumley St George Lyster (for whom the *Illustrious* acted as flagship). Lyster has been forthright in his views: an attack on the Italian fleet at harbour in Taranto – recently allocated the code-name 'Operation Judgement' – would be within the capabilities of the Fleet Air Arm. While not wholly convinced, Admiral Cunningham nonetheless has been encouraged by his rear-admiral's optimism and even the First Sea Lord, Admiral Sir Dudley Pound, an unashamed member of the old school, has not been altogether against the idea, despite his expressed view that 'the operation always appeared as the last dying kick of the Mediterranean carrier before being sent to the bottom'.

Lieutenant Sutton reflects that an attack was planned initially to coincide with the anniversary of the Battle of Trafalgar, 21 October. However, some days before this date an inadvertent spark from a maintainer's tool had caused a fire in the *Illustrious*'s hangar. The sprinkler systems and the armoured fire curtains had operated as designed, but two Swordfish were destroyed and five others were damaged. Operation Judgement had to be postponed; a provisional new date was set for the last day of October. Just three days from the new date, however, it was realized that there would be no moon – hardly ideal for a night-time attack when the Swordfish crews would have to rely on flares to illuminate the enemy fleet. The attack was postponed again, this time to the night of 11 November, when the moon was forecast to be three-quarters full. Lieutenant Sutton now ponders the exhaustive periods of training for the Swordfish crews as they worked up towards the new date. There have been intensive periods of night flying, night navigational exercises, night-time routines. Captain Boyd and Commander Robertson, in conjunction with the two Swordfish squadron commanders (Lieutenant Commanders Williamson and Hale), have insisted on high professional standards. As their training for Operation Judgement has progressed, all the crews have been made aware – painfully so – of the importance of the outcome.

Despite everyone's awareness that nothing must be allowed to go wrong, the rising tension of the last few days has not been eased by a series of accidents and unfortunate incidents. The original plans to mount the attack with thirty Swordfish using crews from 815 and 819 Squadrons from HMS *Illustrious*, and 813 and 824 Squadrons from HMS *Eagle*, had to be abandoned when the *Eagle*'s aviation fuel system broke down a few days ago, on 4 November. With the elderly carrier's boilers prone to giving trouble, it was decided to proceed without her. Six Swordfish – four from 813 Squadron and two from 824 Squadron – were moved from the *Eagle* to the *Illustrious* and the total number of aircraft allocated to Operation Judgement was reduced to twenty-four.

Lieutenant Sutton remembers that when the *Illustrious* set sail from Alexandria on 6 November 1940 accompanied by the ships he now observes, all in the Mediterranean Fleet were aware that surprise was an essential part of the operation. If the Italians got wind of a possible attack they were bound to move their fleet north to the safer harbours at Naples, Genoa and La Spezia. Elaborate steps, therefore, were taken when the Mediterranean Fleet left Alexandria, a port teeming with Axis spies. Admiral Cunningham deliberately pointed his fleet towards Malta rather than further north towards Taranto. The *Illustrious*'s Fulmar fighter aircraft were ordered to fend off prying Italians and yesterday, Friday 8 November, they repelled Italian reconnaissance aircraft on two occasions: just after midday, and again three hours later. About one hour after that, at 1620, three Fulmars were scrambled when seven Savoia-Marchetti SM79 bombers approached the fleet. They managed to shoot down two of the enemy bombers and to drive off the remainder which were seen, in the haste of retreat, to jettison their bombs.

'A willing foe and sea room?' Two members of aircrew remain in earnest discussion as they enter the goofers' gallery.

'That was yesterday, don't forget.'

'What do you make of it, Alfie?' asks one of the newcomers, a pilot.

'I think the foe seems far from willing.'

'He'll be even less willing when he finds out what's in store for him. Have you seen the latest air force recce photos, Alfie?'

'I'm on my way to inspect them now.'

'They are, shall we say, quite revealing.'

'So what were you saying about yesterday?' asks Sutton.

'We were discussing yesterday's naval toast. As it was a Friday, the toast was to "a willing foe and sea room". Today is Saturday so it means . . .' the pilot falters.

'It means,' says Sutton, ' that today's naval toast has to be a special one.'

'Aren't all of them special?'

'Saturday's has to be extra-special: a toast to sweethearts and wives.'

'May they never meet,' says the pilot with a laugh.

'Is that the point, though?'

The pilot is about to respond but hesitates when he glimpses Sutton's sombre expression. There is a moment of uncomfortable silence but the pilot sounds sincere when he says: 'Just put your trust in the Stringbag, old chap.' He tries to soothe the atmosphere as he goes on: 'She'll see us through, don't you think?'

Sutton shrugs. 'Let's just hope you're right,' he says quietly.

'Bound to be, old fellow.' But now, despite his attempt at bravado, the pilot's expression, too, has become sombre. With a sigh Sutton turns to head for the door. The others remain silent but their uneasy looks indicate thoughts similar to Sutton's as he casts a backward glance. He then hastens from the goofers' gallery with an uncharacteristic lack of further comment.

CHAPTER TWENTY

Briefing

MONDAY, 11 NOVEMBER, 1940

Forty-two Swordfish pilots and observers, including Lieutenant Sutton and his pilot Lieutenant Torrens-Spence, crowd into the wardroom of HMS *Illustrious*. Joined by other officers directly involved with Operation Judgement and by an unofficial observer, Lieutenant Commander Opie of the United States Navy, they are about to receive a final briefing before tonight's execution of the twice-postponed operation. It is early evening, the air is smoky, the mood tense: men sprawl in armchairs, sit on table edges, lean against bulkheads. There is a low hum of conversation while they wait for the briefing officer, the ship's operations officer, Commander George Beale, to commence. On display in the wardroom is a large-scale map of Taranto, which highlights the arrangement of the harbour's breakwaters and the layout of the *Mare Grande* and the *Mare Piccolo*. Also on view is a collection of RAF reconnaissance photographs which update the pictures inspected by Lieutenant Sutton after his brief visit to the goofers' gallery the day before yesterday. The latest, taken by an RAF Martin Baltimore aircraft, were collected from Malta by Lieutenants Sutton and Torrens-Spence yesterday – Sunday, 10 November, 1940 – when they flew to that beleaguered island.

The ship's photographic interpretation officer, Lieutenant David Pollock (a solicitor in civilian life), has used stereoscopic lenses for detailed analysis of the recent reconnaissance pictures. As he glances at Lieutenant Pollock, at present perched in one corner of the wardroom, Lieutenant Sutton remembers that this officer is respected for his initiative as well as for his expertise. Pollock managed to circumvent inter-service rivalries a few days ago when he visited the RAF headquarters in Cairo to scrutinise reconnaissance photos. However, when he asked if he could take them back to the *Illustrious*, his air force counterpart said he was very sorry but permission would have to be refused: the pictures were air force property and he was duty-bound to ensure that

163

they remained in the building. When the flight lieutenant wasn't looking, however, the resourceful Lieutenant Pollock displayed the enterprise to be expected of a graduate of Cambridge university and 'borrowed' the photos regardless. He managed to sneak them back to the *Illustrious* where the photographic section made copies. The next day he returned the originals and the RAF remained unaware of the subterfuge. His resourcefulness earned him a pat on the back from the captain, and his analysis of the latest photographs revealed startling information.

When Lieutenant Sutton looks around the wardroom, he notes the apprehensiveness of his colleagues. Some men yawn, some cross and uncross their legs, others fidget anxiously with their hands. A forced jauntiness afflicts the room as men recognize that for some, at least, this will be their final briefing in more than one sense. Perhaps there are feelings of personal invincibility, but the men's mannerisms reveal nagging thoughts of a type best put to the back of the mind. On their minds, too, will be the difficulties that have plagued the operation from the start. Men realize that the aircrew head-count in the room should be forty-eight, not forty-two: in the last few days the number of available Swordfish has fallen from twenty-four to twenty-one. The men do not know it now, but by take-off time this evening a taxiing accident on the flight deck will reduce the number to twenty. Shortly after the second wave's take-off, an aircraft with fuel tank problems will be obliged to return to the carrier, thus reducing the final tally to nineteen (the machine involved with the taxiing accident will be repaired in time to reach Taranto just as the second wave has completed its attack).

As he waits for the briefing to begin, Lieutenant Sutton recalls the drama of yesterday when two of his colleagues from 819 Squadron had to ditch in the sea. Their Swordfish, part of an air patrol searching for enemy ships and submarines, was about 20 nautical miles ahead of the *Illustrious* when the engine suddenly cut out. The machine entered a glide and the pilot, Lieutenant Clifford, turned towards the carrier, but the distance was too great: he was forced to ditch in the sea. He pulled a toggle to release a rubber dinghy from the centre of the upper wing and grabbed flame floats to enable him to alert passing ships or aircraft. The observer, Lieutenant 'Grubby' Going, threw away his bulky Bigsworth chart board, unhooked his retaining 'monkey' strap and dived over the side before the Swordfish sank. After this rush of activity, the aircrew languished in their dinghy until, after a short period, they saw two cruisers in the distance. They managed to light a flame float which was spotted by look-outs on the cruisers, *Gloucester* and *York*. Both ships altered course to pick up the aircrew who, having been rescued, were given a hearty breakfast in one of the wardrooms before being taken back to the *Illustrious* in a Supermarine Walrus amphibian aircraft.

Unfortunately, that incident was not the end of the present run of bad luck. Lieutenant Sutton muses on the commotion caused this morning when another Swordfish had to ditch in the sea, the third aircraft to be lost in as many days. An urgent investigation has just revealed that one of the *Illustrious*'s aviation fuel tanks is contaminated with sea water, probably as a result of the use of the carrier's sprinkler system during the hangar fire. All the aircraft are now in the process of having their fuel systems drained before being refuelled from the remaining – uncontaminated – aviation fuel tank.

The hum of background chatter momentarily quietens as those present observe the two squadron commanders confer together. Lieutenant Commander Kenneth 'Hooch' Williamson of 815 Squadron and Lieutenant Commander J. W. 'Ginger' Hale of 819 Squadron are in the front row, near the briefing officer. The aircrew look enquiringly in the direction of their leaders, but the squadron commanders remain discreet: their conversation cannot be overheard. Those present look for possible signs of significance, but the expressions on the faces of these two men remain impassive. Lieutenant Commander Williamson, who took command of 815 Squadron earlier in the year, is known to be a dedicated naval aviator. Curiously, the same cannot be said of his observer, Lieutenant Norman J 'Blood' Scarlett. Lieutenant Scarlett is a Dartford graduate who has described himself as a reluctant aviator, someone ordered to become a Fleet Air Arm observer as 'one of ten pressed men'. He has made little secret of his eagerness to return to general naval service on the grounds that he 'wants to be in destroyers, not bloody aeroplanes'.

Lieutenant Commander 'Ginger' Hale, the commander of 819 Squadron, is an experienced pilot whom Lieutenant Sutton remembers from his days on HMS *Glorious*. Regarded by his colleagues as being as unshakeable as the Rock of Gibraltar, he is a keen rugby player who, before the war, represented the Royal Navy and England. His observer is Lieutenant G. A. Carline, who joined 819 Squadron at the beginning of the year and who was an observer on a Swordfish squadron attached to HMS *Courageous* before the carrier was torpedoed and sunk by a U-boat at the early stages of the war. In a different part of the wardroom Lieutenant Sutton can spot the crew who will follow his commanding officer's aircraft, Lieutenants G. W. L. A. Bayley and H. J. Slaughter. These two men served with Lieutenant Sutton on HMS *Glorious*; now they are among the crews detached from HMS *Eagle* to support the *Illustrious*-based squadrons. Near Lieutenant Sutton is his pilot, Lieutenant 'Tiffy' Torrens-Spence, a qualified test pilot who by reputation is one of the Fleet Air Arm's most talented flyers. Next year, during the lead-up to the naval action off Cape Matapan, Lieutenant

Torrens-Spence will press home an attack on the Italian cruiser *Pola*, slowing her down so that the Mediterranean Fleet can bring the enemy to battle. His actions will produce this comment from the *Pola*'s captain: 'Either that pilot is mad or he is the bravest man in the world.'

'Gentlemen . . .' the buzz of conversation peters out as Commander Beale stands up to speak. He climbs onto a chair before he continues: 'Gentlemen, I think everyone is present now, so perhaps we should press on.' People shuffle their chairs as an expectant hush falls across the wardroom. The commander glances at the large-scale map of Taranto, then turns back to his listeners before he opens his briefing with a short description of the operation's background. He explains that contingency plans to attack the Italian fleet at harbour in Taranto were first drawn up some five years ago, in 1935. Three years later, as war loomed, the commander-in-chief of the Mediterranean Fleet, Admiral Sir Dudley Pound, asked Lumley St George Lyster, then a captain, to re-examine the plans and to offer his views on their feasibility. He dusted them down and together with two Fleet Air Arm commanders set about revising the original concept. Swordfish squadrons were ordered to mount a series of dummy attacks against the Mediterranean Fleet in the Grand Harbour at Malta where, for added realism, arrangements were made for the ships and the harbour to be blacked out. Following these exercises, Captain Lyster reported that in his opinion their success proved their viability. Nonetheless, Admiral Pound remained sceptical (he lacked faith in the Swordfish and, frankly, he had scant understanding of the potential of naval aviation) and as a consequence the plans were locked away.

However, when Captain Lyster was promoted to rear-admiral and when he was sent to the Mediterranean Fleet in charge of aircraft carriers, the plan was revived. 'And now, gentlemen,' says Commander Beale, 'it falls upon us to try again to implement those plans which, as we all know, have had to be postponed twice in the last few weeks.' He gazes at the sea of faces before him. 'Tonight's weather conditions look reasonable, the moon should be three-quarters full, and Operation Judgement, gentlemen, is set to proceed as planned.' He pauses before he goes on: 'As you must realize, photo recce has been a vital part of the build-up to the operation and despite the odd hiccup—' he glances at his photographic interpretation officer, '—we are indebted to our Royal Air Force friends and to the excellent efforts of the Martin Baltimore pilots. More of this in a minute.' The commander looks down for a moment while he refers to his notes. When he looks up, he goes on to explain that the operation will be conducted in two waves, with 815 Squadron the first to launch at 2030, followed about an hour later by 819 Squadron. The flight time to Taranto is expected to be some two and a half hours for the first wave, a little less for the second wave (the *Illustrious* will continue to steam due west). The squadrons will fly in formation to the target area, at which point they will turn to head towards the outer harbour. The aircraft will split up as they assume their different roles: flare droppers will illuminate the battleships, torpedo bombers will set up for attack, bombers will head for the inner harbour to strike at the cruisers and destroyers.

Commander Beale explains the call-sign system. *Illustrious*-based Swordfish will have their call-signs prefixed with the letter 'L', *Eagle*-based aircraft with the prefix 'E'. After the appropriate prefix letter, crews will be allocated the number 4 or 5. The third part of the call-sign will be another letter. Thus the leader of the first wave, for instance, will adopt the call-sign 'L4A'. At the appropriate moment, a brief 'attack completed' should be transmitted by the wave leader, otherwise radio silence will be maintained throughout. This should ensure security to prevent the Italians being forewarned and to make it harder for them to locate the aircraft or the carrier after the attack.

'You will observe from the recce photos now being circulated,' says Commander Beale, 'that we are faced with a mixture of good news and bad.' He goes on to explain that as the aim of the raid is to inflict maximum damage on the Italian fleet, the operation's planners need to see as many Italian ships as possible concentrated within Taranto's harbours. The latest photographic reconnaissance has revealed that the outer harbour (*Mare Grande*) now contains all six of the Italian battleships moored in a semicircle, four of the Cavour and Duilio class with their ten 12.6 inch guns and two of the new Littorio class with their nine 15 inch guns. In addition, the pictures show three heavy cruisers in the *Mare Grande*, the *Zara*, *Fiume* and *Goriza*, each with 8 inch guns. In the *Mare Piccolo* two more heavy cruisers are moored in the centre of the harbour, as well as four light cruisers and seventeen destroyers. In typical Mediterranean fashion, the ships in the *Mare Piccolo* are moored stern-to at the quays. 'So we can deduce from these photo recce images,' says the commander, 'that the Italians have placed all their eggs in one convenient (if unfriendly) basket. The enemy fleet is ours for the taking.'

He now moves on to the matter of harbour defences. 'The Italians possess all the necessary skills to protect one of the biggest fleets in existence,' he says. He again refers his audience to the reconnaissance photographs which highlight the facilities spread around Taranto's vast set-up: machine workshops, a floating dry dock with the capacity to accommodate a 35,000 ton battleship, several armouries stockpiled with weapons and shells, massive docks with cranes, loading bays, slipways, railway sidings, engine sheds. Pointing at the photographs, he draws attention to the anti-aircraft guns that line the breakwaters of the *Mare*

Grande. Then he shows the other guns placed strategically to safeguard the ancillary installations which combine to make Taranto a port of such significance. 'To offer the Italian fleet a port where men can rest and carry out repairs in security,' he says, 'the set-up has been designed to be virtually impregnable. Literally hundreds upon hundreds of anti-aircraft guns, multiple pom-poms and close-range weapons have been mounted all over the area. Taranto is one of the most heavily defended ports in the world.'

The wardroom's atmosphere is electric as he continues: 'On top of all that is the matter of the barrage balloons and anti-torpedo nets.' He explains that the RAF's reconnaissance pictures feature what looks like a series of maggots – white blobs set against a background of grey. 'These blobs are the tell-tale signs of barrage balloons,' he says, 'and careful examination shows that they're tethered to barges moored along the mole which shelters the *Mare Grande* from the sea.' He describes the scene beyond the immediate harbour area, where additional barrage balloons have been attached to barges along the shoreline. He says that the hazard, though, is surmountable: the wingspan of the Swordfish is 45 ft 6 in; the balloons have been set 300 yards apart.

'Now we must talk about the problem of the anti-torpedo nets. In normal circumstances these would present us with considerable difficulties. This evening, however, we have a surprise in store for the enemy.' He describes how the Italian ships use booms to support weighted anti-torpedo nets which reach into the water as far as the ship's keels. For tonight's operation this problem will be overcome by use of the Royal Navy's new and still highly secret Duplex pistols. Operated by a magnetic device, these pistols will detonate a torpedo as it passes beneath a keel; a ship's own magnetic field will lead, therefore, to her demise. The term 'Duplex' is used because a torpedo can be exploded in one of two ways: by passing within a ship's magnetic field or on impact with its side. When the commander points this out, the senior pilot of 815 Squadron, Lieutenant Neil McI. Kemp, lets out a low whistle of appreciation: 'Heads we win,' he mutters, 'tails they lose.'

Commander Beale reminds aircrew that, Duplex pistol or no, torpedoes remain temperamental brutes which require precise flying if they are to run properly. Tonight, they must be dropped within the height band of 100–150 ft. As the Swordfish lack accurate low-level altimeters, pilots will have to use keen judgement. He refreshes their memories about the point-of-release difficulties caused by the heavy weight of a torpedo. When pilots approach a target, they must ensure that they keep their machine straight and level before squeezing the electrically operated torpedo release switch located on the top of the aircraft's throttle. At the point of release, pilots must anticipate the tendency of the Swordfish's nose to pitch up violently, otherwise the torpedo will enter the sea with a splash, like a diver performing a belly-flop. The commander emphasizes the need for the aircraft to be kept steady so that the torpedo enters the sea at the correct angle, without a splash, thus allowing the device to speed smoothly towards its target.

In view of the exceptionally perilous nature of tonight's operation, the two squadron commanders have been permitted to choose their own preferred method of attack. Lieutenant Commander Williamson has decided that, for the first wave, the torpedo droppers will make a low approach from beyond the harbour entrance. His pilots, therefore, will have to spot the barrage balloons early enough to avoid them. Lieutenant Commander Hale has opted for a different approach: he will take his second wave over the top of the barrage balloons, then the torpedo droppers will dive down within the confines of the *Mare Grande*. This is a method of daylight attack not normally used at night.

Commander Beale waits for the buzz of conversation accompanying this information to quieten before he proceeds with the final part of his briefing: 'And now,' he says, 'we'll cover the procedures for your return journey.'

'Don't let's waste valuable time talking about that,' booms out the voice of Lieutenant Scarlett amidst nervous laughter from colleagues. His remark will prove regrettably prophetic.

When the commander has finished his briefing, he hands over to the ship's meteorological officer, Instructor Lieutenant Bill Watts. The aircrew note the forecast conditions of cloud, wind and weather, then the meteorological officer steps aside as Admiral Lyster stands to face his men to offer words of advice and encouragement. The scene is watched by the ship's chaplain, Padre Henry Lloyd, who later will say: 'I listened with a heavy heart for I was convinced these brave young men were being sent to their deaths.' When the admiral has finished, the two squadron commanders muster their aircrew for separate squadron brief-ings. The men then disperse to prepare for the evening's operation. Meanwhile, Admiral Cunningham orders cruisers to detach from the main force to reconnoitre the Straits of Otranto and to seek targets of opportunity to distract the Italians when the Swordfish fly towards Taranto.

By 1800, HMS *Illustrious* receives a signal from Admiral Cunningham: 'Take escorts and proceed in execution of previous orders.' When the ship has altered course, he sends a further message: 'Good luck then to your lads in their enterprise. Their success may well have a most impor-tant bearing on the war in the Mediterranean.'

Two hours later, with the carrier force bearing 270 degrees at a range of 40 nautical miles from Kaddo Point, Cephalonia, the *Illustrious* is just 170 nautical miles from Taranto. The last of twelve Swordfish is manoeuvred off the carrier's forward lift, the wings are unfolded, and the machine is ranged in front of the other aircraft. Twenty-four pilots and observers dressed in bulky Sidcot suits and Mae West life jackets now appear on the carrier's darkened deck. The men head for their allocated aircraft and clamber into their cockpits. Helped by maintainers, they strap in. Observers then struggle with their Bigsworth chart boards; pilots start the engines to run them at steady revolutions for warm-up. Anxious eyes monitor engine temperature and pressure gauges; Gosport tube communication between pilot and observer is tested.

Just before 2030, Captain Boyd calls for a change of course to catch the small amount of available wind. He orders full speed ahead to provide maximum lift for the heavily laden Swordfish. A shaded green light from Lieutenant Commander Williamson's aircraft, L4A, is answered by a green light from flying control. The lieutenant commander has a last check of his cockpit instruments before he smoothly and firmly advances his aircraft's throttle to full power.

While the first wave launch into the Mediterranean darkness, Lieutenant Sutton and his colleagues endure an apprehensive wait in the ready room. For these men there remains just one hour in which to make final preparations before their squadron must follow.

CHAPTER TWENTY-ONE

Supermarina, Rome

Commander M. A. Bragadin of the Italian navy frowns as he studies charts that depict the Mediterranean theatre of war. He stands in the main operations room of the Italian admiralty in Rome, the *Supermarina*, and as he begins his period as tonight's duty officer, he uses specialist maps and blueprints to help him conjure an overall picture of the operational scenario. He knows that strong British naval forces are active in various parts of the Mediterranean and he is aware that unusual enemy activity will require him to keep a watchful eye. However, his task has not been helped by the latest intelligence reports which have presented *Supermarina* staff with conflicting information.

Two main groups are the focus of Commander Bragadin's attention. To the west is Force H, British ships which have left Gibraltar recently and which have been seen to reverse their course in keeping with classic British procedures. Such Royal Navy tactics, though, are to be expected and *Supermarina* staff assume that the vessels' eventual destination will be Alexandria. To the east is another large force of British ships, elements of the British Mediterranean Fleet. The situation with this force is less predictable. The commander has been told about reports that fighters from the aircraft carrier *Illustrious* have shot down Italian reconnaissance aircraft in the last day or so, and that others have been driven off. He suspects, however, that the crews of those driven off have not been properly debriefed. This is a matter of concern. Commander Bragadin is conscious of poor inter-service co-ordination within the Italian military, and of the consequent impact on the overall standard of intelligence-gathering.

Just now, reflects the commander, good intelligence information is of crucial importance. In recent talks with his superior officer, *Ammiraglio* Domenico Cavagnari, Commander Bragadin has been party to discussions about the navy's role in top secret plans to invade the Island of Corfu. Minister of Marine Benito Mussolini – *Il Duce* himself – has emphasized to his chief of naval staff and secretary of the marine ministry, *Ammiraglio di Armata* Arturo Riccardi, the importance of naval back-up for this operation. Commander Bragadin has been briefed that the planned attack on Corfu will be a follow-on to his country's invasion of the Greek mainland last month. The commander is familiar with the background to that operation, how the Greek government was given an ultimatum on 28 October which demanded right of access for Italian forces. He knows that when the three-hour period of the ultimatum expired, ten divisions of Italian soldiers subsequently crossed the Albanian/Greek border and large numbers of Italian aircraft launched simultaneous bombing raids on Athens.

The commander muses how the British (the bloody British) became directly involved when informed about the Italian action, and how Churchill (bloody Mister Churchill) was swift to pledge his support to the Greek government. What a tedious man, he thinks, and what a different character to his predecessor, the fellow Chamberlain who died just the day before yesterday. Commander Bragadin has heard how Chamberlain seemed haunted to the last by the saga of the Munich agreement – or theoretical agreement; pathetic pact would seem a more apposite description. When Churchill took over as British prime minister last May, the commander and his fellow officers were warned about the new man's infamous rhetoric. Not that the 'new man' is all that new: apparently Churchill is well past pension age already. The new/old man may have been correct when he lectured his compatriots about offering them nothing but blood, sweat and tears, but he was out of order, in Commander Bragadin's view, when he articulated all that nonsense following the fall of France. The newspaper reports of the waffling speech remain clear in the commander's memory. 'Let us brace ourselves to our duty,' said Churchill, 'and so bear ourselves that if the British Empire and its commonwealth lasts a thousand years men will still say: "*This* was their finest hour."'

Thousand years, finest hours. Yes, yes, yes! What hope do they have against Herr Hitler's Germany? Churchill may have talked about fighting in the hills, on the beaches, 'we will never surrender', all that stuff, but to Commander Bragadin's way of thinking, *Il Duce* has got it right. He is a leader to be admired; someone who will support the winning team, the side destined to triumph. Even though he may have irritated certain naval echelons by his surreptitious infiltration into the navy of fascist political officers, and even though he may dress himself a little eccentrically from time to time (and so what?), the man is no simpleton. He sees the way the world is headed; how Hitler's resolve is mighty, mighty enough to overwhelm the body of Europe. Look at France. When faced with the full force of Hitler's storm-troopers, even that great country caved in with astonishing rapidity.

Which leaves those tiresome British to struggle along on their own. In spite of their claim of victory in the Battle of Britain, it is just a matter of time, in Commander Bragadin's opinion, before they fall as well. He ruminates how his own country is about to deliver a further blow to British morale, and a well-deserved one too he thinks. The Royal Navy's efforts to lure Italy's fleet into a major engagement have been persistent – aggravatingly so – but the British have misjudged the situation. *Il Duce* is not so easily fooled. He will bide his time, conduct the war his own way, on his own terms, and quite right too. Instead of being forced into some absurd version of the chaotic Battle of Jutland, he will ensure gainful use of his navy. His notion of strong naval support for this planned invasion of Corfu is a case in point.

With this line of thought, Commander Bragadin gives a spontaneous nod of approval. He is confident about the outcome of the Italian action against Corfu, and he knows that the British will be in for a surprise. He looks forward to the praise that is bound to filter down from *Il Duce* when he congratulates his naval officers for their good planning and for their foresight.

The commander glances again at the *Supermarina* charts, at the strategic situation they portray. Although concerned about the conundrum of air reconnaissance, about the imperfect system of intelligence-gathering, he realizes that at least he can feel confidence in the robust nature of the defensive measures in place at Taranto. He sits down, and with a sigh sinks deeper into his chair as he ponders Taranto's defences, the high standards of protection they afford the Italian fleet. These, he thinks, are bound to ensure a quiet spell of duty in the night ahead.

CHAPTER TWENTY-TWO

Ready Room
Anxiety

O n board HMS *Illustrious*, pilots and observers in the aircrew
ready room make out the distant but distinctive racket created
by the hangar lifts. A sense of the inexorable breathes into the
room's atmosphere as individuals grasp the sound's significance:
Operation Judgement's first-wave aircraft have departed and now
maintainers will be hastening to prepare the second-wave machines.
The aircrew picture the scenes of activity around the ship, the aura of
urgency as personnel manipulate 819 Squadron's Swordfish into hangar
lifts, struggle at deck level to manoeuvre the aircraft, summon available
hands to range the machines for take-off. Meanwhile, with less than an
hour before launch, the second wave's pilots and observers endure an
apprehensive wait in their ready room as they undergo last minute
briefings.

When he glances around the room, Lieutenant Sutton notes his
colleagues' inevitable air of anxiety. In charge of the current briefing is
819 Squadron's commanding officer, Lieutenant Commander J. W. Hale.
He reminds his men that the requirement to maintain radio silence
throughout the operation is mandatory, although crews must memorize
call-signs in case of emergencies. He and his navigator, Lieutenant G. A.
Carline, will use the call-sign L5A. Call-sign E4H – prefixed 'E' to indicate *Eagle*-based – has been allocated to the next-in-line aircraft, crewed
by Lieutenants G. W. L. A. Bayley and H. J. Slaughter. Lieutenant R. G.
Skelton and his observer, Sub-Lieutenant E. A. Perkins (one of the few
aircrew members of the Royal Naval Volunteer Reserve), are reminded
of their call-sign L4F. Lieutenant R. W. V. Hamilton and his observer,
Sub-Lieutenant J. R. B. Weekes are L5B. The CO waits for nods of
acknowledgement from these men before he directs his gaze at
Lieutenant C. S. E. Lea and his observer, Sub-Lieutenant P. D. Jones.
These two officers, who lean casually against a bulkhead, gesture assent

when reminded of their call-sign, L5H. As he notes their response, Lieutenant Sutton is struck by the men's youthful appearance. He reflects on Spencer 'Sprog' Lea's unconventional background as an Australian sheep farmer's apprentice, and recalls his cheery acceptance of banter when reminded of his unorthodox route to a Royal Naval career.

'One second please, chaps.' The CO looks down to check his notes. As members of the aircrew start to fidget in the subsequent hush, Lieutenant Sutton speculates on the feelings of those around him. What, for example, will be running through the mind of Sprog? Perhaps the young officer reflects on the curious disparities between his former life and his new situation, fired up and poised to face Mussolini's might. Maybe his mind is a confusion of contrasts: frustration, stoical determination, fear. So what, wonders Lieutenant Sutton, will Sprog fear the most? The unknown factors? His personal conduct against the odds? Perhaps the fears are more fundamental – whether he'll discover untapped reserves of courage or whether he'll become paralysed with terror. He might be mutilated, lose a limb or an eye. Will he die? Or will he – possibly worst of all – fail at some crucial moment and thereby let down his colleagues?

Sutton glances at his pilot, Lieutenant 'Tiffy' Torrens-Spence, as the latter stifles a sneeze. So what about Tiffy and his feelings? Maybe, as with others in the room, he will show determination of another kind – a steely resolve that excludes superfluous thoughts, focuses on the immediate tasks, on the operational plans, on the complexities and details of the night ahead. If Tiffy feels the chill of fear in his bowels, a sense of heightened awareness, a quickening of the blood, his inscrutable expression reveals few signs. Maybe he is making a conscious effort to suppress his personal emotions.

Maybe Tiffy's sense of duty will be sharpened by his awareness of the background to this operation. Lieutenant Sutton frowns as he considers this. He and his pilot, like all the aircrew, are familiar with details of the Italian leader's deeds, the odious activities that have accompanied an iron grip of some eighteen years over Italy. Mussolini's rapid rise from blacksmith's son to dictator, his spine-chilling actions and those of his Fascist Party Blackshirts, his association with the atrocities of the Spanish Civil War, his use of poison gas during the Italian invasion of Ethiopia, his drastic attempts to improve the Italian economy (it is said that Mussolini would make the trains run on time by shooting someone if they didn't) . . . that all of this has been the product of a ruthless, relentless ambition.

'To continue then, gentlemen . . .' the CO looks up from his notes and searches the room for a particular officer. He spots Lieutenant

J. W. G. Wellham settled in one corner. The CO pauses again, as if in contemplation of Wellham's impressive record. The latter officer was a member of 824 Squadron on HMS *Eagle* when he torpedoed and sank an Italian supply ship during a daylight attack on Bomba Bay in Libya. For his courage and tenacity, he was awarded a DSC. His observer is Lieutenant P. Humphreys, another squadron member decorated for his bravery. Humphreys was serving on a destroyer at the time of the Spanish Civil War when his ship struck a mine. In the ensuing chaos, he, together with a petty officer, assisted in the rescue of seriously injured men from a compartment flooded with water and oil. For this notable act of valour, he was awarded the Empire Gallantry Medal (a decoration replaced by the George Cross in 1940). 'Lieutenants Wellham and Humphrey,' says the CO with a nod of recognition to those officers, 'have been allocated the call-sign E5H. And now,' he goes on, 'there are just three more crews to check.' As he looks towards Lieutenants A. W. F. Sutton and F. M. A. Torrens-Spence, he returns their thumbs up signs acknowledging call-sign L5K. Lieutenant W. D. Morford and Sub-Lieutenant R. A. F. Green, allocated call-sign L5Q, make a similar gesture. The CO seems on the verge of some comment when he spots the last of his nine available crews, Lieutenants E. W. Clifford and G. R. M. Going (the crew who yesterday ditched in the sea) but appears to change his mind and merely announces their call-sign, L5F.

The CO has now confirmed the presence and call-signs of all of his crews, and adopts an impassive expression as he says: 'For the remainder of this briefing, I intend to go over the operational tactics detailed earlier.' He holds up the photographic reconnaissance pictures used at the main briefing and points at the barrage balloons. 'As you will recall,' he says, 'the two squadron commanders were allowed to choose their own preferred method of attack. I decided that the priority for 819 Squadron would be to fly to a position that ensured, as far as possible, that an attack could be initiated before anti-aircraft fire could bring us down. We plan, therefore, to fly the torpedo-droppers *above* the barrage balloons, and then to drop down inside the balloon screen. We should end up in a useful position – one that assures an arc of about sixty degrees in which our torpedoes, once released, must hit an enemy battleship.' He re-emphasizes that as this is normally a daylight method of attack, the deployment of the Swordfish flare droppers will need to be judicious in order to give the torpedo droppers effective support.

'The flight up to Taranto will be protracted,' he reminds his men, 'and when we reach the target area, we'll have to face opposition...' he falters for a second before he goes on with a lowered voice: 'The subsequent flight back to the ship will be long and difficult. We're all aware of the potential hazards. Tonight's operation will be drawn out, cold, tiring, and . . . well we can guess what else. Now we should try to prepare ourselves, mentally and otherwise.' He glances at his watch as he suggests that the aircrew have a last perusal of the reconnaissance pictures, a final check of Sidcot suits, underclothing, woollen balaclavas, Bigsworth chart boards – all the paraphernalia needed for the flight ahead. Lieutenant Sutton, as he watches his colleagues, meditates on the magnitude of the task to be confronted. With a sigh, he moves across the room to re-inspect the reconnaissance images. He tries to commit to memory as many details as possible – the lines of the breakwaters, the positions of the barrage balloons, the expanses of the *Mare Grande* and the *Mare Piccolo*, the location of Cape Rondinella to the north-west, the layout of the ships, the anti-aircraft gunnery sites. He reflects on the painstaking precautions taken by the Italians. The enemy appear to have left nothing to chance. The aircrews' task may be daunting but the Italians, he thinks, will be in for a shock all right.

CHAPTER TWENTY-THREE

Supermarina Scheming

As he settles into his period of duty at the *Supermarina*, Commander Bragadin remains upbeat. When he considers the capability of his fleet's six battleships now at Taranto, he thinks of the *Littorio*, with her 15 inch guns and how the diminutive Greek navy with its manpower of just 6,300 personnel will be defeated with ease. There is no doubt in his mind that the Greek naval threat is so slight that it can be virtually disregarded. The Greeks may boast about the cruiser *Averof* with a standard displacement of 9,450 tons but she is thirty years old, her largest guns are just 9.2 inch, and there is an ironic twist: her sister ship is the Italian vessel *Pisa*. The Greeks have a few destroyers, the likes of the *Vasilissa Olga* with 5 inch guns, and the *Coundouriotis* and the *Spetsai* with 4.7 inch guns, the *Aetos*, *Ierax* and *Panther* with 4 inch guns, but all these vessels are minor – in the range of 1,000–2,000 tons standard displacement. Their few submarines, three in the Nereus class, two in the Katsonis class, are hardly a match for Italy's force of over 100. There are a couple of torpedo boats in the Niki class and there is the fleet repair ship *Hifaistos*. Apart from these vessels, muses the commander, he cannot recall any other Greek naval ship of consequence.

Notwithstanding the Italian superiority and its obvious implications, *Ammiraglio* Cavagnari has briefed his officers on the need to avoid complacency. Nevertheless, Commander Bragadin and his colleagues cannot help a certain swagger when they compare Greece's paltry potential (even with British support) against that of the Italian navy. The staff at *Supermarina* feel that the forthcoming action against Corfu is more or less bound to be a walkover; how can it be anything else? He ponders the security of the Italian fleet now tucked up for the night within the confines of Taranto's impregnable harbour. The situation, he thinks, ideally echoes the original intention: a port of safety where the fleet can relax as they prepare for their next action. Commander Bragadin has another satisfactory thought: *Ammiraglio* Cavagnari can enjoy a quiet night at home without the need to concern himself with events at the *Supermarina*. The *Ammiraglio* deserves a break; as his duty officer, Bragadin will do his utmost to oblige. With the bulk of the fleet secure in harbour there should be no reason to disturb the senior officer's pleasant evening.

The commander has a further thought: perhaps the *Ammiraglio*'s own superior officer, *Ammiraglio di Armata* Riccardi, is about to enjoy a quiet night. As he ponders this, Commander Bragadin considers the irony of *Ammiraglio* Riccardi's pre-war friendship with his opponent, the British Admiral Cunningham. In those days the 23,622 tons *Conte di Cavour*, at present ensconced at Taranto with her five fellow battleships, was *Ammiraglio* Riccardi's particular pride and joy. In view of today's circumstances, recollection of the event may seem inappropriate, but Commander Bragadin is aware that just two years have elapsed since the British admiral was invited to dine aboard the *Conte di Cavour*. (Cunningham would later write about the episode: 'Lunched on board the *Conte di Cavour* with Admiral Riccardi and came to the conclusion that he must have embarked the entire catering staff and band from one of the best hotels in Rome, so distinguished was his entertainment. Afterwards, he took us round his palatial and highly decorated private apartments and took some pride in pointing out a book, *The Life of Nelson*, which always lay on a table by his bedside. His subsequent actions during the war showed that he had not greatly profited by his nightly reading.')

Commander Bragadin reflects on the odd rumours he has heard about *Ammiraglio* Riccardi, including one that the current chief of Italian naval staff and secretary of the marine likes to keep a British book about Nelson by his bedside. Maybe the story has become exaggerated. After all, he muses, the *ammiraglio*'s strategic thinking must have moved on, surely, from that of 135 years ago.

'Sir?' Commander Bragadin has a twinge of irritation when he is returned to reality by a junior member of staff.

'Yes? What is it?'

'A call from Taranto, commander. Anti-aircraft defences have just opened up.'

'Anti-aircraft defences?'

'Yes, commander. They're firing at a lone British aircraft, believed to be a reconnaissance flight from Malta.'

'Okay. Keep me updated, please.' Commander Bragadin glances at his watch. He makes an entry in the duty officer's log and he notes the time: just past 1955 hours. He considers the potential ramifications of a lone British reconnaissance flight, but he realizes that these flights have become pretty much routine by now. A concentration of ships such as those presently at Taranto is bound to attract enemy interest. For a moment or two he dwells on the possibility that the reconnaissance flight could presage bigger things to come. He remains conscious, though, that he has received no reliable advance warning from the *Regia Aeronautica* and decides to put such thoughts to the back of his mind. Instead, he will focus on positive matters. He looks forward with satisfaction to the enemy's forthcoming surprise when they learn about an attack on Corfu. The British, he thinks, will be in for a surprise all right.

CHAPTER TWENTY-FOUR

Slow Slog

The second wave of Swordfish are airborne. The time approaches 2215; some forty minutes have elapsed since the machines' departure from HMS *Illustrious*. In the rear cockpit of Swordfish call-sign L5K, Lieutenant Sutton concentrates on navigational dead-reckoning and on the requirement to monitor incoming radio transmissions. Frequent glances at his watch are a sign of his anxiety. L5K should be in company with eight others, but the number was reduced by L5F's unfortunate taxiing accident on the flight deck. Their slender resources suffered a further blow when, some twenty minutes into the flight, call-sign L5Q started to lose height. Other crews watched with alarm as the aircraft began to disappear from sight. However, the constraints of radio silence meant that the remaining seven crews have to continue the operation unaware of L5Q's fate. Later they will learn how the machine's fuel tank problems led to engine cut out; the pilot, Lieutenant W. D. Morford, managed to restart his engine and return to the ship. For now, though, Lieutenant Commander Hale and his men have no knowledge of their colleagues' fate.

In view of the requirement for radio silence, Lieutenant Sutton's role as radio operator is a passive one: he listens to the flows of Morse messages that crackle through his earphones, but he does not respond. He faces aft as he monitors the Mediterranean Fleet's strike frequency, and he fine-tunes the bulky set by easing a frequency adjuster. He has difficulties as staccatos of dots and dashes intermingle with the squeals and whistles created by general air-wave interference. He sometimes struggles to separate relevant information from spurious, but he knows that many of the broadcasts deal with routine matters – standard weather reports and the like. He knows, too, that certain broadcasts will be designed to deceive enemy eavesdroppers – especially, he assumes, tonight. Further confusion is caused by the fluctuating and distant tones of opera from an Italian broadcasting station, although he finds this not entirely unwelcome. The quality of sound from his Gosport tube system may be less than ideal, but he listens appreciatively as the melodic expansiveness of Verdi's *Aida* fills his cockpit.

Verdi's balanced transformation of grand opera, his stress on melodic suavity *bel canto*, adds to the surreal atmosphere in the rear cockpit of Swordfish L5K, but so too does the ethereal cast of light from the moon and stars. Later Sutton will learn how cloud had endangered the first-wave machines, but by now the layers have dispersed and as the second-wave machines follow Lieutenant Commander Hale in a loose formation, they are assisted by a three-quarter moon to the south. The lunar light teases men's strained imaginations. Startled eyes observe the movement of hands, the images created – transient forms that dance across Sidcot suits, gaze into the open cockpits, hide within cockpit instruments. Conversations become brusque as the flight progresses; pilots and observers eventually settle for silence. The men draw woollen Balaclavas closer to their necks and adjust gloves and scarves for maximum warmth. The Arctic temperatures freeze out normality, discourage discussion, the comradeship of small-talk. After his return to the *Illustrious*, a pilot on the first wave, Lieutenant M. R. Maund, will write:

> Six thousand feet. God how cold it is up here! The sort of cold that fills you until all else is drowned, save perhaps fear and loneliness. Suspended between heaven and earth in a sort of no-man's land – to be sure no man was ever meant to be here. Is it surprising that my knees are knocking together? We have now passed under a sheet of alto-stratus cloud which blankets the moon, allowing only a few pools of silver where small gaps appear. And, begob, Williamson is going to climb through it! As the rusty edge is reached I feel a tugging at my port wing, and find that Kemp has edged me over into the slipstream of the leading sub-flight. I fight with hard right stick to keep the wing up, but the sub-flight has run into one of its clawing moments, and quite suddenly the wing and nose drop, and we are falling out of the sky! I let her have her head and see the shape of another aircraft flash by close overhead. Turning, I see formation lights ahead and climb up after them, following them through one of the rare holes in this cloud mass. There are two aircraft sure enough, yet when I range up alongside, the moon-glow shows up the figure (E)5A – that is Olly. The others must be ahead. After an anxious few minutes some dim lights appear amongst the upper billows of the cloud, and opening the throttle we lumber away from Olly after them. Poor old engine – she will get a tanning this trip. The sub-flight is reassembled now

at 8,000 ft. We have come to the edge of the cloud. The regular
flashing of a light away down to starboard claims attention.
'There's a flashing light to starboard, Bull, can you place it?' 'Oh,
yes,' and that is all. The poor devil must be all but petrified by the
cold by now.

An hour or so after this experience, when Lieutenant Sutton sneaks
another glance at his watch it is 2220 hours. An imaginary clock beats
out an interminable message in his head . . . tick-tock . . . tick-tock. His
sense of turmoil is exacerbated by the slow slog of the minutes. He
considers the ironies: his eagerness to proceed, his eagerness not to; his
impatience to learn about the operation's outcome, his apprehension at
the uncertainties. He is plagued by a sense of doubt, of time running out.
There's a gnawing anticipation in the pit of his stomach, an irritation of
the gut that is impossible to ignore. A line of perspiration moistens his
top lip. His mouth feels dry. He checks fretfully around his cockpit – the
position of his Gosport tube mouthpiece, the security of his monkey
harness, the state of his Sidcot suit, the frequency on the aircraft's radio.
He stares at the frequency adjuster. Should he, perhaps, take advantage
of *Aida*? He could enjoy a civilized form of distraction while he monitors
the Morse messages. He decides to tweak the frequency adjuster. The
ambience becomes almost dream-like. Thoughts recur . . . of *Basilisk*, of
Buckfast Abbey . . . of his beautiful bride. The dots and dashes of Morse
clamour for attention; they clash with Verdi, his melodic interpretation,
the non-stop clock . . . tick-tock . . . tick-tock.

He shakes his head and jerks one hand in a gesture of frustration; the
motion is reflected by moonlight as he tells himself to focus on
operational duties, navigational dead-reckoning, interpretation of Morse
messages. Should he attempt to identify the Morse senders – regulars
whose techniques can be recognized? He bemoans the lack of a secret
form of Morse – a special code that could, for example, reveal the location
of L5F and L5Q, the fate of the crews. Poor old Morford and Green, have
they ditched in the sea? Not much hope for them if they have. What about
Clifford and Going? Will their machine be repaired in time to catch up?
And what of the rest of the men on board *Illustrious*? Perhaps, at this
moment, they are enjoying a comfortable dinner. At least they won't be
bothered by freezing temperatures, eerie moonlight, screeching Morse,
quarrels with *Aida*, crazy clocks . . . tick-tock . . . tick-tock. They will
engage in pleasant conversation, laughter, banter. Perhaps they will
speculate on the whereabouts of the first wave, the second wave. With
the time approaching 2225, the first-wave machines should be in the
vicinity of Taranto before long. Have the Italians woken up yet? How

cold it is up here! Tick-tock . . . tick-tock. He wonders how 'Tiffy' is doing. Better talk to him soon. What's that light ahead? It looks like the regular sweep of a lighthouse. Tick-tock . . . tick-tock. It must be the lighthouse at Saint Maria de Levea. I wonder if Tiffy's noticed it yet. Better talk to him before time runs out. Tick-tock . . . tick-tock.

CHAPTER TWENTY-FIVE

Supermarina
Alert

Commander Bragadin glances at his timepiece. The time is approaching 2230. Some two and a half hours have passed since Taranto's anti-aircraft defences first opened up, and the staff at *Supermarina* have received several more calls from the port authorities. On a number of occasions, listening devices at Taranto have picked up the sounds of aircraft engines and as a consequence air-raid alarms have been triggered at least twice during the evening. Gun crews have raced to their posts; civilians have dashed to air-raid shelters. The cause of the fuss, though, has been put down to the same irritant of two and a half hours ago: reconnaissance flights by the tiresome British.

The commander reflects that by sounding the air-raid alarms, the authorities in Taranto have taken necessary precautions. However, with the pride of the Italian fleet holed up there he considers the ships to be less at risk now than in more normal circumstances. He realizes that a full-blown attack on the fleet cannot be ruled out, but he believes this to be so unlikely that the prospect can be virtually ignored. In his view, the Taranto defences are so effective that *Supermarina* contingency plans to cope with such an attack are a mere formality – a hypothetical exercise. A surface action would be madness, impossible to imagine; the full force of Taranto's defences would obliterate an attacker within minutes. Of course, there is the threat that these British reconnaissance flights could precursor some sort of attack from the air, but even that seems unlikely. The commander is convinced that the potential impact of Taranto's fire-power is bound to deter would-be aggressors.

There is a further deterrent: *Supermarina* staff have set up an air exclusion zone of 180 nautical miles around Taranto. Any sign of hostile air activity would elicit a vigorous response from the *Regia Aeronautica*. The commander reminds himself that *Regia Aeronautica* reconnaissance flights have offered no advance warning of large-scale enemy air movements and he reassures himself with another thought: so impressive is 'Fortress Taranto' that others see the set-up as a model. Indeed he understands that an officer from the Japanese navy is presently at Taranto as an observer. Although the Japanese government's semi-Fascist stance strikes the commander as enigmatic, nonetheless *Il Duce* is keen to foster good relations with his Far Eastern allies. This is especially the case after Italy, Germany and Japan signed that tri-national Axis alliance last September. *Ammiraglio* Cavagnari has given orders that the Japanese naval officer should be offered the full benefits of co-operation, the finest examples of Italian hospitality.

Commander Bragadin glances at the young officers and ratings now on duty in the *Supermarina*. He is conscious of their attitude towards him and his ilk; most probably they see him as old-fashioned, someone with a royalist view. However, even if it is true, the commander feels the viewpoint is overdone – certainly unhelpful when it comes to bridging gulfs within the Italian navy. He ponders that, like any institution, the navy has weak points as well as strong. On a positive note, the latter include the operations room for which he has current responsibility. No one would deny that the *Supermarina* is an efficient set-up with good communications to naval units. He surveys the arrangements of charts that give him an overview of the naval situation in the Mediterranean, and notes with approval the impressive banks of telephones, the supplementary communication systems, the diaries, logs, manuals – all the paraphernalia needed to make the Italian navy's nerve centre such an effective organization.

The *Supermarina* is manned twenty-four hours a day, and although daytime periods can be busy, the night-duty spells can become quite wearisome. Commander Bragadin sits at the strategically placed desk allocated to the duty officer but every so often he stands and paces up and down to keep himself alert. Hours can pass with little to do. He thinks about the long night ahead. Before he is relieved, he will receive the odd signal, the occasional telephone call; he will have a few reports and logs to write up, otherwise all is hopefully set to remain calm. He tries to stifle a yawn. He must keep up appearances; he should look interested and attentive. When he spots one of his staff take another telephone call, probably a further message from Taranto, he glances at his watch: 2250. Even if routine, such calls are a necessary part of the proceedings. Suddenly he notices that the young man has become quite agitated. 'Commander . . . sir . . .' he shouts.

'What is it?'

'Sir . . . there's trouble at Taranto.'

'Trouble? What kind of trouble?'

'Sir . . . it seems . . .'

'What is it man?'

'They're under attack.'

'Under attack? Impossible!'

'It's true, sir . . . Listen.'

The commander grabs a telephone receiver. His face drops when he hears the background noises – the crash of anti-aircraft fire mixed with the clatter of close-range weaponry. He is barely conscious of his assistant's voice as the young man persists: 'Commander . . . this is more than a single reconnaissance machine . . . the listening posts have picked up the sounds of massed formations of aircraft . . . The guns are firing at flare droppers . . .'

Now, as Commander Bragadin and his assistants are galvanized into action, the atmosphere at *Supermarina* becomes increasingly frenetic. The staff have problems monitoring the situation at Taranto. Some fifteen minutes pass while officers and ratings make priority telephone calls, execute contingency plans, update logs, further harass the already harassed duty officer. The Commander's haggard looks, his ashen features, betray his growing anxiety. As he deals with another telephone call from the Taranto authorities, he picks up a particular sound – one that drowns the racket of close-range weaponry. His eyes grow wide; hairs tingle on the back of his neck. He gasps when he realizes that what he overhears is the thunder of heavy anti-aircraft armament from a battleship. (Later, he will learn the cause: the exertions of 37 mm anti-aircraft guns on the *Conte di Cavour* before that battleship is sunk by torpedo.) 'My God.' the commander's stare is grim, his voice a whisper. He hesitates for a second or two, then: 'Quick!' he barks an order to a nearby member of staff. 'Get hold of *Ammiraglio* Cavagnari.' The assistant reaches for his telephone receiver; a colleague enters details in a *Supermarina* log: the substance of the order, who gave it, the time it was given: 2314. 'Tell the *ammiraglio* he is needed here urgently,' cries Commander Bragadin. 'Hurry, man.' In his agitation the commander begins to yell. 'Hurry . . .'

CHAPTER TWENTY-SIX

Attack!

'Stand by!' cries Lieutenant Torrens-Spence to his observer. Lieutenant Sutton stares at the luminescent patterns of fire that stream upwards as his pilot manoeuvres Swordfish L5K in a series of weaves. The time approaches midnight – one hour and twenty-five minutes since he first identified the flashing of the lighthouse at Santa Maria de Leuca, two-and-a-quarter hours after the second wave's take-off from HMS *Illustrious*. Now the machines prepare for attack. The first wave has set course back to the *Illustrious* – with the exception of their leader who has been shot down. In order to deceive Italian sound locators, the second wave aircraft cross and re-cross the coastline to the north-west of Taranto's *Mare Grande*. Lieutenant Commander Hale leads four other torpedo droppers; two machines have separated from the main formation in preparation for their flare-dropping roles. Over the last hour or more, Taranto's anti-aircraft gunners and searchlight operators have produced spectacular effects but just now, with the second wave Swordfish at around 9,000 ft, the machines' height safeguards them from the enemy's prodigious volume of fire.

In the cockpit of L5K, Lieutenant Sutton stares down with a sense of detachment. He reflects how the contrasting colours, the carnival of brilliance, adds to the surreal atmosphere aloft. He wonders at the curious lure of the light, an overall greenish glow that embraces the entire area of harbour. Points of brilliance within this glow – the 'flaming onion' effect of tracer shells – reach up as if beckoning in a cruel illusion of warmth. From within the chill of cockpits exhausted eyes struggle to interpret details. Does Lieutenant Commander Hale seriously intend to lead his men down into that spectre of hell? The implications seem impossible to imagine, too dreadful to contemplate. Perhaps the pilots' manoeuvres help them to vent their frustrations, to distract their minds from the hot breath of Hades. Matters, though, are different for the observers. These men must sit passively, monitor events, offer objective advice to the pilots, try not to dwell on the ramifications. Later they will learn the details of the enemy's overall ammunition output: 1,750 rounds of 4 inch shells, 7,000 rounds of 3 inch and 13,489 rounds of high-angle anti-aircraft shells . . . all of this to supplement the ships' armament (details of which remain unrecorded).

Lieutenant Sutton no longer monitors external radio transmissions. He adjusts the volume of his set to exclude the crackle of Morse messages, the squeals and whistles of air-wave interference, even the exertions of *Aida* . . . all must be subordinated to the main task: brief but vital conversations with his pilot. He is braced for a period of intense concentration; his Gosport tube system must be reserved exclusively for inter-cockpit communication. Outside distractions, the abstract atmosphere, the eerie moonlight, operatic interludes must be dismissed from the mind – although in practice he finds this hard to do. The developing situation, the seducing warmth of the light below, the effects of two and a quarter hours of transit flight in sub-zero conditions, all serve to distract his focus from his immediate tasks. He wonders about the first-wave attack. What about the crews? Have all the men survived? Did they achieve the desired results? Does that greenish glow around Taranto signify an enemy in triumph or do those flaming onions conceal a different story?

He cannot know that the first-wave machines have left a legacy of sinking ships, leaking oil, vessels torn apart; that just one Swordfish was brought down; that at this moment Lieutenant Commander Williamson and his observer are stuck in the inhospitable confines of the *Mare Grande* as they cling precariously to the tail of their Swordfish. Later, he will learn that they were at an altitude of just 30 feet at the point of torpedo release – so low that they could feel the splash of the 'tin fish' as it entered the water. The observer, Lieutenant Scarlett, will later write about the violent manoeuvres as his pilot fought to escape the inferno of the *Mare Grande*:

> We put a wing tip in the water. I couldn't tell – I just fell out of the back into the sea. We were only about 20 ft up. It wasn't very far to drop. I never tie myself in on these occasions. Then old Williamson came up a bit later and we hung about by the aircraft, which had its tail sticking up out of the water. Chaps ashore were shooting at it. The water was boiling so I swam off to a floating dock and climbed aboard that. We didn't know we'd done any good with our torpedo. Thought we might have because they all looked a bit long in the face, the Wops.

Scarlett will learn that his machine was downed by the *Conte di Cavour*'s heavy anti-aircraft armament (the source of the thunderous noise picked up by the telephones at *Supermarina*) but not before the Swordfish's torpedo had struck the ship below her number one turret, blasting a hole 40 ft by 27 ft in the port bow.

The demise of L4A was witnessed by the flare droppers in L4P – Lieutenant Kiggell and his observer Lieutenant Janvrin.

> We had a grandstand view . . . We didn't go down to sea level. We dropped our flares at about 8,000 ft. We were still fired at considerably. We had a fair amount of ack-ack fire and most extraordinary things that looked like flaming onions. One just sort of went through it and it made no great impression. One didn't think that they would ever hit you. There was always fear but in the same way that one had butterflies in the tummy beforehand, but when things were actually happening you don't seem to notice the butterflies much. The torpedo aircraft went down and attacked in two sub-flights. The leader took his sub-flight of three to attack a battleship. He launched his torpedo which hit, but he was shot down immediately afterwards.

But now the five torpedo droppers of the second wave are straightening up. Tension rises as the pilots maintain their easterly headings. The final run in has commenced. 'Stand by Alfie!' repeats Lieutenant Torrens-Spence. The Swordfish head towards a line of barrage balloons deep inside the *Mare Grande*. At any second Lieutenant Commander Hale will signal the order to attack. Lieutenant Sutton's personal account records:

> We are ready. We anticipate the leader's signal. His sub-flight consists of three Swordfish; we will lead our sub-flight of two aircraft – E5H will follow us down (Lieutenants Wellham and Humphreys). I have shifted round from my aft-facing position. Now I am braced looking forward, peering over my pilot's left shoulder, my chest hard against the overload fuel tank. Stand by! Here comes the leader's signal. We see the flash of his Aldis lamp, then he enters a steep dive. We follow – a screaming, whistling, tearing, torpedo dive. Down – down – down. We feel pressure changes; ears begin to pop. We're in a power dive almost to sea level. Down – down – down. We pass through a box barrage of fire then a different type – close-range batteries – twinkling, bursting shells. There's an orange flash ahead. An aircraft has been hit! He spins away – out of control. We carry on down. Down – down – down. Everything seems to be coming at us – stabbing groups of fire pouring up tracer. Down – down – down. Still we descend. Down – down – down. But we're nearly there. We're nearly at sea level. Suddenly Torrens-Spence pulls us up – that terrific jolt that

comes at the end of a dive. We're too short: we've ended up away from the battleships. We're over a group of cruisers and merchantmen. Torrens-Spence aims for them . . . He flies up over their masts . . . Steady does it . . . down the other side. Now he must set up for our torpedo drop. He pulls the aircraft a bit to starboard – towards one of the battleships. As we motor in we see tracer, incendiaries, flaming onions (horrible things) – everything streams up at us. Suddenly Torrens-Spence cries out: 'The one to port is too close. What's ahead?'

I peer desperately in front. I'm standing up – tall as I can, held by my monkey harness. My goggles are buffeted by the blast of air-stream. My chin is pressed hard against the top of the overload fuel tank – the bloody thing will blow me to hell if we are hit. I'm trying to direct my pilot into what's going on. 'There's a *Littorio* dead ahead,' I stoop to yell into the voice-pipe.

'Right! We'll go for the bugger.'

The *Littorio* sees us: she opens fire. The flashes of her close-range weapons stab at us. First one, then others – everything opens up along her whole length. We're coming in on her beam; we're in a terrible mass of cross-fire – cruisers, battleships, shore batteries, the lot. The bloody Italians are firing everything apart from major armament. But we're low . . . too low for the enemy gun-aimers. The place stinks of cordite and incendiaries and burning sulphur. Everywhere is wreathed in smoke – thick, choking, foul stuff. Torrens-Spence holds us low. He steadies. He cries: 'Firing!'

There's a pregnant pause. Nothing happens. The torpedo does not come off . . . the magnetic release has failed. He frantically recocks.

'We'll try again!' he yells. But now we're just 700 yards from the battleship – her bulk appears to fill the whole horizon . . . We seem to be looking down the muzzles of close-range guns. Torrens-Spence struggles with the torpedo's manual release system. He strives to hold the aircraft steady . . . hold it . . . hold it. The battle-ship looms. Streaks of flame reach out for us. Suddenly the weapon releases. Success! An agonizing few seconds now follow: Torrens-Spence must hold our steady course to ensure clean disengagement of the torpedo – the control wires need time to unravel. He's satisfied . . . he immediately yanks the aircraft to star-board. A steep turn. Turn – turn – turn. He straightens out right down on the water. We are incredibly low. Then suddenly . . . smack! We hit the water. Bloody great shudder through the whole aircraft. We are down. Are we? Not quite. We have hit with the wheels. Torrens-Spence is a brilliant pilot – he retains control – he

flies the machine out of the water. Ahead I see the mooring rafts of
barrage balloons – two of them. I con my pilot between these two,
then we point towards the moon as we try to make our escape.
There's a temporary lull . . . but now we see defensive ships
blocking the harbour entrance. Torrens-Spence lifts us up . . . over
the masts . . . down the other side. The ships seem to explode under
us: they open up with every gun they've got. We continue to point
towards the moon. Then everything falls quiet. Quite abruptly.
Silence.

The silence lingers. Lieutenant Torrens-Spence holds his aircraft at low
level and now, as each second passes, a curious awareness creeps into
the men's subconscious. They are safe. Unbelievable . . . amazing . . .
awesome. They have done it. But still there's silence – an eerie silence.
The men do not speak; perhaps they dare not.

The silence persists, but at length, when Torrens-Spence judges L5K
to be beyond the reach of enemy fire, he eases the machine up into a
climb. He assumes a south-easterly heading as he aims for the *Illustrious*
and as he awaits detailed instructions from his observer. Now the latter's
navigational skills will be vital. The observer knows that the *Illustrious*
will be steaming south from Cephalonia and that based on pre-briefed
information he will have to plot an accurate course. The correctness of
his calculations could spell the difference between safety and disaster –
between life and death. The Swordfish will be short of fuel when it
reaches the *Illustrious*, but for fear of enemy interception the ship's
homing beacon will be switched off. Any aircraft that fails to find the
ship swiftly will be forced to ditch in the sea.

'Make it one two eight degrees, Tiffy.'

'Okay.'

The dialogue is sparse but the words speak volumes. The silence has
been breached, the spell broken. Lieutenant Sutton checks and rechecks
his calculations as he focuses on his navigational tasks. He tries to shake
off the turmoil in his mind. He feels numb, disinclined to dwell on the
events, but flashbacks persist, though the main reaction will come later
– the shakes, the experience of feeling like a piece of chewed string, the
overwhelming exhaustion.

'Turn starboard five degrees, Tiffy.'

'Right-o.'

The silence resumes. There's a sense of loneliness, of anti-climax.
There are so many questions. The men cannot know that a 'welcome
home' message awaits (the sign erected spontaneously by stewards in
the *Illustrious*' wardroom), that their meal of eggs and bacon at 0300 will
be accompanied by tots of whisky and a cake baked specially by the

ship's cooks. Neither can they realize that RAF reconnaissance pictures will reveal how the Fleet Air Arm's delivery of eleven torpedoes and forty-eight bombs has created an impact of such significance. The photographs will verify that three battleships have been sunk – the *Littorio*, the *Caio Duilio* and the *Conte di Cavour* (the latter will be repaired but it will take years) – that three cruisers and two destroyers have been badly damaged, that two auxiliaries lie crippled, that Taranto's seaplane base has been reduced to flames and wreckage, that the surrounding waters are blackened by oil spillage and that the harbour is a chaos of debris. Men will shake their heads in disbelief when they consider the action of a handful of obsolete biplanes, the courage of the crews, the way such machines could cause more damage than the combined efforts of the British Grand Fleet at Jutland.

On 13 November 1940, Prime Minister Winston Churchill will announce to the House of Commons in London: 'The Taranto result affects decisively the balance of power in the Mediterranean, and also carries with it reactions upon the naval situation in every quarter of the globe. I feel sure that the House will regard these results as highly satisfactory and as reflecting great credit upon the Admiralty and upon Admiral Cunningham, and above all upon our pilots of the Fleet Air Arm who, like their brothers in the Royal Air Force, continue to render their country services of the highest order.'

But just now, as he concentrates on his navigational duties, Lieutenant Sutton tries to disregard the turmoil in his head, the turbulence of his thoughts. With a shudder he glances up at the moon – how cold it seems, how lonely. The flight back will take over two hours and already the time is well past midnight. Even the radio has quietened. Occasional Morse messages tap out through his earphones, but the operatic entertainment has ceased. The order for Operation Judgement's radio silence endures. The formations up to Taranto, the first and second waves, have dispersed as if consumed by the veil of night. Now each machine returns alone, a disparate string of individuals. He wonders how many there will be. Are he and Torrens-Spence the only survivors? Later, he will be saddened to hear of the deaths of the crew of E4H, Lieutenants G. W. L. A. Bayley and H. J. Slaughter. However, he will be astonished to learn that these were the operation's only fatalities. The crews have risked so much. Many will be in line for awards. Or will they? When the lists first appear on the notice boards of *Illustrious*, the dearth of decorations will infuriate the sailors and the lists will be torn down in anger. Eventually matters will be rectified; then Lieutenant Sutton will learn about his DSC and the similar award to his pilot. His bravery in the coming Greek campaign will earn him a bar to that award. His personal war years ahead will be marked by extraordinary hazards, all of which he will be lucky to survive, including the bombing of the *Illustrious* in 1941, the action at Maleme in Crete when the airfield will be taken over by parachutists and the bombing of the RAF headquarters at Benghazi. Subsequently, a long career in the Royal Navy (he will retire in 1964) will see him promoted to the rank of captain, posted as commanding officer of the Royal Naval Air Station at Hal Far in Malta, decorated as Commander of the British Empire.

The future, however, is uncertain from the confines of a frozen cockpit. Just now, the night still feels tortured, the flight protracted. It will seem like hours before the *Illustrious* is sighted. He stares up at the moon again and shivers as it glares back. A three-quarter moon – it was certainly useful tonight. A three-quarter moon . . . a full life assured – a life destined for good fortune if tonight is anything to go by. He ponders. He has been blessed. He adjusts his goggles as he glances down; he spots the moon's silvery pools, the images in his cockpit, the dancing disguises of danger. He must have been blessed with at least nine lives.

Index